BURIED TREASURE

Overlooked, Forgotten and Uncrowned Classic Albums

Dan Hegarty

For Angie, Camille and Rosie
For Mary and Jim

TABLE OF CONTENTS

Contributors' Album Choices

ACKNOWLEDGEMENTS

I am hugely grateful to all of the people who took the time to talk to me, and contribute to this book; it wouldn't have happened without them.

Putting together *Buried Treasure* would have been so much harder without the help of many other people too. Some gave advice, others acted as intermediaries, while others just put up with me plaguing them with requests and questions! My sincere thanks to the following people.

Lia, Paul Russell, Ian Wilson, Larry Mullen, Ciaran Savage at Warner Music Ireland, Pete Murphy at Pete Murphy Publicity, Steve Kemp, Susan O'Grady, Cathal Murray, Liza Geddes at Friction PR, Conor Sharkey at Leinster Rugby, Craig Walker, Matt Ingham at CherryRed, Paul Shanahan, Anthony Mackey, Steve Murray, Emma Harney at Orchestrate Marketing & PR, Tony Clayton-Lea, Kilian Petit, Lindsey Holmes at LHP, Linda Coogan Byrne at Goodseed PR, Dan Healy at 2fm, Brian Roche, Josephine Nestor, Ken Allen at Faction, Tara McCormack at MCD, Gerry Harford, Niall Woods at Navy Blue, Jenny Huston, Bernard O'Shea, Linda Plover and Michael Carr at Blue Monkey PR, Davie Henshaw, Sir Gugai at Roisin Dubh, Charlotte Maher at Solar Management, Marty Raviraj at CoolBadge, Jesse Booth, Alan Corr, Laurel Stearns at Dilettante Management, Bronagh Gallagher, Dave O'Grady and Alison Rogers at Gilded ALM, Alice Dawson at Oxfam Ireland, Stevo Berube, Amy McGovern at Universal Music, Laura Allen at Universal Music, Sabrina Sheehan at Mission PR, Fiacre Gaffney, Lem Oppenheimer at Easy Star Recordings, Sarah Carley at Locket Artists, Darren Reinhardt at Sony Music Ireland, Aoife Kelly, Olaf Tyaransen, Ace Trump, Roisin Dwyer at Hot Press, Sarah Bolshi and Izzy McGough at Sunday Best, Lucy Kilbride, Claire Leadbitter, Gordon McMillan at Glendalough House, Brendan Canty, Sheena Madden at RTÉ Radio Press, Keith Cullen, Lewis Jackson at Heavyweight PR, Adam Dewhurst, Mark Downing at AMA Music, Róisín Russell, Sheelagh Dempsey and Ian Murray in the RTÉ Sound Library, Louise McSharry, Rebecca Pumphrey at Independent Talent, Denis McKenna, Ann Ingle, Jolyn at Brookes Company, Tim Whitehead, Shane Trappe, Ruth Medjber, Edison Waters, Colin McTaggart at Management Operations, Aengus McMahon, Declan Heeney at Gill Hess, and lastly to Seán, Zoë, Sam, Ailish and everyone at Liberties Press; thank you.

FOREWORD

By Larry Mullen Jr.

I've been making music, or noise, in one shape or another since I was nine years of age. Occasionally I have to jog my memory so as not to forget the reason I started on this path in the first place.

Firstly, there's the initial enthusiasm of all recording sessions; working hard, working late. After a while, however, it begins to wear thin, when one idea after another is axed because of too many choices. The car journey back and forth to the studio can grind to a crawl listening to some of the day's mixes, happy with a few, hating parts of others. It's at times like these – in or out of the studio – that I often need to be reminded, compelled or inspired.

That inspiration can sometimes come from the most obvious places.

Driving home late one night, mortally depressed after listening to the day's offerings, I turned to the radio for company and stumbled upon Dan Hegarty's night-time show on RTÉ 2fm.

He was playing a Sugarcubes song. I didn't know the song, but I kept listening to hear what he was going to play next, hoping to know it. It was Bootsy Collins. I figured surely there was some radio law forbidding such opposites in the one beat on a national pop station. I kept listening night after night, slightly irked by my obvious musical deficiencies, eagerly getting to know the voice and his beautifully mad choice of music.

I have never met Dan, but I know him through the music on his show and through the CDs he so lovingly customised for me over the years to take with me all over the world. I missed the show when I was away, so Dan started compiling playlists of music from the very edges of glam, to bands that I'd never heard before, helping me to discover and rediscover music lost through the noise of years and years of bad pop songs. He's still making them for me. Thank you, Dan!

A musical snob he is not. Listening to Dan I get the sense of a man who knows and loves his music. He's a curator, a musicologist, a fan of The Wombles, a musical air traffic controller, who lands one tune after the other on his late-night radio show. In its own unique way, it is itself a little bit of buried treasure.

It's over a year ago since Dan mentioned to me that he was putting together a book about albums that were not necessarily big hits. I was flattered when he asked me to write this foreword, but I wanted to sneak a buried treasure of my own onto the list. We all have these albums in our collections – ones that we've heard about through friends or on TV shows or the radio. One of mine is Richard Ashcroft's first solo album, *Alone With Everybody*. I bought it in New York City in the summer of 2000, when we were on a promotional tour for the album *All That You Can't Leave Behind*. It was one of only two CDs that I had in my apartment at the time. The other was Van Morrison's *Moondance*.

I took my time. I put the CD on. Luscious, melancholic, personal, it got under my skin from the first play and has stayed there ever since. I was a fan of The Verve. They never finished the job, I thought. I wanted a happy ending – this was as close as I was going to get to it. His voice, the melodies, the song sequencing. Everything. I played it over and over again, and I still play it, though maybe not as often. It wouldn't be buried treasure if I did.

I hope you enjoy Dan's first book. More than that, I hope that through the pages that follow and the stories that unfold you may discover even more musical jewels for yourself.

AUTHOR'S NOTE

Forgotten, hidden, buried, overlooked, misunderstood: these are all words that in some way explain why this book came about. Music is a strange art form at times, and the only thing stranger than it are the individuals who listen to it! I happily say this as one of those people who has been a music obsessive for as far back as I can remember.

The whole music world has changed so much over the last number of years, to the extent that a word like 'album' sounds somewhat old. But, aside from a live performance, that format that we call 'the album' is still the best way of telling where a band or artist is at a particular point in their career.

There is always going to be debate over what constitutes a 'forgotten' or an 'overlooked' album. Some of the artists and albums featured in this book are very well known but, in one way or another, they fit the chosen criteria for when the idea for this project was born. Speaking of birth, this book would have been published a year earlier than it was, but the small matter of my youngest daughter's birth, which pushed it into the dustier recesses of my mind for some time!

You will read about brilliant albums by Gavin Friday, John Coltrane and Johnny Hartman, Linda Perhacs, Ash and many others in this book. They all mean a great deal either to me or the contributor that speaks about them. Rather than just me writing a book about a buried treasure trove of albums, I spoke to a number of people from music, sport, film, TV and the media about albums that have struck some sort of connection with them. I would have loved to include many more, but featuring my own initial list of 230 albums did seem a bit excessive.

Everyone remembers the classics – those multi-million selling albums that engulf the musical stratosphere – but it is easy to let others slip by, or miss them entirely. What a documentary film like *Searching for Sugarman* highlighted was that any music, no matter

how good, can be swallowed up and overlooked. How much well-received music gradually drifts out of people's thoughts, and is, by definition, forgotten?

There are countless articles written about albums like *Nevermind*, *Pet Sounds*, *Achtung Baby* or *Thriller* to mark their anniversaries, and deservedly so. They are all classics, snapshots of a time – and indeed times – of your life. This book could not possibly be a definitive list of under-rewarded albums – it is a glimpse at some of the numerous works that artists laboured over and sometimes struggled to create.

The point of this book is not to right any artistic injustices, though you may detect some occasional ranting. One thing that has always bothered me is when people dismiss an artist, song or album by saying, 'Never heard of it.' This implies that it cannot be of any sort of artistic merit, because they have not heard of it. How ridiculous is that? Surely any artist that manages to navigate their way beyond the countless logistical, financial and creative trapdoors to record and release an album has attained success by even reaching that point?

My love for and fascination with music happened in a similar way to many others. School nights had a strict no-TV policy in our house, so I found myself tuning my radio to Dave Fanning, Mike Moloney and, when possible, John Peel. It was a struggle at times to decipher the names of some of the bands through the crackles and shash. This was not due to pre-historic radio signals – the fault lay firmly with my very old and unreliable mono radio!

Putting together this book has been a true pleasure, because it has allowed me to listen to loads of music that I had never heard before, and much that I had not listened to in far too long. There is a constant torrent of new music coming from every angle, which makes it almost impossible to divide the time between the past, present and what will inevitably become the future.

Sometimes, when listening back to music that meant something to you years ago, you will find that it is not anything like what you remember it being, or that you have just moved on. I found this to be the case quite often over the course of putting this book together, but even nostalgia cannot save you from stripping this music of the high praise that you once awarded it with.

At this point I feel the urge to throw in a meaningful lyric, but that is a little too predictable. I will leave that for later. I could also attempt a clever play on words using a classic album title, but that is not what this is about. This is rediscovering, introducing and celebrating.

—Dan Hegarty
24 August 2014

DAN HEGARTY'S
ALBUM CHOICES

(SIC)

(sic), Victor Entertainment Inc, 1997

When acts like Nirvana, Alice in Chains and Soundgarden were emerging in the US during the early 1990s, bands such as Therapy? and The Almighty were doing their own respective things on this side of the Atlantic. The Almighty were fronted by the formidable Ricky Warwick. You would find it difficult to come across a nicer bloke, but when he was on stage, he looked (and still looks) ferocious.

The Almighty scored a great deal of critical and commercial success, over a career that spanned more than two decades with numerous studio albums. When they split in 1996 there was some uncertainty as to what vocalist Ricky Warwick would do next. After a move to Dublin, the idea of forming the band that would become (sic) was born.

The three-piece first gave us the *Eyeball Kicks* EP, the title track of which could easily be a contender for best pop/rock tune of the 1990s. To give you an idea of how good it actually was, think of Foo Fighters writing a song at their very best, and then handing it over to the Sex Pistols to roughen it up. If you don't believe me, have a listen to it on YouTube.

The album that followed was only released in Japan. This would not be a problem if it had happened today, because you could stream or download it, but in 1997 it presented some interesting challenges. Online shopping was not as straightforward as it could have been, and trying to listen to music online was met with a term from the past known as 'buffering'. The only other options were to fly to Japan yourself, or ask someone travelling there to buy you a copy.

The album itself is every bit as good as the EP. In fact, it is better, because you have more songs. It shows the band's full potential not just as a potent alternative rock group, but as an act that could have been massive. You hear this said about many artists, but, as a band, (sic) had everything.

If you think of the power of a band like Royal Blood, combined with the songwriting skill of Dave Grohl and the snarl of Fugazi, then you will have an idea of what level (sic) were operating at around the time that they recorded this album. An EP usually has four or five tracks, so you can only get part of the picture of a band from that, but on an album there are few places to hide weaknesses.

When you hear songs like 'Pocket Rocket' and 'Ya! Ya! Ya!', you begin to understand the ferocity of this band. Having had the good fortune of seeing them play at that time, it is both a pleasure and a relief to hear a band that have captured the power, essence and intricacies of their songs on their debut album. The fledgling combination of Gary Sullivan, Ciaran McGoldrick and Ricky Warwick sound like they have played together for years.

This book contains quite a few mentions of how music has or has not dated. This is not meant as any sort of validation of inclusion, but rather a reflection on the quality and richness of what has been written and recorded. (sic) absolutely nailed their first attempt at an album. There are never any guarantees that a band will do this, regardless of who they count as members; there are so many factors that go into this potion of noise. As an album, *(sic)* is up there with the very best rock and alternative rock records that were released in the late '90s.

For the Record

By Ricky Warwick

After The Almighty split in 1996, Andy Cairns of Therapy? suggested that I move to Dublin for a change of pace. I was living in London at the time and decided that Dublin might be a great place to find new inspiration. So, off I went. Upon arriving in Dublin, Andy introduced me to Ciaran McGoldrick and Gary Sullivan, and we hit it off immediately. We connected on a lot of levels: music, movies, alcohol and drugs. The two of them became bass player and drummer in (sic).

We set about rehearsing in The Factory in Ringsend every day. We were tight, proficient and, quite simply, did not take any bullshit. The chemistry was intense, and our new sound soon developed. Gary is an amazing drummer, and Ciaran has a bass sound that can only be described as crushing!

We recorded our first album in Northern Ireland, produced by Ronan McHugh. We toured relentlessly for two years, gaining favourable press and building a strong fan base. Japan embraced us early on, resulting in us playing four sold out shows there. We ended those shows in a Tokyo hospital, brought on by a combination of blood loss and absinthe. Alas, in the end, (sic) was not to be. A major record deal fell through at the eleventh hour and knocked the wind out of our sails. The craziness finally caught up with us. The album only ever came out in Japan, although we did also release a four track EP in for the UK/Ireland market. I have very fond memories of my time in (sic), and wish we had had the chance to show the world what we had on a bigger stage.

Artwork by Peter Curzon and photography by Steve Gullick

Tracklist

1	Pocket Rocket	8	Walleyed
2	Puck	9	Potshot #117
3	Spacing	10	Describe Your Sound
4	Magic 8 Ball	11	Crumbcrusher
5	Autofare	12	Turn Off The Big Light
6	Young Gifted And Dead	13	Ya! Ya! Ya!
7	Eyeball Kicks	14	Society Finger

ALMANAC

Pugwash, Vélo Records, 2002

Thomas Walsh, who is, essentially, Pugwash, has written more great songs than the world will ever know. Great songs? Yes, that is correct: the kind that you will never forget once you hear them. The thing is, you have to hear them first.

His debut album, *Almond Tea*, appeared in 1999. It did not hide any of its nods or odes, and is a fantastic album that I still listen to regularly. *Almanac* came three years later, and you can instantly hear that Walsh and his fellow players had learned much in the preceding years. The songs are that little more slick than on *Almond Tea*, and Walsh's songwriting had come on tremendously. This man must consume music and the printed word at a rate of knots!

The obvious choices, as stand-out tracks, are 'Anyone Who Asks', 'Monorail' and 'Keep Movin' On'. As you become familiar with *Almanac*, a ballad called 'Omega Man' starts to shine through, not just as a good song, but as a great one. It features Jason Falkner as guest vocalist, and his and Walsh's vocals work wonderfully together.

The story goes that Falkner was touring with Air at the time of their *10,000 Hz Legend* album, which he guested on. They were set to play Dublin's Olympia Theatre, and the Pugwash crew smuggled him out after soundcheck. They recorded the vocals for the track, and dropped him back in time to go onstage. Well, something like that, anyway.

If you love acts like XTC, Big Star and Bob Mould, you will adore this album. The subtleties act as the hooks here. If those do not get you, then the melodies and harmonies will.

If reviews could be measured in some sort of physical way, Cluas.com's would be a standing ovation: 'This is the second Pugwash album (the follow up to *Almond Tea*), and while it may be regarded as 'the difficult second album', the only difficulty that I have with it is leaving it out of my CD player. This album will wash with just about everyone who appreciates original material.'

Pugwash's lack of commercial reward or fame is puzzling and, one would think, disheartening, but it has not dampened Thomas Walsh's creative spirit. He has continued to make what you could call Power Pop gems as Pugwash, while also being one half of The Duckworth Lewis Method.

On *Almanac*, Walsh shows that he has all the craft of Noel Gallagher and Roy Wood at their best. It is an effortlessly strong piece of work that has, for now, faded into the past.

For the Record

By Thomas Walsh

Almanac consumed my life, as I genuinely thought it was to be my last foray into the crazy world of darker sounds, otherwise known as the world that we struggling tunesmiths call 'pop'. I threw the kitchen at it, let alone the sink. It was my own personal *Out of the Oracle*. Mellotrons, buried vocals, dead stops, no hits: you know, a cult album. In true 'cult' album style, it sold nowt, but it damn well saved my recording career. The Americans embraced it, God bless 'em. Find one now, and I will buy you a bucket for your rocking horse shit problem.

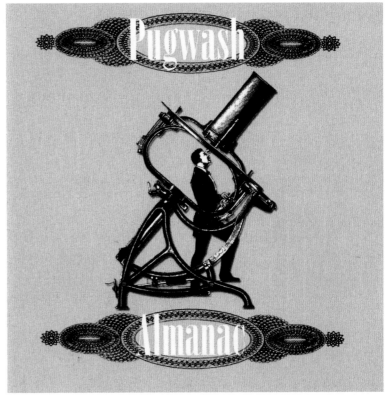

Cover artwork by Michael ua Seaghdha and Thomas Walsh

Tracklist

1 Almanac	8 Anyone Who Asks
2 Keep Movin' On	9 Element Of Fear
3 Everything We Need	10 Following Down
4 Apples	11 Omega Man
5 Sunrise Sunset	12 Weaker Man
6 The Season Of Flowers & Leaves	13 Fix Me For Today
7 Monorail	14 Emily Regardless

ANANDA SHANKAR

Ananda Shankar, WEA, 1970

The sound of the sitar is something that is difficult to confuse with anything else. The instrument has become intertwined with images of 1960s psychedelia in the West. Lest we forget, it is a traditional instrument whose spiralling hypnotic sound was only imported by the West in the 1960s, by acts like The Beatles and Donovan.

Ananda Shankar's self-titled 1970 debut is, in every sense of the word, a classic case of East meets West. His visit to the US in the late 1960s clearly had a profound impact on him. His exposure to music and culture at that time went some way towards shaping his eponymous debut.

Ananda Shankar is striking in so many ways. It features one of the most inventive covers that you are likely to come across. The first time that I heard his take on The Rolling Stones's 'Jumpin' Jack Flash' I nearly jumped out of my skin!

It is not exactly a scientific approach, but you can learn a great deal about a song when you are out at night and you can witness people's reaction to it when it is played. More than four decades on, Shankar's version of The Stones' classic still commands a reaction of surprise, confusion and delight. Some songs transcend time and connect with people of different generations; Shankar's 'Jumpin' Jack Flash' is one of these.

There has to be more to an album than one fantastic track, and there is certainly a lot more to this album than 'Jumpin' Jack Flash'. The stunning 'Metamorphosis' lets you float off for its six-minute-plus duration, as does the mysterious 'Sagar (The Ocean)'. It ebbs, flows and builds like crashing waves, for more than thirteen minutes. His interpretation of 'Light My Fire' by The Doors is something quite special, too.

It is experimentation such as this that has helped countless artists over the years expand their musical boundaries. *Ananda Shankar* helped deconstruct convention, and illustrated that there are no rules. Many albums have been categorised as watershed moments, and you can certainly hear why Shankar's debut has received this distinction many times. It is a brave album in so many ways, because he was working without any sort of blueprint.

Shankar's career went on to have many highlights in the years and decades that followed. The music that he made in the 1990s with State Of Bengal has been widely celebrated, as has his 1975 album, *Ananda Shankar And His Music*.

His appetite for experimentation never diminished, right up until his untimely passing in 1999. The legacy that he and his uncle Ravi Shankar have created should not be underestimated. What Ananda Shankar captured on his debut album was a tremendous joy and energy. It does not seem to be an album that creates much conversation anymore, which is such a shame. In saying that, it is an album that will continue to be discovered for generations to come; the surprise and delight of listening to it for the first time is something that will not be forgotten.

"...I have had a dream to try to combine Western and Indian music into a new form, a music which has no particular name but is melodious and touching, and which combines the most modern electronic devices with the old traditional instrument, the Sitar"

Ananda Shankar

Art direction by Ed Thrasher and photography by John Steele

Tracklist

1 Jumpin' Jack Flash	5 Metamorphosis
2 Snow Flower	6 Sagar (The Ocean)
3 Light My Fire	7 Dance Indra
4 Mamata (Affection)	8 Raghupati

AND SO I WATCH YOU FROM AFAR

And So I Watch You From Afar, Smalltown America, 2009

There are certain world events that make you remember where you were when they took place. To a similar extent, there is music that evokes the same kind of recollection. You can see where this is going, can't you?

The first time I heard And So I Watch You From Afar was in the kitchen of my old house. I was doing the washing up, and wearing a pair of yellow Marigolds. Too much information? I was going through a pile of new music. When I heard 'Set Guitars To Kill' by ASIWYFA, I stopped what I was doing in disbelief.

It was followed by 'A Little Bit of Solidarity Goes a Long Way', which had an equally immediate effect on me. That was it, a two-track sampler, as they were known; I was hooked. From that day forth I always associate ASIWYFA with good quality washing-up gloves!

The two tracks went on to form the foundation of this debut album, which won people over with considerable ease. It was the combination of sheer intensity, volume and classy tunes that made this not only the debut album of 2009, but arguably the best album that year.

You simply have to love songs with titles like 'Don't Waste Time Doing Things That You Hate', 'If It Ain't Broke . . . Break It', and 'Clench Fists, Grit Teeth . . . Go!' Don't go searching here for any secret philosophy to adapt to your life. Do, however, listen at an excessively high volume.

The album was aided by the band's ability to put on amazing live shows. I am pretty sure that my hearing has not been the same since seeing them on one of their early visits to Dublin. Beneath the barbed wire fence of guitars is the tribal pounding from the drums, and beneath that there is a delicate web of noises that bands like Mogwai or Slint would be proud of.

After pulverising you for nine tracks, ASIWYFA end the album with two stunning pieces of music. 'The Voiceless' and 'Eat The City, Eat It Whole' show that the band can live in both the light and the dark. It's like the lapping of the tide after a monumental storm: not quite tranquil, but something close.

This album was not made for your granny or your stuffy uncle, but give them a couple of glasses of brandy, and they might just have the same euphoric moment that I did. One person's poison is another's party, and ASIWYFA's self-titled debut is an album that still makes the hair on the back of my neck stand on end.

For the Record

By Rory Friers

Ourselves and Rocky O'Reilly were introduced by a mutual friend, radio presenter Stephen McAuley, who insisted we make an album together. So, in July 2008, we began tracking at Start Together studios in Belfast. It took around twelve days. We did most of it live, putting the drums in all sorts of strange places – even recording the drums for 'If It Ain't Broke Break It' in the toilets, at one point!

After we had finished tracking in Belfast, we flew to London for twelve more days in September to mix it with Harvey Birell, at Southern Studios. It was pretty amazing to be there, mixing on the desk that so many amazing songs had gone through, from Crass to Shellac to Fugazi. It was a pretty cool time.

Original painting by Julian Friers and design by Tim Farrell

Tracklist

1	Set Guitars To Kill	7	If It Ain't Broke . . . Break It
2	A Little Bit of Solidarity Goes a Long Way	8	These Riots Are Just the Beginning
3	Clench Fists, Grit Teeth . . . Go!	9	Don't Waste Time Doing
4	I Capture Castles	10	Things You Hate
5	Start A Band	11	The Voiceless
6	Tip of the Hat, Punch in the Face	12	Eat the City, Eat It Whole

AT THE MERMAID PARADE

Katell Keineg, Honest Jon's Records, 2010

When you think of folk music, there's a tendency to look to the past, to the 1960s or 1970s. And quite rightly, too. Those decades were fertile times for creativity and new sounds. It was a time when so much must have sounded new and progressive.

This decade has witnessed some outstanding music being created. When it comes to folk, people like Bon Iver, Laura Marling and Lisa Hannigan are outstanding. Katell Keineg is an artist who never stops making the kind of songs that you'll never want to forget.

She first came to people's attention during the 1990s, with her debut album, *O Seasons O Castles*. The first time I heard her music was through that wonderful TV show, *No Disco*. She was singing a song called 'Franklin', and I remember thinking, 'What an extraordinary voice.'

Fast-forward eighteen years, and Keineg released *At The Mermaid Parade*. Truly talented artists can make things sound like they just fell into place – in music and life in general, though, this rarely happens. It is a simple and remarkably moving album.

Katell Keineg has spent time living in Dublin and New York. It was in the latter that she recorded this album. Her voice has always been very disarming, and seems to have developed to an even deeper level on *At The Mermaid Parade*. Like Robert Plant, like Joni Mitchell, like Jeff Buckley; her vocals move you.

Her track 'Olden Days' is a song that I could listen to, on repeat, for large parts of the day. Mixed with others, like 'I Fell In Love With The World' and 'World Of Sex', it helps make this an album that is right up there with the aforementioned Bon Iver's *For Emma, Forever Ago*.

Nestled in the middle is Keineg's take on one of the most beautiful ballads to have ever been written. Tackling Big Star's 'Thirteen' is a daunting task, but she manages it very well, adding yet another dimension to an album that is already rich with lyrical and tuneful depth.

Any time that I play this album to people or on my radio show, the response is always the same: why isn't this album a lot more popular than it is? This is the question. While it may not top the iTunes download chart, it is one that slipped by too many people who would have been captivated by it. Those who have heard it can appreciate its honesty and quality.

Perhaps a review from the 2uibestow blog sums up how many of us feel about this album: 'I've had a copy of Katell Keineg's *At The Mermaid Parade* for a number of weeks now, and it has been played pretty much non-stop. It's preventing me from getting other reviews done because I can't stop playing the album!'

For the Record

By Katell Keineg

Songs were started in Greenpoint and Malaga, Dublin and Piriopolis. Coney Island loomed large – an ode to a world that has disappeared, now that they've torn the old funfair down. Standing on the beach in Tarifa, watching *Star Trek* at home – the Venus drug. [They were made] chatting in London, driving from north to south Wales, past a place of teenage pilgrimage.

All songs except one were recorded at a friend's analogue studio, in New York City. [It is] a wonderful room, with sublime equipment, but I nearly had a nervous collapse during the making of *At The Mermaid Parade* . . . the spare, off-kilter beauty of the playing is what I hear most clearly when I listen to it now. And the names, they tumble out and are gone.

Art direction by Will Bankhead and photography by Katell Keineg

Tracklist

1	At The Mermaid Parade
2	St. Martin
3	Old Friend
4	Summer Loving Song
5	I Fell In Love With The World
6	The Arsehole Song
7	Thirteen
8	Olden Days
9	Dear Ashley
10	World Of Sex
11	Dig A Pit
12	Calenture

BUTTERFLY EFFECT

Sack, Dirt Records, 1997

If the latter half of 1980s was a golden age for Irish music, then the early 1990s could be called its transitional period. There were many strong albums and singles released, but a lot of what did come out at the time does not stand up so well.

Bands and artists were changing how they recorded and made their music. Access to studio space was expensive, so a lot of material was recorded in alternative locations – bedrooms, sitting rooms, rehearsal spaces and even a few kitchens. While these pop-up studios might not have been technically advanced, it was a case of making do with what you had. Bands like Sack certainly succeeded in doing this, most notably on their second album, *Butterfly Effect*.

Sack had previously been known as Lord John White. The name-change preceded their debut album, *You Are What You Eat*. Listed by many as one of the finest Irish albums of 1997, it gained them a considerable amount of coverage from what were then known as 'The Inkies' (*NME* and *Melody Maker*) in the UK.

What would follow three years later was one of the most underrated Irish albums. It is rare that you'll see *Butterfly Effect* featured in any 'Top 100' or 'Top 50 Irish Albums of All Time' list, but, in every possible understanding of the word, this is an incredible album.

You can hear why Morrissey has been such a champion of Sack when listening to this album. The former Smiths vocalist has never been one to voice his approval or disapproval of something, unless half-heartedly. His gushing comments about Sack were backed up by his inviting them to be his opening act on two tours in the following years.

The album's urgency and impact is still as impressive today as it was on its release day. Not only did it see Sack hitting their potential, it was also an early production credit for a gentleman called Garret Lee (or Jacknife Lee, as he is otherwise known), who went on to work with names like U2, Ed Sheeran, Taylor Swift and R.E.M. The tracks may come in the form of would-be indie anthems, but they are bursting with essential ingredients for any great pop tune.

The two main singles taken from it are, in many respects, complete opposites, but they illustrate the album's diversity in both tempo and texture. 'Laughter Lines' could nearly be described as a ballad, while 'Latitude' sounds like The Smiths transported to the late 1990s, with a point to prove.

'Bumble bees in a jam jar jail/Towering trees drinking warm brown ale', is delivered by vocalist Martin McCann, on one of the album's stand-out tracks, 'Climb Mine Powerhouse'. Here is another musical injustice – McCann is one of the most gifted and unique vocalists that Ireland has ever heard.

For the Record

By Martin McCann and John Bereton

Our two weeks of pre-production for *Butterfly Effect* was actually spent building the studio (in Dublin's North Lotts), along with engineer Paul Tipler (of Stereolab) and co-producer Garret 'Jacknife' Lee (who would go on to produce albums for U2, R.E.M, Snow Patrol). It was an inauspicious start, but when the tape started to roll, it all clicked in to place.

At this time, we had lost a keyboard player but gained a guitarist, so the songs were more focussed and dynamic than on our debut album, *You Are What You Eat*. Most notably, 'Laughter Lines' (the second single from the album) was famously quoted by Morrissey as a song that 'should be Number One forever'. The band were subsequently invited by the man himself as his special guests on two tours throughout Europe and the west coast of the USA, in 1999 and 2001.

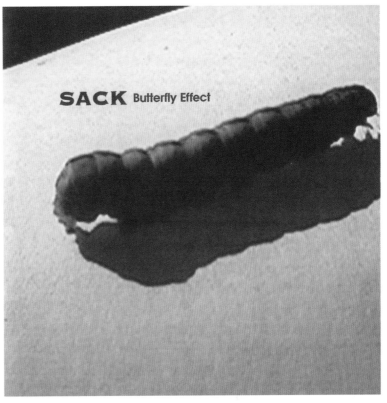

Sleeve design and layout by Martin McCann

Tracklist

1 Climb Mine Powerhouse
2 Latitude
3 Laughter Lines
4 Sleeping On The Floor
5 Nothing Stays
   The Same Forever
6 Blood Lover
7 I've Heard You Singing
8 Latter Day Saint
9 Beginners Luck
10 Angel
11 Shopsoiled
12 Talafornia
13 Wish You Were Here
14 A Sunny Day

CHINOISERIES

Onra, Label Rouge, 2007

What am I listening to? How did he come up with these sounds? Who is this guy? These are the kinds of questions that race through your mind when you listen to something this random, that you know absolutely nothing about. That feeling that you get when you discover something special is one of life's pure joyous pleasures. Take it for granted at your peril – you may not experience a moment like it again for quite some time!

The word 'curious' is one of the many that describes *Chinoiseries* by Onra. He is a prolific artist and DJ, and the first of his *Chinoiseries* albums shows him at his most adventurous and inventive.

The story behind the album is one as colourful and interesting as the album itself. Onra travelled to Vietnam in 2006 and, as he puts it, bought '30 vinyls, most of them in poor condition' along the way. He used these to make some beats, and what started out as a bit if fun morphed into an entire album.

Most music fanatics will find some sort of gem when they visit a foreign land. There are not many, though, that would be able to make two albums from it – or one, for that matter.

Chinoiseries is as much made up of Onra's curiosity as it is of the exquisite sounds that he extracted and contorted from the vinyl gathered on his trip. The self-confessed vinyl junkie made music that lives both in the old world and the present. Chants, noises and rhythms, somewhat alien to our time, are transformed and rediscovered through Onra's experimentation.

'Smoking Buddha' is the most conventional track, but even saying that does not make it a straight up pop tune. Imagine DJ Shadow, Justin Adams and Jah Wobble collaborating, and you will have an idea of the stratosphere that a track like this comes from.

Chinoiseries is an album that must have helped Onra discover a great deal about himself. As he says on the sleeve notes, Vietnam is 'The land of my grandparents.'

One of the other great things about this album is that Onra left all the crackles and blemishes from the old vinyl that he used. So much music these days is so clean and airbrushed that you cannot hear any sort of blemish that may indicate that it was made by a human being! There is nothing wrong with some music sounding pristine, but having that familiar vinyl crackle makes this a heartwarming album. This is not a nostalgic thing; it just adds to the overall aural aroma that Onra has cooked up.

The song titles alone would make you want to listen to this album. 'Boundless Boundaries', 'Chop Your Hands' and 'Here Come The Flutes' may give you some idea about what you are about to hear, but, if *Chinoiseries* does anything, it constantly throws you off whatever course you might think you are being taken on. Simply put, it is a fascinating album, steeped in retrospect, adventure and experimentation.

For the Record

By Onra

The album came out in 2007, but it was made in 2006. Back then, I took the decision to move out of France. I thought it was going to be my third – and final – album. I did not really care if people were going to like it or not. I thought that there was no way to make it in the music industry for me, and then, suddenly, gigs and press attention came in. I think that I underestimated the 'uniqueness' of this project. I did not realise that it was something that people had never heard before and were, for sure, never going to forget.

Artwork by Rekick (Musique Large)

Tracklist

1	Introduction
2	The Anthem
3	Chop Your Hands
4	Relax In Mui Ne
5	Naughty Hottie (Interlude)
6	Eat Dog
7	Last Tango In Saigon
8	Apocalypse Now
9	I Wanna Go Back
10	Full Backpack
11	War
12	Lesson With The Master
13	Dark Sea
14	Phuoc Dat (Interlude)
15	Boundless Boundaries
16	What Up Duyet?
17	Welcome To Viet Nam
18	Here Come The Flutes
19	The Vallee Of Love
20	Smoking Buddha
21	Clap Clap
22	Bounce (Interlude)
23	Live From Hue
24	Where's My Longan?
25	Take A Ride
26	Raw
27	The Ritual
28	Cymbal Oelek
29	The Third Sword (Interlude)
30	One Day
31	The Got Breaks Too
32	Hope

CIDDY HALL

Nine Wassies From Bainne, Numnum Records, 1998

You've heard it a thousand times or more: there is nothing truly original in music anymore. There are, however, albums that are so unusual that you will be scratching your head, enthralled, even in trying to place their varied reference points.

Ciddy Hall is an album that brings together many different themes and styles, so much so, that it may take you a few listens before you are fully taken with this unusual piece of work. This is not meant to be in the least bit derogatory – quite the contrary.

It is strange the way that your mind can alter your recollection of things over time. I had not listened to this album in many years, and my memory of it was of having some sort of a trad aspect. In addition to that, the sound that they came up with, on 'Whahi Whahi Did' and 'Fan', for example, is much heavier than I remember.

When it comes to recording music, so many artists are more conservative than they should be – they end up stripping the soul and energy out of their songs. How many times have you found that an artist's live show makes their album sound almost stagnant? Nine Wassies and their cast of friends and guests went for an all and out assault on the senses, and give us an album with no incomplete measures or ideas.

In the mid 1990s, there were a number of acts with a County Cork connection that forged their own path and completely ignored any trends. Along with Nine Wassies, you have people like Hyper (Borea), Interference and Cathal Coughlan (in a solo and with The Fatima Mansions).

People often make reference to albums that 'could be the soundtrack to a dream'. *Ciddy Hall* fits this slightly vague reference almost perfectly. The songs are distinctly Irish, but it sounds like the band went on tour with The Butthole Surfers and The Jim Rose Circus just before they recorded them! Surreal is not a word that one would often use to describe music. However, there is not another word in the English language that captures what Nine Wassies have done here.

Ciddy Hall never saw Nine Wassies From Bainne fill stadiums around the world, but it is unlikely that this was ever the objective. It is an unusual album that still stands out from almost everything else from the later stages of the last century. It never fails to surprise how and where *Ciddy Hall* pops up in conversation – that is, after all, the reward for making something that can truly be called individual.

For the Record

By Giordai Ua Laoghaire

The album was named after a funny experience that a friend of Peter's had in Cork. One weekend when this young (part-French, part-English) man was wandering the streets of the southern capital, looking for the City Hall, he committed the mistake of asking someone where the 'Town Hall' was to be found. 'IT'S A FUCKING CIDDY 'ALRIGHT, LANGER! CIDDY HALL IS WHAT YOU'RE LOOKING FOR! CIDDY FUCKIN' HALL ALRIGHT BOSS!' Of course, Laurent was none the wiser after this encounter as to the location of the 'CIDDY HALL' as the guy just marched off in a fit of pique.

I was surprised to find how much I enjoyed the album after not listening to it for such a long time – I would do it again if I had the money. The people who brought something special to the recording were bassist Eddie Lee, singer Miriam Ingram and sound engineer and mastering specialist Aidan Foley. Eddie's playing gives the album depth. He remains the finest bassist that I ever played with.

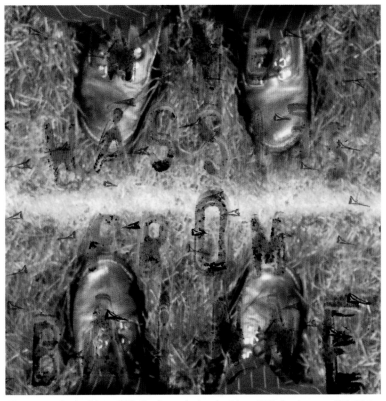

Photography by Liam O'Callaghan, design by Liam O'Callaghan and Mat May

Tracklist

1 the Day Got Mustrad got death
2 fan
3 mr and mrs Lapsipah
4 whahi whahi did
5 under the moon-mumhan under
6 níos
7 connie balltie
8 shop at fleadhworld
9 the wassie in me
10 the bucks of bladdermore
11 not burma

COPING MECHANISMS

Si Schroeder, Trust Me I'm A Thief, 2006

There are two reactions that you will get about Si Schroeder's *Coping Mechanisms*. Many will not have heard of it, but those who have are often passionate about it to the point of obsession. It is an album that could be justifiably described as having cult status.

Rollerskate Skinny's *Horsedrawn Wishes* was one of 1996's most unique albums, and the same thing can easily be said of *Coping Mechanisms* from 2006. It did not sit with any particular trend or style at the time, and when you first heard it, you could not be quite sure if this was marvellous or misguided.

In hearing some of the tracks that make up this album you hear the sound of an outsider or, at least, someone with their own vision. 'Lavendermist' and 'A Little More' sound so very different from everything else that was being made in Ireland at the time.

The kind of albums that one could equate this to are releases by acts like Sigur Rós, Godspeed! You Black Emperor and Spacemen 3. Over the nine tracks, you can hear the pedigree of an artist that has developed over many years. It was quite rightly shortlisted as one of the Irish Albums of 2006 at the Choice Music Prize, a list that included Fionn Regan, The Immediate and – the eventual winner – The Divine Comedy.

Si Schroeder (whose real name is Simon Kenny) has experimented with various sounds over the years. From the somewhat basic yet effective drum machine and dual guitars of Schroeder's Cat, to the more refined Schroeder Sound, what you hear on *Coping Mechanisms* has not sprung up over night.

His performance at the Eurosonic festival in 2008, clearly impressed a number of foreign media attending the show. It is brought up at the festival almost every year since, the moment that someone's hears that you are from Ireland. That is quite something, when you consider the number of acts that have passed through the host city of Groningen in the years since.

I have often struggled with the description of 'night-time music'. It always, I felt, sounded a bit stupid, or a fit-all for music that wasn't upbeat and jolly. Here comes the 'but': *Coping Mechanisms*, though, is indeed an album that slots into that rather vague description.

There is an uneasy beauty about what Si Schroeder has made here. It is not what you would call haunting, but it is not angelic or ethereal either. Listen to a track like 'C4', and you will instantly get what I mean. I am not usually that curious about how specific music is made, but I am with this.

There are all sorts of influences evident on *Coping Mechanisms*. You can hear his leaning for guitars, but there is also a strong electronic sound here, too. Throw in some psychedelic, folk or even classical, and you have one individually complete piece of work.

For the Record

By Simon Kenny

I was sitting in an empty Japanese restaurant one night in central London, February 2006. I had just come from a day's mastering at The Exchange, in Camden. I was carrying the masters for *Coping Mechanisms* and eating sushi. The record was finished. There was no sense of accomplishment or achievement, just total exhaustion.

I had come to London with Jimmy Eadie, the engineer and producer with whom I had worked, for what seemed like years, on the album. The intensity of the work had burnt us both out. We had parted company quietly that evening after a noisy pint. I sat in the restaurant, and contemplated the strange feeling of anticlimax that was setting in – as though the record was not mine any more, just something that I had been looking after for a while, and that had now left home forever.

Later, Jimmy called me to ask if I wanted to go to a 'performance knitting' gig in Brixton. I said no.

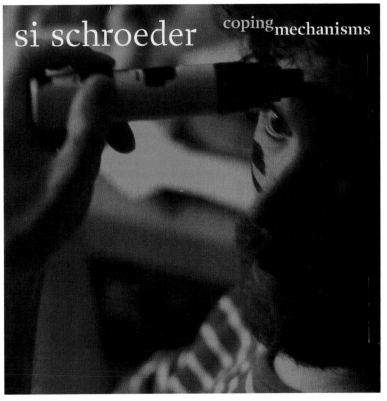

Design by Dara Ní Bheacháin

Tracklist

1	The Reluctant Aviator	6	Elaine'sPorsche/Poor Hélène/Céline Pours
2	Lavendermist	7	Duck!
3	C4	8	A Little More
4	Eyes-Wide	9	Here, After . . .
5	(Apology)		

DANCE THE DEVIL . . .

The Frames, ZTT Records, 1999

The mid and late 1990s were very fertile years for Irish music. The sheer amount of material from that time in this book should give you some sort of indication. There are not many bands that the word 'enduring' could be applied to, but The Frames are one such act. Their career has had more ups and downs, more twists and turns, than an episode of *Breaking Bad*.

By the mid 1990s the band had released two albums: *Another Love Song* in 1991 and *Fitzcarraldo* in 1995 (with a second version the following year). Line-up changes had not destabilised things like it could have; in many ways, it battle-hardened The Frames, and made them even more determined to progress.

At that point in their career, *Dance the Devil . . .* was their most complete album. In many ways, it is still their most accomplished, though you will not have to look for long to find someone that will tell you that 2001's *For the Birds* can lay claim to that distinction.

'Perfect Opening Line' opens *Dance the Devil . . .* , and what follows is a set of songs that can match nearly any song from any album. 'God Bless Mom', 'The Stars Are Underground', 'Rent Day Blues', 'Hollocaine', 'Star Star', 'Pavement Tune' – it is a wildly impressive album.

Can an album be described as iconic if it has not sold millions? If it can, then Glen Hansard and his Frames cohort came up with some iconic tunes here. One of the reviews in *Melody Maker* certainly thought so, hailing it as sounding like 'Mercury Rev meets dEUS meets Will Oldham in heaven, only better.'

There was a big leap in standard between the band's debut album, *Another Love Song* (which Glen is not a fan of), and their follow-up, *Fitzcarraldo*. The same can be said for the progress that they made both as a band, and as a group that understood the subtleties needed when recording in a studio.

The Frames's popularity really started to grow following the release of *Dance The Devil . . .* While it did not signal a major international breakthrough, the possibility of this happening did not seem impossible. As their fan base grew, their detractors began to shout louder – being a member of The Frames required having thick skin.

The album was to be The Frames' US breakthrough. While it did not achieve what it should have, it solidified their own particular sound. Third albums can often be the point at which artists find their sound, but it is not always the case. Musically, this album was the band's most strategically produced, something that worked well on the batch of songs that they had written for it.

Dance the Devil . . . saw the end of their second record deal and the beginning of their independence, another rebirth for a band that have become renowned in Irish music. In the years that followed, songs from this album have always made up the heart of The Frames's live show. Granted, 'Revelate' from *Fitzcarraldo* is still their centrepiece, but, as a sequence of songs, The Frames's third studio release remains their best and most important album.

For the Record

By Glen Hansard

We had figured out some kind of independence on *Fitzcarraldo*. With *Another Love Song*, we were signed to a major label and did exactly what they told us. It was a dreadful record, and we all came out of it burned. *Dance the Devil...* was the first murmur of confidence in The Frames, where we went, 'We can go and make a record any way we want.'

It was the first time, as a band, that we were finding a voice. This was where we went into the studio and we started making music for the love of the sound of it. On *Dance the Devil...* it was a meeting of decent tunes that had been written at the time, and then finding a sound. Craig Ward from dEUS came in and played some guitar, and had a big influence.'

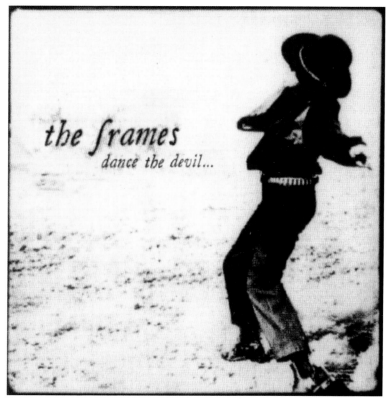

Cowboy by Joe Egan

Tracklist

1	Perfect Opening Line	7	God Bless Mom
2	Seven Day Mile	8	Rent Day Blues
3	Pavement Tune	9	Hollocaine
4	Plateau	10	Neath the Beeches
5	Star Star**	11	Dance the Devil Back into His Hole
6	The Stars are Underground		

DIASPORA

Natacha Atlas, Nations Records/Beggars Banquet, 1995

The saying, 'There are only so many hours in the day', excuses many human failings. It is probably one of the most utilised self-justifications that we can come up with for missing music, books or movies, that we end up discovering and loving years after they were first made available.

It was only when I was putting this book together that I quite literally stumbled across *Diaspora* by Natacha Atlas. It is an album that I had read about a couple of times over the years, but I did not hear it in its entirety until June of 2014 – almost two decades after it was first released. In retrospect, I would happily swap the time that I had spent listening to countless other albums in place of this, if that were possible.

Released during a time when acts like Oasis and Michael Jackson ruled the music world, it is an album that could slot into any year since its release. At times, you feel like you could be listening to Massive Attack at their very best, while at other moments, Atlas's distinctive vocals are such that she seems like the one vocalist who can hit notes in quite that way.

There are a number of artists and albums that will always remind me of this book, and *Diaspora* is definitely one of them. As I wrote this piece, it was playing in the background, competing with the sound of The Netherlands playing Costa Rica in the World Cup – quite an audio montage!

Opening with 'Iskanderia', there isn't a dull moment on *Diaspora*. The sounds and orchestration are extraordinary.

'Dub Yalil' and 'Leysh Nat'Arak' are two highlights; both are different kinds of tunes, but go far in illustrating the quality and diversity of this album.

Atlas is often referred to as a 'world music' artist. What exactly constitutes world music these days? In a time when genres and categorisations seem so blurred, 'world music' sounds like too vast an expanse to put anything in.

There are vocalists like Jeff Buckley, Nina Simone and Bobby Womack, who had that soul and power that move you. Natacha Atlas is another who manages this. Her lyrics are lost in translation for some, but this does not dampen their impact. There is a long list of artists who came together to make this special album, and they deliver a big sound, in an unconventional sense.

At certain times, you don't need to know a huge amount about an artist to thoroughly enjoy their music. These days, we have, in seconds, the resources available to find out every possible fact about almost anything. Allowing for something to retain its mysticism is sometimes refreshing. The finer details of *Diaspora* will remain unknown to me; that is a conscious decision. It is a cliché, but music is well able to speak for itself, without the aid of Wikipedia or numerous articles archived in that electronic ether.

Call this album world music, call it ethnic, call it electronic(a); it does not matter what you describe it as. This is an album that has been discovered by many, but is one that many more will uncover and thoroughly enjoy, as I have.

NATACHA ATLAS
DIASPORA

Design by Alison Fielding and photography by Mary Farbrother

Tracklist

1   Iskanderia
2   Leysh Nat' Arak
3   Diaspora
4   Yalla Chant
5   Alhambra Part 1
6   Duden
7   Feres

8   Fun Does Not Exist
9   Dub Yalil
10 Iskanderia (Atlas Zamalek)
11 Diaspora
    (Ballon Theatre Mix)
12 Fun Does Not Exist
    (Dolmus Mix)

DOS DEDOS MIS AMIGOS

Pop Will Eat Itself, Infectious Records, 1994

Much has been made of the impact that The Prodigy's *Music for the Jilted Generation* had on music in the mid 1990s and thereafter. Alongside others like *Leftism* from Leftfield and The Chemical Brothers's *Exit Planet Dust*, it heralded a new sound and attitude.

In the years prior, Pop Will Eat Itself had built an arsenal of noise with albums like *This Is the Day ... This Is the Hour ... This Is This!* and *The Looks or the Lifestyle?*. But it was not until 1994 that they made an album that became, for some, a landmark record. It may not have made a mainstream splash, but it was not a million miles away from doing so.

It also worth mentioning that PWEI supplied their writing strength to help create the thunderous sounds on The Prodigy's 'Their Law', from the aforementioned *Music for the Jilted Generation*. This was one of the songs that helped The Prodigy attain that crossover appeal, and it is still a live favourite to this day.

Dos Dedos Mis Amigos and Curve's *Doppelgänger* were the first albums on which I heard those fused guitars and processed beats that we would all become accustomed to just a couple of years later. It had elements of the industrial sound that Nine Inch Nails (who they toured with in the US) had made a big impact with.

The thing about PWEI was they were not a bunch of pensive looking dudes, simply wanting to make music that you could dance to. These guys looked like they would impale your head with a bass guitar if you were not freaking out enough at their gigs.

Viewers of RTÉ's *The Late Late Show* may remember their live performance of 'Ich Bin Ein Auslander'. If you have not seen it, it is on YouTube, and definitely worth watching. Seeing it on TV, as it happened, was quite something. It brought the band a great deal of media coverage, which did their credibility no end of good. Suddenly, they were the band that your conservative relatives disapproved of – now there's a band to tell your mates about!

The impact that *Dos Dedos Mis Amigos* had, and still has, is immediate. Impact is the correct word, too, because they have managed to make their trademark pop songs into monsters. Seeing this band live back in 1994 or 1995 would have probably scared the shit out of me, but I would have been willing to take the risk had the opportunity arisen!

PWEI knew what they were doing by the time they were in studio with *Dos Dedos Mis Amigos*. They made an album with many shades. The temptation to have everything with the accelerator to the floor must have been hard to resist, but they knew better.

The band split soon after, and the follow-up album was shelved. It was eventually released as part of a *Dos Dedos Mis Amigos* re-issue in 2013. PWEI have reformed, and have made some really impressive new material, but their 1994 album remains their most impactful. It brought the band much success, but nowhere near as much as they truly deserved.

For the Record

By Graham Crabb

Dos Dedos Mis Amigos was our fifth (and last with the original line up) studio album, and probably most equal to *This Is the Day . . . This Is the Hour . . . This Is This!*, in my opinion. While that album was more inventive, *Dos Dedos Mis Amigos* hit the mark, sonically, with its big crunching sound, dark, brooding intensity and a new maturity in the songwriting that put previous criticisms to bed – of PWEI lacking the conviction on record that we showed live.

Sleeve by The Designers Republic

Tracklist

1	Ich Bin Ein Auslander	7	Cape Connection
2	Kick to Kill	8	Menofearthereaper
3	Familus Horribilus	9	Everything's Cool
4	Underbelly	10	R.S.V.P.
5	Fatman	11	Babylon
6	Home		

DREAM ON

Scala & Kolacny Brothers, PIAS Recordings, 2004

Certain albums come, as the cliché goes, 'like a bolt out of the blue'. To describe *Dream On* in this way does not fully reveal the unexpected reception that this album received. This was not the first time that a choir tackled contemporary rock or pop songs, but Scala & Kolacny Brothers differentiated themselves by selecting a wonderfully diverse list of songs.

The choir and the two brothers (Steven and Stijn) had been doing this for a number of years, however, *Dream On* brought them the international attention that they deserved. Perhaps it was my own preconceptions of what a choir does that caused my pleasant surprise when I was introduced to this album.

What would you expect a choir of sixty young women to sing? Honestly, Christmas carols seem most likely! Scala & Kolacny Brothers smashed this ridiculous idea with *Dream On*. They tackled a broad array of songs, from the straightforward to the slightly more complicated.

Their reworking of Depeche Mode's 'Dream On' fittingly opens the album, and is soon joined by the Red Hot Chili Peppers's 'Under The Bridge', and 'Walking After You' from Foo Fighters. This may sound strange if you have not heard any of these, but it is a case of it working better in reality.

Hailing from the town of Aaraschot in Belgium, Scala have gone on to release many albums of both interpretative and original material. The logistics of getting the songs that make up *Dream On*, recorded to the standard as they appear on the album, must have caused a few sleepless nights. At times, the pitch-perfect 14-track album really does make the hairs on the back of your neck stand on end.

It is the versions of The Verve's 'Bittersweet Symphony', 'I Touch Myself' by The Divinyls and the title track that really stand out. Initially, when I played these during the late hours on 2fm, the reaction was either one of absolute joy or unreserved disgust. People can be strange about someone re-doing a classic, but the fact that it gets such a strong reaction really shows you that it made an imprint on people. A song that makes no impression on people is, by definition, doomed.

Like any album made up solely or largely of covers or interpretations, *Dream On* will not be taken seriously by some, purely because is not all original material. In a similar way to *Radiodread*, by Easy Star All-Stars (featured elsewhere in this book), some people will just look on this as a novelty album, which is unfair, because that word often implies that the 'novelty' aspect is the only redeemable quality.

In the decade that followed *Dream On*, Scala & Kolacny Brothers's notoriety continued to grow and, in 2010, their version of Radiohead's 'Creep' was featured in the trailer to the hugely successful motion picture *The Social Network*. On an international level, their success began with *Dream On*, an album which will continue to serve them well.

For the Record

By Steven Kolacny

The *Dream On* album was produced after 2002-2003, the magic year in which Scala earned golden records and experienced a complete metamorphosis. While *Scala on the Rocks* (Scala's debut album of live recordings) had been recorded in admiration and amazement, the next one (*Dream On*) quickly confirmed the style that my brother Stijn and myself wanted the singers to grow towards.

The whole album rests on the concept of stripping down rock songs (without really modifying the original), to reshape them completely. The selected songs were all songs that I had been listening to for years, and that I liked playing on the piano. When I am listening to *Dream On* again, I am still moved by the emotional purity of our version of the song 'With Or Without You', as well as by the dark side of *Dream On*.

Artwork and photography by Jo Clauwaert

Tracklist

1   Dream On (originally by Depeche Mode)

2   Under The Bridge (originally by Red Hot Chili Peppers)

3   Don't Break My Heart (originally by UB40)

4   21 Things I Want In A Lover (Originally by Alanis Morissette)

5   Wrong (originally by The New Symbol)

6   I Touch Myself (originally by The Divinyls)

7   Go Where I Send Thee (originally by Stephen Hatfield)

8   Exit Music (For A Film) (originally by Radiohead)

9   Bittersweet Symphony (originally by The Verve)

10   With Or Without You (originally by U2)

11   Walking After You (originally by Foo Fighters)

12   Daddy I'm Fine (originally by Sinead O'Connor)

13   Perfect Day (originally by Lou Reed)

14   Underneath It All (originally by Nine Inch Nails)

DRIFT

The Devlins, Capitol, 1993

There are certain bands that you do not click with straight away. Maybe it is because the tone of the music does not fit with your mood at the time. Sometimes, it is as simple as you not being very receptive to something new when you first hear it.

I remember the unmistakeable sound of Gerry Ryan's booming voice, introducing a song by the name of 'Almost Made You Smile'. After around twenty seconds in, a band called The Devlins first made a lasting impression on me. The words, 'In my hand, you might see, something special that she gave to me . . .' came piercing through my clapped-out stereo. Shazam did not exist back then, so I had to scramble to find a pen and write down the band's name.

Like *The Unforgettable Fire* by U2, *Drift* is a clever album, with a seductive undercurrent that grips you like few others. It is late-night music that manages to straddle the very different world of 'daytime mainstream'.

At this point in their career, The Devlins had just about everything going for them. They were getting all the right nods and winks in the US, and intrigue was growing in their native Ireland. The Newry band, led by brothers Colin and Peter Devlin, had songs that melted their way onto American FM radio.

It is not just good songwriting that makes *Drift* such a strong album, it is the way that they were recorded and produced. Would-be pop/rock anthems like 'Someone To Talk To' and 'I Knew That', sit alongside the beautiful and atmospheric 'Every Time You Go'. The latter is as good as anything produced by acts like The Blue Nile or Talk Talk in their prime.

If you listened to this album for the first time today, you would guess that it is from the early or mid 1990s, but it has aged gracefully. There is something almost subliminal going on in *Drift*, which makes it easy to admire; it has a quiet confidence, much like someone who is comfortable with who they are. That said, The Devlins keep you guessing, as *Drift* does not give too much away. It is an album that reveals itself over a period of time – you have to live with it a little bit.

Some albums are ruined by attention to detail. This is a strange thing to say, but it is true. Sometimes the fun, adventure and edge can be sucked out of music when precision is brought to an extreme. There is no doubt that great care and attention to detail went into *Drift*, but there is a freedom to these songs that makes them that little bit more magnetic. Recorded in Dublin, New Orleans and London, this album was – and remains – quite a statement from The Devlins.

For the Record

By Colin Devlin

The expression 'lost in music' is the one that comes to mind when thinking back to the recording of *Drift*. When you play in a band, things are constantly changing: surroundings, people, inspirations, influences. As with all art, you are constantly searching. It is easy for one year to run into the next, without really ever stopping to see how much time has passed.

As I write this, I cannot help but realise that it really was quite some time ago when we started to roll the tape in Dublin for the recording of *Drift*. And yet, the intervening years have not changed the way I feel about the music, and how proud we are of the record.

The DEVLINS. Drift

Sleeve art and design by Michael – Nash Associates

Tracklist

1	I Knew That	7	Someone To Talk To
2	Everytime You Go	8	Necessary Evil
3	Turn You Around	9	As Far As You Can Go
4	Drift	10	I Don't Want To Be Like This
5	Almost Made You Smile	11	Until The Light Shines Through
6	Alone In The Dark		

EARTHQUAKE DUB

The Revolutionaries, Earthquake/Hot Pot, 1978/2005

Thank God for reissues! Thank God for Wikipedia! It is through both of these that The Revolutionaries and Ossie Hibbert were introduced to me. Hibbert has contributed to and made an incredible amount of music. To say that The Revolutionaries's *Earthquake Dub* is their finest release would be unfair, because you would need to set aside the best part of a year to work your way through all the music that Hibbert has brought us.

To the average music fan, the name Ossie Hibbert may not be as recognisable as that of Marley, Toots or Cliff, but his influence on reggae and dub is far greater than you would imagine. It is hard to comprehend how prolific he was, particularly in the 1970s.

Earthquake Dub was originally released in 1978, but, for years, the likeliest way that you would have heard any of the album would have been by trawling through various audio files that people had uploaded. Then, in 2005, it was finally reissued with loads of additional material.

The original album featured ten tracks that were recorded between 1975 and 1977, in one of Kinston's best-known studios – Channel One Studios. Ossie Hibbert produced, recorded, arranged and mixed the album. Hibbert was in charge of sessions at the studio, and also acted as arranger. In addition, he operated his own label, which was very active during the 1970s.

The Revolutionaries were an extraordinarily talented band that, at one point, featured the revered Sly Dunbar on drums. On *Earthquake Dub* each note melts into the other. The album that they put together cannot sufficiently be described simply as 'inspired' or 'moving'.

Under the guidance of Hibbert, the album opens with the title track, capturing you immediately. It is a case of 'once it has you, you are engrossed', right up until this album closes, with 'Pain Land Dub' (or 'Conscience Version' on the expanded, re-issued version of 2005). Other tracks, like 'Black Diamond Rock', 'Rasta Foundation' and 'Secret Agent', stand out as remarkable individual pieces of music too.

At some point during *Earthquake Dub*, you wonder how many other treasures have evaded us. The list of albums and singles recorded in Channel One Studios in the 1970s is difficult to comprehend. Names like Dennis Brown and Dillinger worked with Hibbert during this time, along with seemingly countless others.

If this album could be put into context, it is like the first page of the opening chapter of the kind of book that will leave an indelible imprint on your life. That is a pretty emphatic statement to make, but it underlines the hugely overlooked quality of the music that was created for *Earthquake Dub*. Albums like this make you want to dig deeper, to see what other treasure that you can uncover.

Design by Smith & Smith

Tracklist

THE EIGHT LEGGED GROOVE MACHINE

The Wonder Stuff, Polydor, 1988

When you think of the great British rock bands, names like The Beatles, Led Zeppelin, Oasis, The Cure and Rolling Stones flash through your mind instantly. But what about the ones that did not go global?

Perhaps 'forgotten' is too strong a word when thinking of Supergrass, Lush, The Wedding Present and Mansun. They are bands that have put out some remarkable material over the years. Add to that list The Wonder Stuff: they had huge success, but, for some reason, many people seem to gloss over their glory days.

Hup, *Never Loved Elvis* and *Construction For The Modern Idiot* are probably their best remembered albums, but it is their almost flawless 1988 debut, *The Eight Legged Groove Machine*, that was their boldest venture. It was musically anarchic at the time, and still holds much of its individuality years later.

When you think of anarchy, you will probably think of punk, but what The Wonder Stuff gave us with this record was something much more subtle, but still leaving an impression. You can pick up on their humour and mindset, too – on the sleeve of the CD version, it reads 'Enjoy your CD (you paid enough).'

The Wonder Stuff's second album, *Hup*, had more songs that you could call anthems, but *The Eight Legged Groove Machine* has a distinct lack of self-consciousness to it. There is not a track longer than three minutes and fifteen seconds on this album, so, suffice to say that if they had any ideas for any blousey guitar solos, they dispensed with them.

Songs like 'A Wish Away', 'Red Berry Joy Town' and 'Give, Give, Give Me, More, More, More' were born during a different time, and hold a potency that is not fuelled by any sort of obligatory nostalgia. The Wonder Stuff have always known how to have crowds hopping, only to hit them with ballads like 'Some Sad Someone' and 'Rue The Day'.

Around the time that The Wonder Stuff were promoting *The Eight Legged Groove Machine*, vocalist Miles Hunt would nearly overwhelm his audience with his seemingly limitless charisma. He added to this a biting sarcasm, that was both brash and clever. It really gave the band an edge over most of their peers.

There was not another band like The Wonder Stuff in 1988. The world was being governed by hideous glam/stadium rock bands at the time. Manchester's 'Baggy' band's, like The Stone Roses, Inspiral Carpets and Happy Mondays had made an impact, and the Seattle influx had not happened yet. The Wonder Stuff never called any of these so-called 'scenes' home, they plotted their own course.

To say that The Wonder Stuff were ahead of their time would be wrong; rather, they were one of the changing faces of music at that time. They were one of the acts that helped bring a bit of disorder and fun back into music at the end of the 1980s, and call in a new decade that would see them score some major commercial successes. It started with *The Eight Legged Groove Machine*, and that is always the best place to begin listening to The Wonder Stuff's back catalogue.

For the Record

By Miles Hunt

We recorded *The Eight Legged Groove Machine* between February and April 1988 in east London, with producer Pat Collier. It took twenty-eight days. We would spend no more than a week at a time in the studio before heading out to do more gigs, and that kept us tight as a band. It also meant that there was never enough time spent in the studio for us to get lazy or bored with what we were doing.

Most of the songs had been written, played and demoed prior to recording with Pat, but we wrote, 'No, For The 13th Time' and 'Grin' during the our time in the studio. I only have good memories of recording the album, Pat was exactly the mentor we needed to help us focus, and Polydor Records, the label that would release the album, pretty much left us to our own devices throughout all of the sessions. I still think the album stands up today.

Sleeve by Hazel

Tracklist

1	Red Berry Joy Town	7	The Animals And Me
2	No, For The 13th Time	8	A Wish Away
3	It's Yer Money I'm After, Baby	9	Grin
4	Rue The Day	10	Mother And I
5	Give, Give, Give Me More, More, More	11	Some Sad Someone
6	Like A Merry Go Round	12	Ruby Horse
		13	Unbearable
		14	Poison

THE END IS HIGH

Blink, Mutant Sound System, 1998

The End Is High, by Blink, is another release that gets glossed over when it comes to uncrowned, classic albums. It is strange that this has happened, because the album catches one of Ireland's best bands of the past 20 years at their finest.

Released in 1998, *The End Is High* quickly gathered the kind of reviews that you would usually need large suitcases of ash to acquire! They had learned a lot from recording and touring their debut album, *A Map of the Universe by Blink* (August 1994), as was evident on this, their second release.

'Sporting an explosive sound, a knack for memorable melodies and attitude to spare, Irish rock quartet Blink brings to mind an updated version of the best of the '80s British synth-pop bands – notably, New Order, Eurythmics and Frankie Goes To Hollywood.' This how US music bible Billboard summed up *The End Is High*, just before the Dublin band relocated to New York City for their full-on assault upon America.

'Planet Made Of Rain' and 'Would You Kill For Love?' had the right balance between guitar pop and what had become known as electronica. 'Cello', which had appeared on their debut album, was reprised for this release, and, once again, proved to be the jewel in Blink's would-be crown. Also reappearing was 'Fundamentally Loveable Creature', closing the album in a seismic fashion.

To this day, 'Cello' still sounds in equal parts epic and mysterious, when played alongside the very best of the new crop of synth-pop purveyors; you could play it after or before any song, and it would still strike you as outstanding.

The Eastern influences add much to the measured, whispered vocals, while the orchestration melts away like a setting sun.

With all due respect to *A Map of the Universe by Blink*, the band managed to beef up their sound on *The End Is High*. While their debut contained slick pop tunes, their second brought us songs that were much bigger and, in some cases, brasher. It comes back to that word attitude: they had found a way to meld it into their songs, and they were all the better for it. It's like the tracks had been sent off to boot camp, and came back packing a considerably larger amount of muscle.

When it came to performing this album and their other material, Blink could really deliver. Dermot Lambert had a 'Joe Strummer meets Phil Oakey' (of The Human League) thing going on, which added an additional edge. There are always artists that struggle with their live sound, but Blink managed to roughen things up, which made you appreciate what they had done in the studio that little bit more.

The album's commercial impact cannot measure its artistic merit. If songs like these show us anything, it is that not every exceptionally good album gets that sought after universal endorsement. It has gotten lost over the years, and has (like the album *Butterfly Effect*, by Sack, mentioned elsewhere in this book) regularly been overlooked in various 'Best Irish Albums' lists. Blink went on to record another fine album: *Deep Inside the Sound of Sadness*, in 2004. *The End Is High*, however, remains their golden artistic moment, and what a moment it was.

For the Record

By Dermot Lambert

It took three years to put this album to-gether, mostly because of the amount of touring we had begun to do in the USA. A bunch of very radio-friendly songs, meant to be the second Blink album, were re-placed one-by-one with odd songs that we just could not resist.

It is an album of very mixed canvasses, from straight techno to straight rock, and even has a harmonica solo thrown in. Some of the recordings are ultra lo-fi, cre-ated on a four-track in an office in South Anne Street in Dublin, and some other recordings have bits missing, because the technology did not exist to fix things the way we wanted.

We got what we wanted though, in mak-ing a true album as opposed to a collection of songs – with patches of work from differ-ent moments over a three-year period, mostly through quite difficult and challeng-ing times. The fact that Blink persevered and actually got the album finished re-mains the biggest accomplishment.

Sleeve design by Aiden Grennelle at B'Zerk For Holly, Dublin

Tracklist

1	A Planet Made of Rain
2	Would You Kill for Love?
3	Cello
4	Dead Little Bird
5	The Luckiest Man Alive
6	This One Is Wild
7	The Girl With the Backward Skin
8	Sky Land Scraper Paper Fly
9	The Raven
10	The House That Illuminates Your Thoughts
11	Baby You Broke My Heart But You Know . . .
12	I'm Not Sorry Now
13	Fundamentally Loveable Creature

EXPLOSIVE

The Shades, Grade Records, 2004

The city of Cork has given us a lengthy list of musical talent over the decades. Whether it is Microdisney, Nun Attax, The Sultans Of Ping FC, Stanley Super 800 or more recent acts like The Altered Hours or Echogram, the south-west corner of Ireland has offered up some riches.

As with so many bands, The Shades formed out of a love for and curiosity of music. Their music and line-up grew over the years, and they released their debut album in 2004. The album, *Explosive*, was just that – it had an immediate impact on anyone that heard it, and picked up some very positive coverage.

It was not typical of the sounds going around at the time. Many bands had opted for a more raucous guitar sound, like that demonstrated by The White Stripes or Von Bondies. What The Shades came up with would not be far removed from what The xx did on their own debut album, six years later.

When you look at the dynamics of any band, everything is weighed against obtaining commercial success. It is not even artistic friction – it often comes down to making some sort of financial return. The more people you have in a band, the more delicately balanced that dynamic becomes. This is not to say that either of these factors contributed to The Shades's demise. They do, however, impact upon the everyday existence of any band.

Explosive managed to find a subtle sound that seduced you rather that slapped you across the face. One of the striking things about it is that it sounds like it cost a fortune to record. The reality is a different story; it was a case of imagination over finance.

The album was made available as a free download last year, introducing it to a new audience. Let's not get into the contentious debates surrounding downloading or streaming, or issues concerning physical format. Surely, at this stage, the most important thing is that people hear the music?

I have listened to *Explosive* so many times in the years since The Shades released it. It would have been easy to see it do very well for the band, and the fact that it did not have more of a commercial impact must have definitely shortened their career altogether. While they did put out an EP a year later, it would have been fascinating to see what they could have come up with on a second album.

That, unfortunately, did not happen, but one indication of what direction The Shades might have is revealed in one of their offshoots. Graham White formed Freezer-Room a couple of years later. They captured much of the magic that The Shades propagated, and added a more electronic edge.

There are many criteria that albums must satisfy to feature in a book such as this, and *Explosive*, in all its subtle beauty, meets just about all of them. If you have not heard it, it is an album that is certainly worth the time to seek out.

For the Record

By Graham White

I will always be very proud of The Shades's album. I grew up with Ray Scannell in Monkstown, County Cork, and we spent our teenage years in his family's basement writing songs. Ray is an amazing piano player and vocalist. I was messing around with a sampler and keyboards. We were both going to Sir Henry's every weekend, and it was a great time in Cork to be involved with music.

Explosive was the result of a couple of years working together from an early age, jamming with a bunch of great musicians. To this day, I always enjoy playing it for people who have not heard the album. Every song has a story in the music and the lyrics!

Sleeve design by Mr Fork and Mr Who, art by Mr Who

Tracklist

1	Taking My Time		6	Tripping Tune
2	Explosive		7	Breathe
3	Shine On		8	How To Find A Hobbo
4	Cider Horizon		9	Out On A Limb
5	Made In Five Minutes		10	Long Time

EVERYBODY IS FANTASTIC

Microdisney, Rough Trade, 1984

There have been many great song writing partnerships throughout the existence of this thing we know as music. From Lennon and McCartney to Pharrell Williams and Chad Hugo, Robert Forster and Grant McLennan to Carol King and Gerry Goffin; these combinations have amassed multi-millions in sales and, in the process, their work has reached an immeasurable number of individuals.

One inspired partnership that you do not hear about as much that of two gentlemen by the names of Cathal Coughlan and Sean O'Hagan. As members of Microdisney, they brought some unusual shades and textures to what was often a glaringly neon 1980s. You could say that they were different from all of their contemporaries at the time, but the truth is that they would have been unique for any decade that they had existed in.

For a debut album, *Everybody Is Fantastic* has many of the qualities that one would associate with a third or fourth studio venture. It is a solid unit of songs with a distinct identity, not to mention an eccentric charm. Many people will tell you that later albums, like *The Clock Came Down The Stairs*, are better and, in truth, they are probably right.

It is Microdisney's work following this debut album that got the majority of praise, but it is the foundation that this album established that helped them develop. Take, for example, a song like 'Sleepless': it shows its age, yet the fundamentals of a great pop tune are captured in it. The same can be said of 'Before Famine', which encapsulated the kind of sound that the band would come to be known for in later years.

Every now and then you hear of people who have just been introduced to Microdisney, usually through the songs 'Town To Town', 'Birthday Girl', or 'Singer's Hampstead Home'. It is then that they can go back through what the band did, over a creatively rich but relatively short career. It is only the opinion of one, but if you want to work your way through the catalogue of music that Coughlan and O'Hagan made as part of Microdisney, as well as their subsequent solo careers and differing paths with The Fatima Mansions and The High Llamas, the best place to start is at the beginning.

For the Record

By Cathal Coughlan

On (what felt like) a boiling-hot July afternoon in 1983, Sean O'Hagan and I got off the train in Paddington Station. This was the big time: burnt bridges back home, giant vaulted imperial ceiling above us now, all of that.

Our previous single had had a lot of play in the evenings on BBC Radio 1, mainly on John Peel's show. This took us from two-piece-with-a-rhumba-machine ridicule (in Cork, some folks still speak with derision of our 'Hall & Oates delusion') to the point where people wanted us to make an album.

We recorded from August to early September, in a converted chapel near the mythic Ladbroke Grove (of Roeg, Astral Weeks and Moorcock fame). The owner was the ex-drummer of Curved Air, the manager was a very nice lady, and the whole thing was way more salubrious than the places we'd worked in previously, or (mostly) afterwards.

The drum machine still sounds like shit, and most of the songs flail about without getting to any point, melodically, dynamically or lyrically. The 'personal' aspect of most of what I wrote is artless fabrication and self-absolution – there is neither wit nor underlying honesty, with the possible exception of 'Dolly'. It's a shame it took an LSD-driven confrontation with myself to produce it. The lyrical results are probably obtuse to most ears, but it has something lacking elsewhere in my part of the work from that time.

It's not as bad, though, as some other things I've done. Without it, we wouldn't have gotten to the next point, which was much better, and so one must be thankful. It came out, and some people thought we fancied ourselves a sort of Steely Dan. Fuck them. And the drum machine.

Album sleeve produced by Barker Dave at Assorted Images

Photography by Richard Haughton

Tracklist

1	Idea	8	Sun
2	A Few Kisses	9	Sleepless
3	Escalator In The Rain	10	Come On Over And Cry
4	Dolly	11	This Liberal Love
5	Dreaming Drains	12	Before Famine
6	I'll Be A Gentleman	13	Everybody Is Dead
7	Moon		

FAR FROM REFUGE

God Is An Astronaut, Revive Records, 2007

When most people think of instrumental music, they conjure up images of being stuck in a lift listening to music that is so bland it offends just about everyone. There is that kind of instrumental music, but also many other kinds which, in most cases, have more of an edge!

God Is An Astronaut have made numerous albums, all of which are highly recommended. Their debut *The End of the Beginning* was a statement, as was its follow-up, *All Is Violent All Is Bright*. However, it was their 2007 album *Far from Refuge* that gave us a much broader picture of what kind of band they were, and would go on to develop into.

Listening to it over the years has given me a much greater appreciation of what GIAA achieved with it. At the risk of sounding overly poetic, listening to *Far from Refuge* is like looking at a slow-moving river; all seems calm on the surface, but you soon realise that there are many undercurrents and submerged activity taking place.

Some of the tracks that feature on this album are still the foundation of most of the God Is An Astronaut live shows. 'Radau', 'Tempus Horizon' and 'Sunrise In Aries' are three of the most brutally beautiful pieces of music that you may ever hear.

In a review published on ultimate-guitar.com in June 2007, the reviewer says: 'Despite this lack of mainstream appeal, the record exudes a fantastically positive vibe. It's a happy journey, and this is something which marks a departure from earlier works that felt a lot more nostalgic. Tracks such as "Grace Descending" create moods that translate very well indeed to a live setting.'

Having seen the band play a lot over the past twelve years, I can begin to understand the high standards that they place on themselves. If that's the case for live shows, it's not hard to appreciate how intensely hard they work to produce songs in studio.

Not that they'd want to, but God Is An Astronaut will never rid their sound from having that metal undertone. There is menace mixed with the melody, which creates an unease that hooks in the same way that a thriller keeps you on the edge of your comfort zone.

Someone once asked me how I'd describe what GIAA sound like. What I came up with isn't entirely accurate, but it might give you an idea of their power and pedigree: imagine Tool playing Edvard Grieg's 'In the Hall of the Mountain King', and you're not a million miles off.

The Wicklow band have made better albums since *Far from Refuge*, but it remains a staggeringly impressive document of a band hitting their stride. It also set a standard that they have maintained ever since.

For the Record

By Niels Kinsella

Far from Refuge was in part influenced by Pink Floyd's *Live in Pompeii*, which Lloyd brought to our attention. We wanted to create a more live sounding album, but still have experimental sounds and ideas.

I remember recording some of the bass parts in the living room with a huge SVT bass amp – the place was vibrating with plaster falling from the ceiling. As a whole it was the first album that we really performed and wrote as a band with all three of us contributing equally.

We are still very proud of the *Far from Refuge*, and it stands as a unique sounding album in our catalogue. We remastered all of our albums in 2011 and some of the albums were also mixed as part of the process, but *Far from Refuge* was one of the albums that still has the original mixes. We didn't feel the need to change anything.

Artwork and design by Niels Kinsella

Tracklist

1	Radau		6	Darkfall
2	Far from Refuge		7	Tempus Horizon
3	Sunrise in Aries		8	Lateral Noise
4	Grace Descending		9	Beyond the Dying Light
5	New Years End			

FEEL NO SHAME

Aslan, EMI, 1988

There are certain artists and certain songs that become knitted into the very culture of their country of origin. Aslan, and, specifically, their ageless anthem 'This Is', fits this description perfectly. If you looked at radio airplay statistics in Ireland, the song would easily be in the Top Five Most Played Songs over the past three decades.

The year 1988 was the year that Aslan were forecast to attain global stardom. The fact that this did not happen is a shame, but, in another way, it is also a blessing. There are few bands that remain a solid unit after the white-knuckle ride to worldwide success. The countless tours, the blurred lines between artistic versus commercial pressure and the numerous fame-related frustrations can make things complicated. After their break-up in the late 1980s, Aslan regrouped and went on to become one of the most enduring and loved Irish acts ever. Would they have had such a lengthy career had things exploded for them with *Feel No Shame*? No one can definitively answer that, but it is less likely.

As an album, *Feel No Shame* marries songs with choruses that are hard to forget, revealing a tender side that the band would later be renowned for. From the frantic pace of 'Loving Me Lately' to the concluding track, 'Book Of Life', Aslan made their intentions clear, with a debut album that matched the best of what was being released internationally at the time.

When the album was released, everything suggested that the band's steep upward trajectory would continue at the brisk pace that it had gathered. Their tours across Europe and the US had exceeded expectation, and reviews of *Feel No Shame* had been very favourable. The circumstances of how things unravelled must have been extremely hard for all involved. Much of it played out in public, too, which could have only added to the torment.

Listening to *Feel No Shame* over the years revealed a number of things. Here were a band in their prime, waiting to showcase themselves to as wide an audience as possible. It became a reference point for future albums, serving as a compass, and setting a high standard that they needed to match with everything that followed.

They made it clear that they hadn't reformed to live off their past and, after they reformed in 1993, were a new band for many younger fans. New songs such as 'Where's The Sun' and 'Crazy World' mixed well with their old songs. To this day, there's a special energy that engulfs a venue when the band plays 'This Is'. The song connects with people as much as it did when it was written in the 1980s.

In a sense, it is strange writing about *Feel No Shame*, even though it has been an album that I have written about many times before. It is strange in the sense that it is such a fixture in Irish music's past, but is still very much a part of many people's present. You could say that it has received its fair share of praise, but, for the album that it was in 1988, and for what it still is today, it never came close to reaching the horizon that it should have ventured far beyond.

For the Record

By Billy McGuinness and Christy Dignam

When it came to recording our debut album, *Feel No Shame*, there were two conditions that we insisted on. The first was that we record the album in Ireland, and the second was that we wanted Mick Glossop to produce it. The reason to record in Ireland was because we were sick of Irish bands who, as soon as they got a record deal, would get out of the country, and deprive the Irish music industry of much needed revenue. We wanted to put something back. Even to this day, we have recorded all of our albums and videos here.

The reason we insisted on Mick Glossop was that he had just finished The Waterboys's *This Is the Sea*, and it sounded magnificent. In the middle of recording the album we heard that David Bowie was going to play at Slane. We are all big Bowie fans, so you could not believe the buzz in the studio when we heard we had got the support.

I remember recording 'This Is' and Mick Glossop saying: "That song will always be played on radio." He was right; here we are, thirty years on, and it still features in polls for the best Irish song ever. Last year, U2 recorded a version of it.

Feel No Shame remains an album that we are very proud of. Even now, we still perform songs from it in the set. 'Don't Look Down On Me', 'This is' and 'Pretty Thing' are being listened to by people who probably were not even born when the album was released!

Photography by Amelia Stein and design by Steve Averill

Tracklist

1	Loving Me Lately		7	Please Don't Stop
2	Pretty Thing		8	Down On Me
3	This Is		9	Sands Of Time
4	Been So Long		10	Feel No Shame
5	The Hunger		11	Book Of Life
6	Heat Of The Cell			

THE FUTURE IS MEDIUM

Compulsion, One Little Indian, 1996

Who is this band? Where are they from? These are some of the questions that I remember asking myself when I first heard them. It was a track from their 1994 debut album, *Comforter*, called 'Mall Monarchy' that I heard through a friend in college, and it rocked like a . . . well, you know the rest.

It was pre-internet era, or, at least, was not widely available, so all you had to go on were magazines and, in Ireland, Dave Fanning's radio show on 2fm. Someone told me that Compulsion were from Chicago, so I believed them.

Word of their second album's imminent release, *The Future Is Medium*, was big news for me. I was doing reviews for a local newspaper and a show on a local radio station, so I asked the record label for a copy of the album to review and play. They said no!

As an album, *The Future Is Medium* is a juggernaut of a record. It is jammed with songs that I truly believed would be massive. In my mind, this was an album to sit alongside *In Utero* by Nirvana, the Sex Pistols's *Never Mind The Bollocks* . . . and the masterful self-titled debut from Rage Against The Machine.

It was not just straight up rock either, these guys were quirky. Their song titles had humour sewn into them. The album opened with 'All We Heard Was a Dull Thud', joined by 'They're Breeding The Grey Things Again' and 'Lost On Abbey Road'.

Allmusic.com gave it a three-and-a-half out of a five-star rating. In a review on the site, it commented: 'One of the more interesting albums of the year, it is sort of like the Guided by Voices LPs, in that it covers so much territory and gathers a sort of mad momentum with its different converging styles. And certainly, *Future* is chock-full of hot moments, such as "Juvenile Scene Detective". Don't miss; even if the import route turns out to be the only one.'

One of the things that can alienate music from what we call 'the mainstream' is if it is perceived as too complex, or if it lacks those pop-tune ingredients. *The Future Is Medium* is like a wave of guitar terror, but it is tempered with clever and catchy songwriting. You actually do not come across it done as well as this very often.

This was to be Compulsion's second and final album, and it still pisses me off that they did not get to make more. Everything about it screams huge commercial potential – it is just such a shame that it was not realised. Listening to it at high volume works best, but don't expect to maintain a warm relationship with your neighbours.

For the Record

By Jacknife Lee

I do love *The Future Is Medium*. Its failure to connect in Britain knocked the wind out of me. It was a time of self-love there, with Britpop and Blair and football, and we were not a welcome addition to the party. In the US, we were supposed to be the next Nirvana (Bush did that), but the label thought the record was too European, and dropped us. Rightly so – we were contrarians and self-saboteurs. That was the indie in us.

Design by Garret Lee and Andrew Sutton at ThinkElectric.com and photography by Mike Diver

Tracklist

1 All We Heard Was a Dull Thud
2 Question Time for the Proles
3 Juvenile Scene Detective
4 It's Great
5 They're Breeding The Grey Things Again
6 Fast Songs
7 Western Culture Collector
8 Happy Monsters
9 Belly Laugh
10 Is This Efficient Living?
11 Down The Edifice
12 Happy Ending
13 Burst
14 Lost On Abbey Road
15 Spotlight Into Space
16 Me

A GRAND LOVE STORY

Kid Loco, East West/Yellow Productions, 2007

I still vividly remember the circumstances of when I first heard this album. It was exactly two years after the album had been released, and I was working in a record store at the time. I was in the middle of serving a customer, when a friend who I was working with said, 'Listen to this, you'll love it.' They were right – I did!

The opening and title track to Kid Loco's *A Grand Love Story* came drifting through the speakers, and completely threw me off from what I was doing. I could have handed the customer back the entire contents of the till for all I knew (note to employer: I can assure you that I did not!).

Like many great albums, *A Grand Love Story* does not stick to any sort of blueprint or previously trodden path. The sampling is subtle, and the impact that the tracks have on you is almost contradictory; they grab your attention with a snappy vigour, yet, simultaneously, have you gliding along in a trance, like bubble. How does that sound, you might ask? It sounds like *A Grand Love Story*.

Katrina Mitchell's vocals on 'Love Me Sweet' have a hypnotic tone, like that Hope Sandoval, of Mazzy Star. Combined with the stylish instrumentation and tune, this track alone never fails to evoke curiosity. But perhaps the real magic of this album can be explained by the sleeve notes: 'Produced and mixed with incomparable taste and perception by the still handsome but real stoned Kid Loco at the Lafayette Velvet Basement.'

Joking aside, Kid Loco (whose real name is Jean-Yves Prieur, and who hails from from Belleville, Paris) made the sophisticated sound natural and accessible. You could categorise what he had done on *A Grand Love Story* as lounge, which may set off alarm bells in people's minds. Does it vanish into the obscure, where only a select few can navigate their way to? Is it highbrow, too clever for its own good? The answer is that it cannot be found guilty on either of these.

Getting a reference point for this album is like drawing up a weekly shopping list; it is lengthy and, inevitably, you'll forget some of the key ingredients. There are two particular albums that always stick out when I hear *A Grand Love Story*: Air's *Moon Safari* and *Fresh* by Sly & The Family Stone. Musically, these are three very different pieces of work, but there is a staunch individuality and subtle power to each, that draws them together.

There is a school of thought that anyone can write one good song. But to put together an album like this involves a great deal of skill and vision, so it is not the case that this was a fluke. Since the release of *A Grand Love Story*, Kid Loco has produced work for Jarvis Cocker, and a particularly strong album called *Too Late To Die Young*, for UK band Departure Lounge, in 2002. His remixing résumé is also impressive, but, as yet, he has not made something quite like his 1997 masterpiece.

Sleeve design by Benoit Gibert, graphic design by R. Pépin

Tracklist

1 A Grand Love Theme
2 Relaxin' with Cherry
3 Love Me Sweet
4 The Bootleggers
5 Calling Aventura King
6 Sister Curare
7 She's My Lover (A Song For R.)
8 She Woolf Daydreaming
9 Alone Again So
10 Cosmic Supernatural

THE GUNNER AND THE GHOST

BlackboxRed, Geertruida Records, 2013

Every now and then you come across music that is so intense and immediate that it is like an aural left hook. BlackboxRed have been constructing their own brand of noise for a number of years, and perfectly captured what they are about on their 2013 debut album, *The Gunner and The Ghost*.

Far from relying on an arsenal of guitars, the duo (Eva van Netten and Stefan Woudstra) do just fine by themselves. They are from Leeuwarden, which is situated in the north of the Netherlands, and is the capital of the Dutch province of Friesland.

It was in January 2011 that I accidentally saw them play at the Eurosonic festival in Groningen in the Netherlands. It was coming towards the end of a long day, and I was walking back to my hotel after finishing one of 2fm's annual broadcasts from the festival.

I passed by a bar where a few people were coming out, and caught the blast of something that I could not resist investigating further. The first thing that hit me when I walked through the door was the condensation falling from the ceiling. The place was packed, and the duo on stage were incredible. Eva had an undeniable presence on vocals, and Stefan was giving the drums a beating of John Bonham-like proportions.

Fast forward two years, and BlackboxRed were recording their debut album in a haunted 17th century mansion in the north of France. After being snowed in for much of their stay, they left with an album of intense and ferocious beauty. They captured the isolation of the location, along with an unease that is hard to put into words.

Bands like Nirvana, The Doors and The Melvins all have something in their music that is best described as incendiary. There is an initial sense of menace, and then a calm moment before everything explodes onto another octave. BlackboxRed have something quite similar happening in *The Gunner and The Ghost*, which keeps you guessing.

You get the impression that BlackboxRed were prepared to record this album with an open mind. From a live point of view, they do not let any so-called rules stand in their way. There is no messing about: the songs are straightforward, but incredibly intense.

'Howling Wolf' and 'The Wild' and 'Stripper' are three of the tracks that stand out in their live set, and they have captured them well on *The Gunner and The Ghost*. Something particularly noticeable about the album is that it sounds like they have recorded everything at maximum volume, which suits the songs perfectly. Certain music is made to rattle your brain, and there are few duos that can do this better than BlackboxRed!

For the Record

By Eva van Netten

We don't like recording studios; they make us feel uncomfortable. We can't build anything from a bunch of million-dollar microphones all set up and ready to go. We want bricks and cracks and fuses that break when we make too much noise, forcing us to record in the dark. We want struggle and a challenge. That is exactly how this record was created.

In March 2013, we went to an idyllic place in northern France called Bival – a big, haunted 17th century house. We spent nine days in there, making music twenty-four-seven. For four of those days we were snowed in, with the closest village eight kilometres down the road. It was a true survival challenge, which also gave us a lot of time to spend on writing and recording. Inspired by the isolation and cold, we came to a sound on this album that we call 'ghostgrunge'.

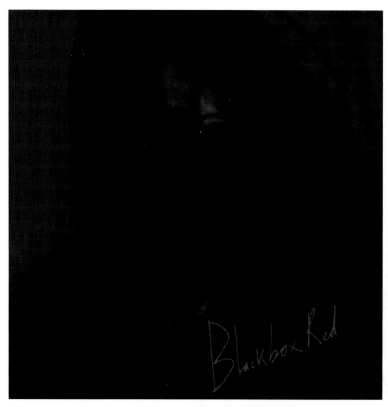

Photography by Milena Wilkat and design by Diggy Smerdon

Tracklist

1	Victim I		7	Marauder
2	Stranger		8	Frances
3	Stripper		9	Louisiana
4	The Wild		10	The Swallow
5	Hungry For Bones		11	Mist
6	Howling Wolf		12	Victim II

HAUNTED LIGHT

Cap Pas Cap, Skinny Wolves, 2010

There is more than a touch of mystery – and even mysticism – about *Haunted Light* from Cap Pas Cap. It is an album that I played constantly on my radio show when it came out, but knew very little about the band. Even now I still do not know that much, and, in some ways, that is the way I would like it to stay.

If you were being unfair, you would categorise this as an alternative rock or indie album (whatever 'indie' means anymore). In actual fact, *Haunted Light* does a lot more than the first listen will tell you. 'Friends' is the kind of synth-pop tune that, if manipulated, could pass as something that Lady Gaga would put to tremendous effect. The band will likely disagree with this unexpected compliment!

'Hearts' still ranks as one of the most enchanting tracks that I have ever had the pleasure of hearing. 'We can learn a lot from fighting time, but when all the clocks stop it's not fine.' The lyrics always make me stop what I am doing and become reflective. I am not even sure whether that is their aim, but that is the effect.

In his 'Top 50 Irish Bands right now' article in *The Irish Times* in 2010, Jim Carroll wrote: 'Dublin band Cap Pas Cap play a hugely alluring post-everything game. There have only been a handful of releases to date, but each one has seen them pulling new shapes from the bag. Their best moment to date was last year's hypnotic and spacey We Are Men single on the Skinny Wolves label, a pointer to the new-wave-no-wave-what-wave terrain they're calling their own. Cap Pas Cap's debut album should be one of this year's highlights.'

As so many excellent Irish albums are, this was produced by Stephen Shannon. Whatever he does to the music that he works with, it quite simply works. Streamlines is not the right description, but he leaves the music with its edge, sending it – flowing – in the right direction.

The reference points for Cap Pas Cap are often the same: Yeah Yeah Yeahs, Ladytron and, at times, Arcade Fire. But they don't tell the whole story. As you move further into this album, the visual power of the songs really takes hold. As bizarre as it may sound, they are like the soundtracks to great short films that you have not yet gotten to sit down and enjoy.

Most people who are into music have their sacred list of albums and, over the last number of years, *Haunted Light* has worked its way onto mine. It joins Jeff Buckley's *Grace*, Led Zeppelin *III*, U2's *Achtung Baby* and a number of other albums featured in this book.

It is an album that gives one contradictory feelings – you grow close to it, yet it has a distinctly isolated feel. How can that be? *Haunted Light* always leaves me with a number of questions, but long may they remain unanswered.

For the Record

By Grainne Donohue

Haunted Light was our debut album, and over a year in the making. The songs were developed in the practice room and through live shows over our previous years together, first as a four-piece, and then as three.

The recording process lent them an unintentionally darker intonation, which may have been a result of the first attempts at recording in an eerily large, empty house in Ashtown, and then ultimately finishing in Stephen Shannon's studio in west Dublin. This splintered process was hard on us as a band. We were eager to release our debut, and wanted to control and develop the live sound as much as possible.

Ultimately, though, the mood of the band and the frustrations felt within were perfectly captured in the ten songs that became *Haunted Light*. The band split some time later, but this still stands as a perfect document of the good times and memories we shared as Cap Pas Cap.

Photography by Eoin Williams

Tracklist

1	Mirrors	6	Can't Say
2	We Are Men	7	Brand New Town
3	Ship Shadow	8	Y Lies
4	Friends	9	Save Our Sights
5	Hearts	10	Night Tribes

2 HELL WITH COMMON SENSE

Power Of Dreams, Polydor Records, 1992

For a long time, the letter 'U' and the number '2' were never far away when Power Of Dreams were the topic of conversation. It was not because the two bands sounded alike; it simply came down to people looking for 'The Next Big Thing', or 'The Next U2'. In the late 1980s and early 1990s, these infamous phrases were thrown in the direction of many young Irish bands that showed potential. What started out as a compliment turned into a millstone, and unnecessary pressure.

By the time they were ready to record their second album, Power Of Dreams had developed from being a promising young act into a group that could make a major international impact. They had released a number of well-received singles and EPs, along with a very strong debut album, *Immigrants, Emigrants & Me*. One of their songs even featured in a scene in *Eastenders*, and another on *Football Focus*.

Where *Immigrants, Emigrants & Me* won people's affection in its youthful energy and vigour, *2 Hell With Common Sense* was the sound of Power Of Dreams hitting their prime. The songs had a hunger and urgency about them that made a lot of what was around at the time sound, by comparison, translucent and flimsy.

This was a million miles away from 'grunge', and a substantially removed from defining albums like *Songs Of Faith And Devotion*, *Achtung Baby* and *Screamadelica*. Power Of Dreams had more in common with acts like House Of Love than with any of the above.

Having an introduction that gets your attention is important on any album, and the first three songs on *2 Hell With Common Sense* are absolute killers. It opens with 'Rain Down', and then moves to the explosive 'There I Go Again', followed by 'On and On'. These were pop tunes with an edge, demonstrating a confidence mixed with determination to move on to bigger things.

Many Irish bands at the time did not relocate to the UK, but Power Of Dreams based themselves over there at that time. Their touring schedule, prior to recording *2 Hell With Common Sense*, was non-stop. There is a saying that you have years to write your debut album, and months to write your second. This was true in Power Of Dreams' case, but there are few signs of haste when listening to it.

Music, at that time, was changing in a big way. The US grunge invasion was still at full strength, but electronic acts like The Shamen, Altern 8 and The Prodigy were beginning to make a significant impact. This electronic influence is evident on *2 Hell With Common Sense*; it is guitar music, with sub-bass from a club lurking in its midst.

This is an album that has always been overshadowed by their debut. Power Of Dreams had more success and recognition with *Immigrants, Emigrants & Me*, but *2 Hell With Common Sense* is more progressive, and more adventurous as a collection of songs. In many ways, the albums compliment one other: one is the sound of a young band's excitement for adventure, while the other is a more rounded, experimental group, crafting some of their defining songs.

For the Record

By Craig Walker

For the six-month period that we spent recording the album, the band lived together in a house in north London – Monkees style! We recorded during the day, and at night embraced the hedonistic acid house scene that was exploding at the time.

There seemed to be landmark albums getting released every week: *Nevermind*, *Screamadelica*, *Laughing Stock*, *Loveless* – each had a unique influence on the album we were recording. It was a beautifully creative period for the band, and for music in general. It felt like anything was possible. I still get that feeling of possibility when I hear the album today.

Illustrations by Alan Carroll, photography by Huw Thomas, concept by Alan Carroll and Power Of Dreams, design by Chippy Minton

Tracklist

1	Raindown	7	Understand
2	There I Go Again	8	Slowdown
3	On And On	9	100 Seconds
4	She's Gone	10	Happy Game
5	Untitled	11	Metalscape
6	You Bring Me Flowers	12	Blue Note

HI-LO

The Walls, Earshot Records, 2000 (Second Edition 2004)

There are some songs that are stitched into a country's culture. The Stunning gave us two: 'Brewing Up A Storm' and 'Half Past Two'. But what happens after your popularity peaks? Do you carry on, or do you split and move on to the next thing?

All sorts of stories started circulating after The Stunning broke up. The main one was that Joe and Steve Wall had moved to London and become a 'dance act'. These were the days when any music that had the faintest trace of anything electronic in it was labelled dance music.

This turned out to be partially true – the Wall brothers had reinvented themselves, and had a new crop of songs awaiting us. The first was a single, 'The Night I Called It A Day', and proved quite a starting point.

Hi-Lo was a departure from what everyone knew of Joe and Steve, yet it is one that sounds perfectly natural. Their ability to pen quality songs had not diminished, they just changed the way they went about making their music. Rather than make them conventional pop or rock tunes, they messed about with them and gave them a new identity. You could say that it sounded like they were remixing their own work, and, in a sense, they were.

Everything about this album was the sound of the present. 'Broken Boy' is a track that is as instant as anything that you will hear from anyone. A touch of Beck, but mostly Walls, it goes: 'Sold my 750, sold my bass guitar, and then when I had nothing, I sold my daddy's car . . . ' It combines clever lyrics with a tune that bounces around your mind for hours after hearing it.

In retrospect, you could hear the Wall brothers leaning this way as far back as when they released 'Heads Are Gonna Roll' and 'Tightrope Walker' as singles with The Stunning. Other tracks that really stand out on *Hi-Lo* are 'Bone Deep', 'Get Wild', 'Earthling' and the album's opener, 'Some Kind Of A Girl'.

'Something's Wrong' is more of a straight-up ballad that sits midway through the album (when you are listening to it on its original CD format), and draws in those – perhaps more conventional folk – that were not quite sure whether they were enjoying the proceedings.

This album definitely is not The Stunning II. It is a different chapter to a different story. The best parts of *Hi-Lo* still sound strong after the passing of years. This is the true test for music. That spark and energy that The Walls bring to their live shows is encapsulated perfectly over the thirteen tracks of *Hi-Lo*. Your own introduction or revisit is in order very soon.

For the Record

By Steve Wall

The Walls take years to make an album. Circumstances always seem to conspire to trip us up, and each record becomes a bit of a saga. After The Stunning split in 1994, Joe and I started writing new songs in a home studio in Galway.

The Stunning's sound had become dated, and we wanted to try something new with The Walls. We started experimenting with samplers, sequencers and loops, combining these with organic sounds, like live drums, organ and guitars. Beck's 'Loser' was a big hit at the time, and we loved the way he blended hip hop loops with live instruments.

After a major label stint in London went askew, we moved to Dublin, where we started our own imprint, built another studio in a dingy basement, and got down to finishing our debut. We released a few singles, but nothing clicked with radio until 'Bone Deep' – the last track to be recorded.

When I listen to it now, I see a journey that took us from Galway to London to Dublin, and all the dreams, disappointments, frustration, elation and madness along the way. Basically, all the highs and the lows. When it came out in 2000 it was a bit of an anomaly, as the scene was mostly singer/songwriters and dance music. *Hi-Lo* is for people who like edgy guitars, good lyrics, hooks and melodies. People who own it say they keep going back to it. That is all that counts.

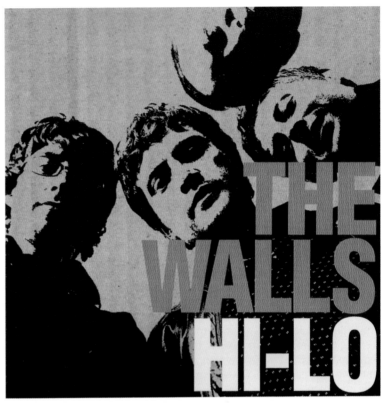

Sleeve design by Gareth Jones, band photo by Gareth Jones

Tracklist

1	Bone Deep	7	New Born Baby
2	Broken Boy	8	Earthling
3	Some kind of a Girl	9	Love Eluded Me
4	Chestnut	10	Hartland Road
5	Something's Wrong	11	One of those Days
6	February's Gone	12	If I had You + hidden track

I TO SKY

JJ72, Lakota Records, 2002

Don't be tempted to believe anyone that tries to tell you that JJ72 only released one good album. Yes, it is true that their self-titled debut was quite something, but so was their second, *I to Sky*, that arrived in 2002.

Hindsight shows mixed fortunes for JJ72. From the early highs to the extreme disappointment which led to their demise, it is a story that is unfortunate, but not unique, in the world of music. The Dublin three-piece had become the first Irish band, in quite a long time, to make a breakthrough in both the UK and Europe. They had made the cover of (the now defunct) *Melody Maker*, something that few Irish acts had ever managed to do.

'Formulae' was the first single released from the album, and it remains one of the band's best songs. It is not an anthem like 'Snow' or 'Long Way South', but it has an alt-pop undertone, much like Smashing Pumpkins did with '1979', and 'House of Jealous Lovers' from The Rapture.

The band received much love from the media for their debut album. But by 2002, when *I to Sky* arrived, part of that love had dissipated. The album did receive a lot of positive coverage, but some reviews went beyond the regular scope of what would be considered 'reviewing', underlying the fickle relationship between the music media and artists.

I to Sky illustrated both JJ72's improvement as a band and vocalist Mark Greaney's growth as a songwriter, singer and figurehead for the band. '7th Wave' was a prime example of the band's progression, and 'Oiche Mhaith' showed a softer, even sweeter side to JJ72.

Bringing up a band's age can sometimes imply that you're trying to make excuses for them. JJ72 have never needed any excuses or concessions, but the transition from a celebrated debut album to making its follow-up must have been daunting for a band that was still very young.

From listening to *I to Sky* then and now, you hear how the band revealed a much broader potential than you may have previously realised they were capable of. 'Nameless' and 'Always and Forever' illustrate how JJ72 were not a one-trick band. The frustrating thing, from a listener's point of view (and, no doubt, the band's), is that they didn't have the opportunity to show us how far they could go.

Hilary Woods left the band, and Sarah Fox joined Mark Greaney and Fergal Matthews. There was a third album recorded, but it was never released. The two singles – 'She's Gone' and 'Coming Home' – that did come out are excellent, which makes the story all the more disappointing.

Some have labelled *I to Sky* an ill-fated album, but it is a fine album from a band whose career ended years before it should have. There is little, if anything, on *I to Sky* that has dated much, which is in itself is a testament to how good this album really is.

For the Record

By Mark Greaney, from an interview in Hot Press, *September 2002*

I think this little baby is well able to speak for itself. Just with its eyes it can convince people that it needs to be hugged. I think this record will work on people who actually give it time. And the reason there's no doubts about the record is there's not one note on it I played and sang that I didn't mean, and that's the truth from start to finish. I think really very few songwriters would say that. On the first record there's a few songs I would throw away now without a second thought, but this record I think I'll have a place in my heart for it for a long time.

Artwork concept by Mark Greaney and design by Phil Lee

Tracklist

1	Nameless	7	Sinking
2	Formulae	8	7th Wave
3	I Saw a Prayer	9	Half Three
4	Serpent Sky	10	Glimmer
5	Always and Forever	11	City
6	Brother Sleep	12	Oíche Mhaith

KINGDOM OF GHOSTS

Humanzi, The First Born Is Dead Recordings, 2010

Humanzi never broke any new musical ground, but, at times, they did manage to make a few of their influences sound somewhat wimpy in comparison. Call what they did indie rock or electro rock, or whatever genre – it comes with a swagger and a slap in the face!

By the time the Dublin band got around to recording their second album, *Kingdom of Ghosts*, they had relocated to Berlin. Many bands that go through 'the major label machine' never manage to survive to record an album independently, or at least on their own terms.

Kingdom of Ghosts was the polar opposite of its 2006 predecessor – no hype, no fanfare and little financial backing, but yet a much more complete album. From being selected to being on the cover of the first issue of the sadly short-lived *NME Ireland* magazine, to being unfairly relegated to what you could call outsiders, you really get the impression that Humanzi had a point to prove. They retained the thunderous sound that was a striking characteristic on their debut album, *Tremors*, and added a serrated, even sinister edge. If *Tremors* could be described as having a bite like a snarling Rottweiler, then *Kingdom of Ghosts* was a pack of rabid wolves.

Perhaps this dangerous creative edge was borne out of frustration, but whatever the reason, it gave the album the kind of power that MC5 or The Stooges had in their prime. There is little that you could call self-conscious about the songs that Humanzi wrote at this time, but there is clearly a pop tune in the midst of the chaos and fury that is hard not to admire.

Berlin is a city that inspired many artists looking for change. U2 found it when they recorded *Achtung Baby* between 1990 and 1991, and David Bowie's Berlin experience inspired what's become known as 'The Berlin Trilogy': *Low*, *Heroes* and *Lodger*, between 1977 and 1979. Humanzi blossomed as a band, and made an explosive statement with the songs which made up *Kingdom of Ghosts*.

A review on State.ie fittingly captured *Kingdom of Ghosts*: 'Stronger and more assured than before, tracks like the Joy Division influenced "Black Sunrise" and the Primal Scream-esque "Neu Tune" show that the Dublin four-piece have learned the power in creating a menacing atmosphere with sparse arrangements.'

There is an impressive list of artists and acts that left their natives shores to find inspiration, or simply a new audience. In Humanzi's case, they didn't manage to find a wider audience, but they did prove their critics wrong in a striking fashion. Although the band never officially split, they all moved on to other projects and bands.

For the Record

By Brian Gallagher

Upon our red-eyed arrival to Schöenefeld airport, in the early morning light of 15 April 2007, Berlin looked beautiful. It was a feeling of magic and mystery. The majority of the second Humanzi record did not yet exist. The demos of the songs that had been written so far were in their infancy. We spent the coming summer and autumn on the outskirts of the city, writing what would eventually become *Kingdom of Ghosts*.

It was recorded in the first weeks of the following year, during what Berliners were calling a 'Siberian winter'. We had a lot of fun producing the album with Rob Kirwin in Radio Funk Haus (the huge abandoned complex of the old East German radio station). Looking back on the album, I think we successfully captured exactly where we were at as band. I feel it's a solid piece of work that said what we wanted to say, both musically and lyrically – 'Every year is getting shorter' but the songs remain the same.

Sleeve design by Gav Icon

Tracklist

1 Hammer	7 Straight Lines
2 Just Like Bukowski	8 Ill Repute
3 Bass Balls	9 Step Into The Shadows
4 Black Sunrise	10 Baby I'm Burnin'
5 Neu Tune	11 Shorter
6 Amsterdamaged	

KYLIE MINOGUE

Kylie Minogue, Deconstruction Records, 1997

It is hard to think of any part of Kylie's career in which you could legitimately say that she was struggling commercially. In the mid 1980s she was one of the onscreen soap darlings, from her part as Charlene in *Neighbours*. A bigger career beckoned, and she chose music as her vehicle to becoming a worldwide name.

As history will show, she has had huge success with more hit songs than even she can probably remember! In the early days of her music career, her teaming with Stock, Aitken and Waterman was an instant success. It started with 'I Should Be So Lucky', and mushroomed from there.

By the late 1990s, Kylie had changed as an artist. *Impossible Princess* (or *Kylie Minogue* as it was later renamed, following the death of Diana Princess of Wales) was a departure from the pure pop sound that had served her so well in years past. People started calling her 'Indie Kylie' during this period, which represented the sound of some of what she was doing. In truth, there is a lot more than guitar rumblings going on this album; you can clearly hear a curiosity with electronic music, and what was labelled trip hop at the time. While the overall style was not a complete axis change, it was obvious that she had moved on musically.

The singles taken from the album have much more of an edge than anything that she had released prior to this.

'Some Kind Of Bliss' (co-written by James Dean Bradfield of Manic Street Preachers) and 'Did It Again' are what you might call 'indie', while 'Breathe' has a much more laid back, electronic feel about it, which wasn't hugely dissimilar to what Olive and Morcheeba were doing at the time.

This album may seem like it stands out when compared with many of the others featured in this book. However, it is one that found its creator at that critical point in their career, where they embraced change and development. Generally, this either flies or loses you fans at an astonishing rate.

If one were to be cynical, you could say that this was Kylie trying to second guess what many of her fans from the early days were into at the time. You would have to be very cynical to think that though – it was her biggest musical risk, and had mixed fortunes in store for her.

Impossible Princess / Kylie Minogue is very much like Madonna's *Ray of Light*, in that it is a really impressive album, but one that is overshadowed by other parts of the artist's catalogue of music. You can say this about any artist, and often it is those areas where you find the most interesting and challenging music. This is certainly the case with Kylie – you may not rate it as her best album, but you would have to agree that it is her most diverse.

Sleeve by Farrow Design, photography by Stéphane Sednaoui

Tracklist

1	Too Far	7	Drunk
2	Cowboy Style	8	I Don't Need Anyone
3	Some Kind of Bliss	9	Jump
4	Did It Again	10	Limbo
5	Breathe	11	Through the Years
6	Say Hey	12	Dreams

LEGION

Bantum, Eleven Eleven Label, 2012

Most albums have a time and place attached to them, but when you listen to *Legion* from Bantum, it is hard to figure out where or when it is from. Is this the mark of a great album? Perhaps. It certainly fits the description of a timeless one.

The mysteriously named Bantum is actually a guy called Ruairi Lynch. Originally from Cork, he has been based in Dublin for many years. The migrated Rebel County man has come up with edgy material for a long time, but on this, his debut, he had clearly grasped everything that there was to making an album of serious quality. It can be difficult writing about albums and artists like this, because you can end up using far too many superlatives.

Bantum's selection of guests on the album is one of its strengths. Benni Johnston supplies gothic vocals on 'No More' and 'Send Me Under'. Elsewhere, Eimear O'Donovan brings a rare kind of joy and light to 'Oh My Days'. It always makes me wonder about the consideration – even torment – that an artist goes through when trying to figure out who should do which track. And then, if things do not work, do you just bin it and start all over again?

Legion is an album that knits together many sounds. In isolation, tracks, like 'Dice', 'Roll Pt. II' and the album's title track sound very different, but, put together, they make complete sense. Every band and every album is the sum of its parts, and the components that are placed together here are done so with precision.

In its review of *Legion*, *Totally Dublin* magazine agreed that: 'The album is a collection of sounds and influences that span many genres. Some parts hint at Lynch's rock influences as well as some beautifully crafted IDM sections, with elements that would not be out of place on a Death in Vegas or Tycho album.'

Without wanting to sound too muso, the binding compound on *Legion* is one that seems largely based around rhythm. Any of these tracks could have been international super hits in another lifetime! Bantum has made a set of pop songs, and then taken an angle grinder to them.

In the two years that led up to the release of *Legion*, Bantum had released a number of EPs and singles. Each one saw a steady progression from the other, so the expectation for his debut album was considerable, from those who had come across his music. It is evident that no one had higher expectations for this album than Bantum himself. Everything flows, and works wonderfully.

So, how am I doing on the superlative count? *Legion* is, in many ways, an individual album. Not in the sense that it was made by one guy (with the aforementioned guests), but in that it does not share many characteristics with much else that came out around that time. Yes, there are the reference points that you may pick up on, but as a piece of work, it stands by itself: impressive, and, in many ways, addictive.

For the Record

By Ruairi Lynch

The *Legion* album was tough work. Fittingly, it took nine months from conception to arrival, with relatively few bumps along the way. After work, I would usually be up into the small hours working on album tracks, but it was never a chore, and never will be. I'm proud of the fact that everybody who I collaborated with on the album can be counted as a friend – from vocals to artwork, drums, mixing and even getting it released. I would like to think that it will still sound good in years to come, not linked to any particular genre. *Legion* is the sum of many parts that each mean a lot to me.

Design by Shane O'Driscoll and photography by Sean Breithaupt

Tracklist

1. No More (ft: Benni Johnston)
2. Roll Pt. II (ft: Eimear O'Donovan & Owensie)
3. Oh My Days (ft: Eimear O'Donovan)
4. Legion (ft: Margie Lewis)
5. Pretty Words
6. Send Me Under (ft: Benni Johnston)
7. Dice
8. Pretty Little Interlude
9. Fedora (ft. Margie Lewis)
10. For the Day (ft. R.S.A.G)
11. Frenzy

MAGICO MAGICO

Lir, WAR/Vélo Records, 1993/1994

If you knew nothing about the history of Lir, and someone sat you down and played you *Magico Magico*, you'd be forgiven for thinking that this was one of the biggest records from the 1990s that you had forgotten about. Everything about this album lent itself to becoming something that people were going to be singing along to en masse.

There have been many twists and turns in Lir's story – unfortunate complications that would have been the undoing of any band – but many amazing moments too. There are two versions of *Magico Magico*, but this focuses on what is known as the US version. Both are wonderful albums, but this second version captures the band as they were when they played live at that time.

There are those albums that have that ingredient that makes you feel as if the artist is in the room with you. Lir captured this on many of their recordings, but never to quite the same extent as they did on this album. There are the obvious reference points, like Led Zeppelin, for instance, coupled with less evident ones, like Nick Drake and Sly & The Family Stone.

You may have heard of a description for music known as light and shade. *Magico Magico* encompasses this perfectly, as it slides from the big riffs of '3 Legged Guy' and 'New Song' into the beautiful balladry of 'Some Folk Are Truly Evil' and 'In A Day'. You cannot help but hear the sound of a band that knows its strengths and frailties all too well.

The chemistry that Lir had at this stage of their career was unmatched by any other band in Ireland. Their musicianship was exceptional, and when you add this to strong songs, the result, evident here, is stunning. The criticism at the time was that Lir didn't have enough songs that were deemed singles.

This critique never had any foundation, as their single 'In A Day' picked up a respectable amount of airplay on radio, and support from Irish TV shows 2TV and No Disco. The definition of what a 'single' was at the time was changing, as it does with every new decade and chapter in music. Bands like Nirvana and Pearl Jam had helped this a few years previously, as did The Stone Roses and Happy Mondays before them.

Constructing songs in a studio environment and playing them live is a very different process. Whatever balance that you have to maintain while in studio cannot be straightforward, but Lir managed it wonderfully well with *Magico Magico*, and their second album, *Nest*, released in 1995.

Songs like 'Traveller', and 'Dog Rhythms' had (to pardon the pun) a real bite to them, while 'Good Cake Bad Cake' and 'House of Song' were more subtle yet potent nonetheless. Did Lir realise that they had made an album of such quality at the time? Like so many bands, they probably weren't sure. If they ever did doubt this album's class, they should not have; it is, without any doubt, remarkable.

For the Record

By Dave McGuinness

The genesis of *Magico Magico* started in 1991, I guess, at a time when we were rehearsing five days a week. It is an album of fond memories and hard work, and of a time when music was changing.

It was released in 1994 on an Irish label (Vélo Records) and then later in the US (on the W.A.R. label), with some new tracks added. Some of the songs used were actually remixed demos or with overdubs added in. We worked with a great engineer, Aidan Foley, who was integral to the sound and chemistry of the recordings.

Twenty years later I had a listen, and it warms my heart to hear five young lads aged between twenty-two and twenty-five live their dream. It may not have sold, but it is there on tape for future listeners; Magico Magico indeed!'

Design and photography by Liam O'Callaghan, typeface by Enda Roche and colour separations by John Forde at State Of The Art

Tracklist

1	Traveller	7	The House of Song
2	Dog Rhythms	8	In a Day
3	Not to be Overlooked	9	Good Cake Bad Cake
4	New Song	10	Two Worlds
5	Some Folks are Truly Evil	11	In the Parlour
6	3 Legged Guy		

MONO BAND

Mono Band, gohan recordings, 2005

Regardless of what their critics say, The Cranberries's success is something that most people cannot even begin to grasp. They sold millions of albums and became household names; that is the dream for so many bands, isn't it? It is even the objective of many of those acts that claim that artistic and creative excellence is their sole aim.

After more than a decade of lengthy tours and recordings, The Cranberries took some time out from being The Cranberries. During that period, Noel Hogan undertook an unexpected project. Combining world music, alternative folk ballads and aspects of electronic music, he came up with Mono Band.

The opening track, 'Brighter Sky', still enlists curiosity to this day. It sounds like the offspring of a relationship between Led Zeppelin and Transglobal Underground, with some Tinariwen bloodlines thrown in there too. As is so often the case with albums, *Mono Band* is as diverse as the list of guests, but all makes sense as a sequenced unit.

Where and how Hogan found many of the contributors may well be quite a story in itself, but it is great for us that he did. Like Leo Abrahams's *The Unrest Cure* (which you'll read about elsewhere in this book), *Mono Band* has an identity that is as unique as a fingerprint. That is not to say that it is not without blemishes, but once you become familiar with it, you will realise that all its intricate lines and curves are perfectly formed and often fascinating. It is a vague way to describe music, but once you hear the adventure that is *Mono Band* you will understand the unusual description.

If you ever had any doubts about Noel Hogan's ability to put together music that can move you, his Mono Band guise will answer them emphatically. 'Waves', featuring vocals from Richard Walters, and 'Run Wild', with Alexandra Hamnede as guest, are what could be described as more conventional, guitar-based tracks that bring balance to an album that swings and weaves in unpredictable directions. The more adventurous side of *Mono Band* is evident in the aforementioned 'Brighter Sky', along with 'Miss P' and 'Invitation'.

Without trying to guess what Noel Hogan's hopes and objective were for this album, it is likely that matching his band's sales figures wasn't one of them. This allowed him to do things that people making albums with commercial targets would be hesitant to do. In every way imaginable, *Mono Band* is as free spirited as any collection of songs could hope to be. While there is great diversity, you never get the impression that these songs were simply placed together in an attempt at appearing random.

Much was made of the stylistic gulf between *Mono Band* and the material released by The Cranberries in previous years, but there are subtle links between some of the *Mono Band* and Cranberries tracks, like 'Daffodil Lament' and 'How'. Perhaps this is me looking for links, but a similar thought process can certainly be registered in areas of the two bodies of work.

In the context of what the music world has become, *Mono Band* is part of one of the infinite number of courses of a feast that you could never come close to finishing. It is, however, worth locating and sampling, as it has one of the most unusual tastes you will ever encounter.

For the Record

By Noel Hogan

In 2003, I began the Mono Band project. I had the idea of mixing guitar-based music with more electronic programme-based music together. After speaking with Cenzo Townsend, he suggested that I meet with a programmer called Mat Vaughan.

Over the following two years, Mat and I met several times, working on and expanding tracks that I had written. I was also very keen to work with as many vocalists as possible. After spending many years in one band, this idea seemed like a new and exciting way of working.

By 2005, I had built up a collection of songs with vocalists from various countries. These vocalists had all come from different musical backgrounds and, in this, varied the overall sound of the album.

Design and artwork by Candida Bhoopongsa

Tracklist

1	Brighter Sky	8	Hollow Man
2	Waves	9	Miss P
3	Why?	10	Indecisive
4	Run Wild	11	Release
5	Home	12	Coyotes & Helicopters (Hidden Track)
6	Invitation		
7	Crazy		

NEW ADVENTURES IN HI-FI

R.E.M., Warner Bros, 1996

R.E.M. have written many classic songs and sold many multi-million selling albums. Songs such as 'Losing My Religion', 'Orange Crush', 'Everybody Hurts' and 'What's The Frequency Kenneth?' are instantly recognisable classics that you've heard hundreds – if not thousands – of times over the years.

Their back catalogue of albums rivals that of any other artist or band: *Green* (1988), *Out Of Time* (1991), *Automatic For The People* (1992) and *Monster* (1994). You will rarely hear, however, anyone mention the album that they released in 1996. Or, at least, *New Adventures in Hi-Fi* is an unlikely contender to the first name that rolls off someone's tongue when R.E.M. are the topic of conversation.

It is often said that R.E.M. altered their course at this point in their career. This is both true and untrue. As different as *New Adventures in Hi-Fi* might be from *Monster*, that album – and their previous opus, *Automatic For The People* – is also radically different, so, it was more a time of constant change and tweaking for the Athens, Georgia band.

With *Monster* they had developed a rougher edge, upon which they continued with *New Adventures in Hi-Fi*. It was not a complete rebirth, like U2 had undertaken with *Achtung Baby*, but to call *New Adventures in Hi-Fi* R.E.M.'s own *Zooropa* or *Rattle & Hum*, would not be completely inaccurate.

There is no denying that the band took a more experimental approach with this album, but their flair for writing pop tunes was still very much evident. They showed us this on the wonderful *Electrolite*, and the anthem that never quite was – 'New Test Leper'.

New Adventures in Hi-Fi is the sound of a band wanting to challenge themselves, musically. Their four previous albums had been mammoth; songs like 'Out Of Time' and 'Automatic For The People' were MTV staples in the early 1990s.

Recording an album such as this, after the huge commercial success that they had enjoyed, was an incredibly brave step to take. When a successful band experiments with their sound it can provoke fairly divided reactions. Some bands do not alter what they do at all – they have a template from which they would not dare deviate. As hard as it must be for an artist to expand their creative boundaries, it is sometimes even harder for fans to accept or understand any kind of shift in style or sound.

When you look through the album's credits, you see where some of the songs were recorded:

'Zither' (Dressing Room – Philadelphia), 'Bittersweet Me' (Memphis Soundcheck) and 'Low Desert' (Atlanta Soundcheck). If the band were looking to shake off the perception that they were a giant hit-making machine, you would have to say that they succeeded.

When looking back over the band's long, distinguished career, it is a fair point to make that there has been little you could call 'conventional' about their career path. R.E.M. took steps that most 'big' bands would not have had the courage or insight to take. Rather than remaining static and living off songs from the past, R.E.M. made their bravest, most challenging album when they were at the very height of their popularity.

Packaging by Chris Bilheimer and Michael Stipe, printing by Ian McFarlane (WB Ally), and Tom Recchion (Marcel Duchamp)

Tracklist

The Hi Side
1 How the West Was Won and Where It Got Us
2 The Wake-Up Bomb
3 New Test Leper
4 Undertow
5 E-Bow the Letter
6 Leave

The Fi Side
7 Departure
8 Bittersweet Me
9 Be Mine
10 Binky the Doormat
11 Zither
12 So Fast, So Numb
13 Low Desert
14 Electrolite

NIGHT HORSES

Super Extra Bonus Party, Self Released, 2009

Could have and should have are phrases that come to mind when I think of Super Extra Bonus Party's second album. Was it a difficult second album to make? Who knows, but it is as complete an album as you're likely to find. It's packed with killer tunes, and the list of guests is pretty impressive too.

Night Horses followed SEBP's Choice Music prize-winning debut album, *Super Extra Bonus Party LP*, which they released in 2007. The Choice Music Prize has become an established part of Ireland's music calendar, awarding Irish artists on artistic merit. The much sought after award has been won by the likes of Two Door Cinema Club, Jape, Adrian Crowley and The Divine Comedy.

SEBP's debut album is like a burst of youthful energy, full of strong ideas and fearless experimentation. *Night Horses* impresses in a different way – it's just a far more potent outing that its predecessor. The band sound confident on this album, aware of the opportunity it is giving them of making a bigger name for themselves, both nationally and internationally.

If you wanted to highlight any serious flaws in *Night Horses*, you'd find it hard to isolate any legitimate ones. Here is something that you could put on at a party, and it would eradicate 99% of the whining to change the music. It jumps seamlessly from the tranquillity of 'Sonora', featuring Ann Scott, to the ferocity of 'Eamonn', which has vocals from MayKay of Fight Like Apes. The brilliant Cadence Weapon lends his rhymes to 'Radar', Heathers sound exceptional on 'Comets' and SEBP show a very different side with the traditional/folk-influenced track, titled '2'.

So, is this too much praise for an album that didn't command the commercial or critical acclaim that was expected by many? Not one bit. Comparing the band's two albums is slightly unfair, but let's do it anyway. As good as their first album, *Super Extra Bonus Party LP*, *Night Horses* is better in every way. It's an album that is as good as anything that LCD Soundsystem released. It would appeal to anyone who is a fan of what James Murphy and his LCD Soundsystem comrades created.

Super Extra Bonus Party gave us a concerto of sounds that outshone most of what was released in 2009. Here is a collection of songs that people will discover in coming years, and scratch their heads, wondering how this band didn't become one of those names of note. This tells you everything that you need to know about this band during a period when they were at their very best.

For the Record

By Cormac Brady

The recording sessions in Waterford, Dublin and Kildare brought *Night Horses* together and made it feel real for us. That's when we really shared ideas, made loads of noise and ultimately made a disparate bunch of demos feel like, and eventually turn into, an album. Before we started recording *Night Horses*, we were used to playing a few of the demos live and hearing them loud as fuck on massive sound systems. So when it came to recording, we re-amped practically every synth and left a lot of imperfections and distortions in the mix. We wanted everything to feel as real as possible.

As the deadline for mastering the album got closer, everything got a bit more frantic. At the same time, the album was becoming a lot clearer in our minds. There were so many recording sessions as a band or with the collaborators, cooked up in bedrooms and kitchens for hours on end, everyone wide-eyed at what was unfolding. When I think back on the ways we might have made things easier for ourselves, or on what we could have done differently, I think that to change a single aspect of what we did would be to have the album lose its charm. *Night Horses* is a perfect snapshot of where we were and the great times we had.

Illustration by Stephen Mooney, concept by Super Extra Bonus Party and Nialler9, design and layout by Nialler9

Tracklist

1 Superteam Go!
2 Radar (ft: Cadence Weapon)
3 Who Are You And What Do You Want? (ft: R.S.A.G.)
4 Thin Air (ft: Mr. Lif)
5 Night Horses
6 Comets (ft: Heathers)
7 Eamonn (ft: MayKay)
8 Do Inicio Ao Fim (ft: Rodrigo Teles)
9 Tea With Lord Haw Haw (ft: Captain Moonlight & White Noise)
10 Sonora (ft: Ann Scott)
11 2
12 Mark Huges Top Corner
13 A Midsummer Night's Cricket Disco

OCTOBER

U2, Island Records, 1981

The difficult second album is something that has reached an almost mythical status. Surely making your first, third or even twentieth is difficult, too? *October* was U2's second album, and it is one that always seems to get swept to one side when the topic of U2 is up for discussion.

Along with 1993's *Zooropa*, *October* rarely gets mentioned. It is a strange situation, because there are plenty of the band's finest moments captured over the eleven tracks. The title track is crushingly beautiful, melancholic and touching, while 'Gloria' is like a roar from the suburbs, that would later be heard in stadiums and arenas across the globe.

There are two things that you will hear from most people if you ask them about *October*. The first is, 'If U2 were a new act on a major label today, they would have been dropped after releasing that album.' The other is usually something about how run-down Dublin looked in the album photography.

The first claim is debatable, though it borders closer to likely rather than unlikely, while the second is unquestionably true. What is now known as Grand Canal Dock looks like a futuristic space city in comparison to Ringsend Basin, as it was called locally in 1981.

Artistically, *October* is one U2's most important album. It saw them face critical and commercial adversity, which they survived and learned from. The word 'expectation' looms over every U2 album following its release. This must have been quite a learning experience for a band at that stage in their career.

'Rejoice' has to be one of the best U2 songs that people never talk about. It has everything; the trademark guitar sound from Edge, rhythmic bounding from Larry, the steady bass line from Adam and Bono sounding as good as he ever has.

'Tomorrow' is drenched in Celtic mysticism, and features the exquisite uilleann pipes of Vincent Kilduff. The song builds into the kind of epic that made them not just a big band, but an important band. You could quite easily hear this song mixed in with the final tracks on *The Unforgettable Fire*, and it would fit in quality, and, in some ways, tonally.

There is no doubt that U2 have made better albums than *October*, but if there was one U2 album that you have never heard, the likelihood is that it is probably this. A large part of this is because of the mixed comments that have been made over the years. It is also a case of being overshadowed by some of the biggest albums of the 1980s, 1990s and 2000s, which came from a band that grew out of *Boy* in 1980, and *October* a year later.

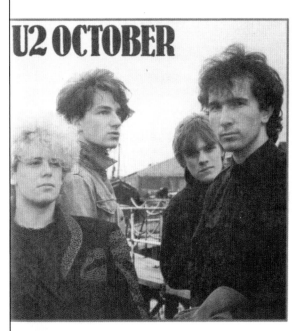

Sleeve layout by Rapid Exteriors, photography by Ian Finlay

Tracklist

1 Gloria
2 I Fall Down
3 I Threw a Brick Through a Window
4 Rejoice
5 Fire
6 Tomorrow
7 October
8 With a Shout
9 Stranger in a Strange Land
10 Scarlet
11 Is That All?

20 ODD YEARS

Buck 65, Warner/WEA, 2011

20 Odd Years is perhaps the most underrated album released in the last five years. This is a big statement, especially in the context of this book! It transcends genres, leaping from place to place, allowing your imagination to run free. While some albums profit on their predictability and reliability, *20 Odd Years* comes at you from a completely different angle. You simply do not know what Buck and his cast of guests will hit you with next.

Despite what the title may lead you to believe, *20 Odd Years* is not a retrospective of the Canadian artist's career, though it was released in the year that marked Buck 65's (real name Rich Terfry) twentieth year of making music. Many of the tracks that appeared on the album were released on a series of EPs the previous year. This sometimes suggests that the subsequent album sounds disjointed and segmented, but it is certainly not the case here.

Style-wise, Buck's back catalogue is varied; it shows all the hallmarks of a hungry creative soul. From 2002's *Square* (which features four long pieces of music) to his 2003 follow-up, *Talkin' Honkey Blues* (perhaps the most like *20 Odd Years*), he constantly develops as an artist. In 2011, his social commentary and off-beat sense of humour had never sounded better.

There is a touch of that late-night radio DJ about Buck 65's voice – easy on the ear, welcoming, and indelibly cool. It may come as no surprise to learn that he is actually also a DJ on Canada's CBS network. Comfort is not the right description, but you can hear that the verse rolls off his tongue, like many of the truly great and inspired vocalists and lyricists of the past.

When I brought a friend to see him when he was touring his *Talkin' Honky Blues* album, they remarked how, 'He sounds like Tom Waits rapping.' Accurate or not, this gravelly delivery has won him much favour over the last couple of decades. There is an intense attention to detail on the tracks that make up *20 Odd Years*, mixed with a playful sense of humour.

What guests like Gord Downie and Jenn Grant bring is that extra ingredient, to make what we call a pop tune. These two guests feature on two of the album's stand-out tracks: 'Whispers of the Waves' and 'Paper Airplane', respectively. Other tracks of note are the blues-infused disco anthem 'Zombie Delight', and the animated 'BCC'.

Calling what he does simply hip hop, would be like saying that what James Murphy did with LCD Soundsystem was 'simply electro'. *20 Odd Years* is an album that draws together sounds and influences from areas of music that you would not normally put together. Categorisations are not important here – all that you need to know is that *20 Odd Years* is a wonderful montage of sounds and tales.

For the Record

By Buck 65

I only realised that it had been twenty years since I had released my first album after finishing *20 Odd Years*. So, I just marked the occasion in the album title. I certainly was not trying to capture my previous twenty years of writing and recording.

My main concern was to record the most melodic songs I had made to that point. Melody, provided by the human voice, was of primary concern. I am not much of a singer myself, so I called in a bunch of talented friends to sing with me.

All of the songs on the album – with the exception of a handful – feature a guest vocalist. Beyond that, if there is a theme to the record, I suppose it is falling in love with my ex-wife: songs about us meeting, of being in a long-distance relationship, of her waiting for me at the airport when I would visit her and of her saying yes when I asked her to marry me. I think it is safe to say it was the happiest time of my life. I'm glad it was documented.

Sleeve design by Kate O'Connor and photography by Kate Greene

Tracklist

1 Superstars Don't Love
2 Gee Whiz (ft: Nick Thorburn)
3 Whispers of the Waves
(ft: Gord Downie)
4 Paper Airplane (ft: Jenn Grant)
5 Stop (ft: Hannah Georgas)
6 Zombie Delight
7 Tears of Your Heart
(ft: Olivia Ruiz)

8 Cold Steel Drum
(ft: Jenn Grant)
9 Who By Fire (ft: Jenn Grant)
10 She Said Yes
11 BCC (ft: John Southworth)
12 Lights Out
13 Final Approach
(ft: Marie-Pierre Arthur)

RADIODREAD

Easy Star All-Stars, Easy Star Records, 2006

Reggae and dub versions of Radiohead songs? Could this be true? Yes, and before you say anything, they're excellent. In truth, *Radiodread* is more about interpreting (or reinterpreting) the songs from Radiohead's iconic *OK Computer*. It sounds like a bizarre concept, but when you hear it, it makes absolute and complete sense.

It wasn't the first (or last time) that Easy Star All-Stars gave a classic album the reggae/dub treatment. In 2003 they reassembled Pink Floyd's *Dark Side of the Moon* with *Dub Side of the Moon*. They also gave The Beatles's *Sgt. Pepper's Lonely Hearts Club Band* (Easy Star's *Lonely Hearts Dub Band*, 2009) and Michael Jackson's *Thriller* (Easy Star's *Thrillah*, 2012) their patent makeover.

With a cast of guests including Toots and the Maytals, Kirsty Rock, Horace Andy and The Meditations, Easy Stars navigate the potentially treacherous waters of *OK Computer*. It follows the same track sequence, and it is in every way fascinating to hear how the songs can be broken down and rebuilt in a different form.

'Airbag' begins much as the original does, but then that familiar reggae beat kicks in, and transforms the song into something very different. It is later transformed into what is best described as a dub wig-out in 'An Airbag Saved My Dub'.

If *Radiodread* highlights anything, it is the true quality of what Radiohead gave us in 1997. You really begin to understand what an outstanding achievement *OK Computer* is. One of the hallmarks of truly great music is that it can be stripped right back, and still holds that special quality.

When you hear albums like this, it does raise the question of why so many cover albums are frowned upon. The word 'novelty' is always lurking somewhere nearby. Often, the assumption is that if it is not original material, then it is not a serious album. Think about that for a second, and you will realise how ridiculous it is to tarnish every cover album with the same slogan.

The album was praised by the members of Radiohead. In an interview with me in 2010, Philip Selway said, 'There are some amazing tracks on that; the version of "Let Down" is stunning.' If imitation is the greatest form of flattery, where does reinterpretation stand?

There is always a strange reaction from people when this is played in a club or bar – that expression of, 'I know this, but wait a minute, it sounds weird!' It is like seeing someone you know who has undergone a complete transformation; you have to double-take to realise who they are and what they have changed about themselves. Perhaps some of the Radiohead purists don't approve of this kind of 'sacrilege', but if it is good enough for the people who made the original album, then it is good enough for the rest of us.

Easy Star All-Stars were not the first reggae act to cover music from other genres, and they will not be the last. Many of the acts that are part of the Trojan Records roster have experimented in this way, as has Little Roy (with *Battle For Seattle*) and The Jolly Boys (the *Great Expectation* album), but there have been none better than Easy Star All-Stars and their *Radiodread* album.

For the Record

By Michael Goldwasser

Radiodread was a really interesting challenge. I had not felt a ton of pressure with *Dub Side of the Moon*, because it was the first album of its kind. *Radiodread* had the weight of *Dub Side*'s success, and we all know critics often look for a sophomore album to flop. So it made sense to choose an incredibly difficult album to do next!

Because of the success of *Dub Side*, it was easier to get guest vocalists. I had the pleasure of producing sessions with some of my favourite artists: Horace Andy, Morgan Heritage and Toots and the Maytals. I remember recording the melodica on 'Subterranean Homesick Alien' with my wife and mother-in-law having a conversation right outside my door – I half expected there to be snippets of their dialogue on the album!

To me, the album was a success: both fans and Radiohead liked it. Radiohead said they appreciated the attention to detail, which meant so much to me. While most people don't understand what goes into making an album, those guys do, so I really took the compliment to heart … sales be damned!

Artwork design and concept by Eric Smith, Lem Oppenheimer and Brian, art direction and design by Brian/Sensitive Guy Design and original painting by Tim Okamura.

Tracklist

1 Airbag (ft: Horace Andy)
2 Paranoid Android (ft: Kirsty Rock)
3 Subterranean Homesick Alien (ft: Junior Jazz)
4 Exit Music (For a Film) (ft: Sugar Minott)
5 Let Down (ft: Toots & the Maytals)
6 Karma Police (ft: Citizen Cope)
7 Fitter Happier (ft: Menny More)
8 Electioneering (ft: Morgan Heritage)
9 Climbing Up the Walls (ft: Tamar-kali)
10 No Surprises (ft: The Meditations)
11 Lucky (ft: Frankie Paul)
12 The Tourist (ft: Israel Vibration)
13 Bonus Tracks
14 Exit Music (For a Dub)
15 An Airbag Saved My Dub
16 Dub Is What You Get (Mad Professor/Joe Ariwa Mix) (Vinyl Only)
17 Lucky Dub A (Mad Professor/Joe Ariwa Mix) (Vinyl Only)

33 REVOLUTIONS PER MINUTE

Marxman, Phonogram/Talkin' Loud, 1993

33 Revolutions per Minute is one of those albums that is impossible to sit still to when listening. If you can imagine the sound of Public Enemy collaborating with Moving Hearts, you will have an idea of where Marxman were coming from.

The idea of fusing hip hop with traditional Irish music was not a new one in 1993, but nobody had managed to concoct something with this level of potency. This kind of experimentation had been attempted prior to this, but, with the exception of Scary Eire, the results had been somewhat underwhelming.

Formed in the late 1980s, Marxman was made up of four key members (Hollis Byrne, Stephen Brown, Oisin Lunny and DJ K One). Their debut album, *33 Revolutions per Minute*, saw them enlist names like Davy Spillane, James McNally and Sinead O'Connor, who delivered stunning vocals on the track 'Ship Ahoy'.

You can hear how this album connected with people through its clever lyricism, which was, at times, controversial. Their single 'All About Eve' bluntly dealt with domestic violence: 'She's got a bruise upon her pretty pretty cheekbone, I asked how she was doing over a cup of coffee, she said the bruise was caused by her stupidity.'

The use of the words '*Tiocfaidh ár lá*' as lyrics in the year 1993 was always going to unsettle and upset some people. It was clear that Marxman understood that hip hop had started as a form of protest, not just a genre around which to bend words, catchy hooks and beats. While the lyrics were never sexually explicit, the band did not struggle to express their views through the music on the album.

33 Revolutions per Minute was released in a climate where grunge and Garth Brooks were at their height, and US hip hop was being nurtured by acts like A Tribe Called Quest, 2Pac and – as he was then known – Snoop Doggy Dogg. As crazy as it may sound, the sound of non-American hip hop was still very new to many people back then. That same year, Marxman were guests on two of the biggest tours of the 1990s: U2's Zoo TV tour and Depeche Mode's Devotional Tour.

I played the track 'Do You Crave Mystique?' on my radio show, and it prompted one listener to comment that it was 'the sound of now'. I didn't have the heart to say that it was actually a sound from more than two decades ago. It proves a number of things, the first being that this music has aged well. The other point it verifies is that things do indeed come full circle, even though this is often dismissed as an older generation trying to be hip!

If music was measured as seismic activity, most of it would not come close to registering on the Richter scale. While Marxman did not score major commercial success with *33 Revolutions per Minute*, they certainly left a small indelible mark on the musical landscape of the early 1990s, one which is certainly worth surveying.

For the Record

By Oisin Lunny

We were lucky – from day one we had a strong idea about what we wanted to say. We self released, made our own PR and demoed half an LP before we signed to Talkin' Loud in 1992. The next four years were intense and a lot of fun. Our first single was immediately banned by the BBC. We supported a lot of causes close to our heart, played anti-racist and anti-fascist gigs and fundraised for Women's Aid. We had a Top 30 hit with 'All About Eve', a song about violence against women. We were resolutely political.

One UK music magazine asked us whether we had put together our second single, 'Ship Ahoy', for a bet, given the mix of Irish trad, hip hop and orchestral samples, in a song about wage slavery with Sinead O'Connor. But it struck a chord. We toured with U2 and Depeche Mode, made a video with Spike Jonze and played everywhere, from Paris to New York to Belfast. To this day I'm proud of what we did, what we said, and how we said it.

Sleeve design by Swifty Typografix, photography by Kevin Westenberg

Tracklist

1	Theme from Marxman	7	Droppin' Elocution
2	All About Eve	8	Dark Are The Days
3	Father Like Son	9	Drifting
4	Ship Ahoy	10	Demented
5	Do You Crave Mystique	11	Spot On My Nose
6	Sad Affair	12	Sad Affair (Bodhrán Mix)

ROAD TO ROUEN

Supergrass, Parlophone, 2005

Supergrass were a band that released a lot of strong material, but never quite got the recognition that they deserved. Yes, you could say that they had their faces on that metaphorical Britpop poster, yet, in retrospect, their time as a big band seems rather short-lived.

'St Petersburg' was the lead single from *Road to Rouen*, and it is one of the best pieces of music that the band has ever recorded. It would not be fair to say that Supergrass's days of being a band of note were over, at this stage. To use a football analogy, their popularity had gone from top four, to just above mid table.

If you were to look at all of their albums from a purely musical, creative perspective, *Road to Rouen* is definitely their finest moment. People will argue that *In It for the Money* is a hard album to flaw (and this is true), but it does not quite have the craft and wonder that *Road to Rouen* does.

There is always the argument that it did not sell as well as other Supergrass albums, but, as I have said elsewhere, this is never a gauge of how good music is. There is so much more than just quality that goes towards major commercial success – money, timing and a lot of good luck play a huge part, too.

Perhaps the question should be whether this was the album that Supergrass fans were waiting for? Whether it was or was not, they received an album of sheer class and beauty. Prior to this, the band had showcased their ability in what is known as, in a musical sense, 'light and shade', but never before to the standard here.

A Pitchfork.com review of the album stated: 'You get the swamp-rocking title track and its companion, "Kick in the Teeth", which together make up the album's late-energy burst. *Road to Rouen* is stuffed with nasty descending riffs and volume pedal swells to back up Gaz Coombes's blue-eyed soul croon. On an album that resides mostly in slower tempos, it becomes clear just what a great singer Coombes is. He has a rich, nuanced voice that sounds great shouting or navigating a delicate melodic phrase.'

Everyone knew that Supergrass could come up with anthems – 'Richard III' and 'Alright' are prime examples. If you followed their career, you would have heard their ability to write heartfelt ballads like 'Late In The Day', but *Road to Rouen* showed a new side of the band. It has a sombre, reflective feel. Above all, it leaves you in no doubt over the band's pedigree.

Some of the post Supergrass solo material that Gaz Coombes released, like 'Buffalo', 'This Time Tomorrow' and 'White Noise' (the latter taken from his debut solo album, *Here Come the Bombs*) have similar tones to much of *Road to Rouen*. Some would say that this album saw the band mellow, but it sounds more like Supergrass reached a new plateau in their songwriting.

Photography by P. Wilson, M. Quinn and POM

Tracklist

1 Tales of Endurance (Parts 4, 5 & 6)
2 St. Petersburg
3 Sad Girl
4 Roxy
5 Coffee in the Pot
6 Road to Rouen
7 Kick in the Teeth
8 Low C
9 Fin

SAUL WILLIAMS

Saul Williams, The Fader Label/Wichita Recordings, 2004

'I got a list of demands written on the palm of my hands . . . ' These words were first bellowed out of speakers in the year 2004. 'List Of Demands (Reparations)' was, for many, the introduction to Saul Williams's self-titled second album.

Williams is an artist who cannot be described as just a lyricist. He is a poet, he is an actor, he is a musician and he is a vocalist. If you want to hear passion in a human being's voice, there are few people in music today who can deliver it better than Williams. Although he had released a well-received debut album (*Amethyst Rock Star* in 2001), it was his second album that grasped many people's attention.

Like many other albums featured in this book, *Saul Williams* stood out from everything else at the time of its release. An inspired Williams sounds like a mix between Chuck D and Gil Scott-Heron; the words stream out of his very being. One description at the time called him a prophet of rage, but angst is only one of the many tones on this album.

The tales that he unveils are gripping and revealing. On 'Black Stacey', he says: 'I used to hump my pillow at night/The type of silent prayer to help myself prepare for the light.' Call it honesty or creative storytelling, Williams sparks interest with words like few others.

Rage Against The Machine's Zack De La Rocha adds his patent howl to 'Act III Scene 2 (Shakespeare)', while Serj Tankian of System of a Down contributes his writing force to the album's opening, a stand-out track, 'Talk To Strangers'.

Saul Williams toured the album in 2005. Some of the shows were as guest to Nine Inch Nails, some with The Mars Volta and others as part of the iconic Lollapalooza music festival. He also played a memorable gig at the dearly missed Crawdaddy venue as part of this tour.

You can often learn a lot about an artist and their music when seeing them perform live. The remarkable thing from this performance was the amount of imagery that Williams creates in his music. At times, you find yourself reaching a point of sensory overload. It is like watching cross-town traffic as it meets, weaving its way around obstacles and gradually sliding into the distance.

Some say that politics and music should not cross paths, but surely it depends on who is mixing them? Williams's social awareness is sharper than most. One gets the impression that this is an important thing fuelling his substantial creative power.

When you think of all the information we process on a daily basis, it is quite remarkable that so many words from this 2004 album stick in your mind. It is a testament not just to Williams's lyrical talent, but to the way that he manages to process his thoughts into verse. *Saul Williams* remains one of the most remarkable albums from the vast musical landscape of the past twenty years.

For the Record

By Saul Williams, from an interview for The Alternative *on 2fm*

I recorded the album for free, primarily at home, so it was a matter of when friends were over, and I would ask, 'Hey, do you want to lay this down real quick?' The one exception was Serj Tankian from System of a Down. He called me one day, and told me that he had been thinking about me, and had written a song. He recorded it, and sent me the music for the opening track, 'Talk To Strangers'. I just wrote to it, and made it the introduction to the album.

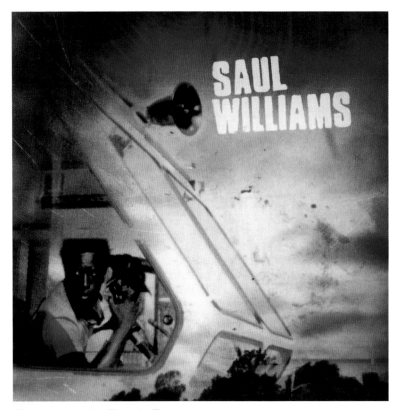

Sleeve design by Brandy Flower

Tracklist

1	Talk to Strangers	7	Black Stacey
2	Grippo	8	PG
3	Telegram	9	Surrender (A Second to Think)
4	Act III Scene 2 (Shakespeare)	10	Control Freak
5	List of Demands (Reparations)	11	Seaweed
6	African Student Movement	12	Notice of Eviction

SELL SELL SELL

David Gray, EMI, 1996

David Gray had been an established name for many years, but before his worldwide success, his career did have points where it stuttered and stalled, that is, until November 1998. We'll get to that date later, though. His third album, *Sell Sell Sell* came out in 1996. It was a change from his previous two, *A Century Ends* (1993) and *Flesh* (1994), as this was more of a full band sound. He did not lose any of his lyrical or vocal edge, but it harnessed a power like nothing that he had made before.

Some said at the time (rightly or wrongly) that *Sell Sell Sell* was a record that was aimed to break through in America. Whether this was the case or not, it showcased Gray's growing strength as a songwriter and vocalist.

I remember interviewing him a year after *Sell Sell Sell* was released. He spoke about some of the frustrations and disappointments the he had experienced with the album. He also told me about the album that he was planning to record. It was going to be a departure from what we had known of David Gray – it would make use of a drum machine and essentially employ a lot of the ingredients that people used to make what people called 'dance music' in those days.

While he was telling me I was thinking, 'What a dreadful idea, this is never going to work!' Just over a year later, in November 1998, he released *White Ladder*, and it sold millions.

Coming back to *Sell Sell Sell*, it was obvious that the record label had big plans for it. The jewel in the album's crown was a song by the name of 'Late Night Radio'. To this day, it is still one of the best songs that David Gray has written. Technically, it has everything that any song of merit needs to have: an intro that grabs your attention, a catchy chorus and a tune that gets stuck in your head.

In 1996, David Gray became an even bigger name in Ireland, where he had already cultivated quite a following. In the UK, things progressed at a steady rate. This was in part thanks to praise from larger acts like Radiohead, who Gray also toured with. Everything about this album screamed major success, a success that would, however, elude Gray for a number of years.

Listening now to *Sell Sell Sell*, and tracks like 'Magdalena' or 'Faster, Sooner, Now', each song seems as if it should have engulfed arenas worldwide. The ballads 'Forever Is Tomorrow Is Today' and 'Folk Song' would command silence from any audience. In short, the *Sell Sell Sell* chapter of David Gray's career is a bit of a mystery, riddled with disappointment and marvellous songs.

Design by Mark Farrow Design and photography by Rankin'

Tracklist

1	Faster, Sooner, Now	7	Smile
2	Late Night Radio	8	Only the Lonely
3	Sell Sell Sell	9	What Am I Doing Wrong?
4	Hold on to Nothing	10	Gutters Full of Rain
5	Everytime	11	Forever Is Tomorrow Is Today
6	Magdalena	12	Folk Song

SHAG TOBACCO

Gavin Friday, Island Records, 1995

Gavin Friday is an artist who, over the years, has always been wonderfully out of step with the dominant trends in music. To call him an individual who cares little for scenes and movements would be a pretty accurate description.

In 1995, when Europe had been swallowed up by Brit-pop, Friday's creative mind couldn't have been further from the 'Cool Britannia' ethos. *Shag Tobacco* tipped its hat to the very different worlds of Jacques Brel, Marc Bolan and the sound of 1930s Berlin. Add in Friday's writing partner Maurice Seezer and producer Tim Simenon (of Bomb the Bass) to the cocktail, and you have a concoction with unpredictable potency.

It is always refreshing to be proven wrong about music. I remember reading a review of *Shag Tobacco* in *The Irish Times*, and thinking it sounded like a load of pretentious rubbish. When I got to hear the album a few weeks later, though, I was humbled and enchanted. From the opening title track to the sinister pop sound of 'Dolls', *Shag Tobacco* undertakes a journey through time and tempo. 'The Last Song I'll Ever Sing' is a ballad like you have never heard before, and Friday's version of Marc Bolan's 'The Slider' is immense.

Simenon's contribution as producer must not be overlooked here. His work with his band Bomb the Bass was well known at this stage, and the two albums that he worked on after *Shag Tobacco* (*Tao Of The One Inch Punch* by One Inch Punch, and Depeche Mode's *Ultra*)

were each excellent in their own way. They were three very different albums, but all still stand as three of the best and most underrated of the mid 1990s.

The fact that *Shag Tobacco* did not reach a substantial mainstream audience is surprising, but, in other ways, not surprising at all. A strong sense of individuality certainly worked for Radiohead's *OK Computer*, but *Shag Tobacco* was perhaps too much of an acquired taste for the time. That said, its brilliance is in its unique, measured sophistication.

The singles 'Angel' and 'You Me And World War Three' serve as appetisers for a collection of songs that have managed to withhold all of their character and charm, even two decades on. Commercial impact is only one side of music – the rest comes down to personal taste, and how the music has aged over time. The idea that something is not any good because it has not been hugely successful is nonsense.

'Music is not a business, it is a way of life', Friday stated, back in 1995. 'The Virgin Prunes were me growing up in public, they were fuelled by a lot of anger and frustration, and I suppose I am still an angry man – happily angry. Real music is when you do not really know what you're doing – it's just your instincts at work. I love that. I love going in at the deep end, and struggling and fighting and hopefully coming out . . . into the light.'

For the Record

By Gavin Friday

It's twenty years ago this summer that we recorded *Shag Tobacco*. Myself, Maurice Seezer, Tim Simenon with his Bomb the Bass crew and a cast of bespoke players spent the summer in Eastcote Studios in London. I usually find recording painful and slow, but making *Shag Tobacco* wasn't overly so. We had worked with Tim on various projects between 1993 and 1994, including Jim Sheridan's *In the Name of the Father*. There was a very strong understanding of each other musically.

Maurice and I had written and demoed most of the material in Dublin, which was a godsend. It left all our time in the studio to make our humble demos into something special. When making an album, I always start with, 'I haven't got a clue what I am doing but I know exactly what I want.' So I am totally open to all experimentation.

I don't see albums as just collections of songs, but as worlds of their own. *Shag Tobacco* . . . the movie, the play, the soap opera, the short story, whatever. And the 'whatever' it takes to create that world – that's where I'll go. I hate explaining how something spontaneous is made, and I truly hate the demystification of how music is made. I don't think anyone can really explain the chemistry between musicians.

I am very proud of what we achieved with *Shag Tobacco*, even though today I can see all its energetic faults and adorable naivety. And I love it, because I know we made something unique and true to itself, something that didn't care if it fit in or not, something true that had created its own world . . . the world of *Shag Tobacco*, where the extraordinary is the ordinary.

Sleeve artwork (crushproof pack) by Rob Crane, Amy, Irene and Calligari on Art Island

Tracklist

1 Shag Tobacco
2 Caruso
3 Angel
4 Little Black Dress
5 The Slider
6 Dolls
7 Mr. Pussy
8 You Me And World War Three
9 Kitchen Sink Drama
10 My Twentieth Century
11 The Last Song I'll Ever Sing
12 Le Roi d'Amour

SHOT IN THE LIGHT

Engine Alley, Independent Records, 1995

The year 1995's *Shot in The Light* was Engine Alley's second studio album, and it captures the band at their very best. If you have ever wanted to hear a band finding their sound and absolutely nailing it, then this album is a great example.

They dispensed with the glam and theatrics that had brought them much acclaim on their 1992 debut album, *A Sonic Holiday*, and made one of the best Irish albums of the 1990s. *Shot in The Light* holds so much depth and character that, even two decades on, it sounds fresh compared to much of what was released at the time.

The Kilkenny band could have taken the slightly less imaginative step, and adopted a Britpop sound that could have won them an instant audience. Although they were still a young band at the time, they had enough character and self-belief to come up with something as exceptional as *Shot in The Light*. You cannot help but feel that there was a degree of soul searching prior, and perhaps during, its recording.

Shot in The Light was the yin to their debut's yang, and it was recorded under very different circumstances. They had parted company with their record label, and entered what must have seemed like the daunting unknown to make a new album. So many bands unravel and fall asunder after events such as these, but the fact that Engine Alley didn't shows how strong the bond between its members was.

Drummer Emmaline Duffy-Fallon had left the band, and Jerry Fehily (of The Hot House Flowers) had taken over drumming duties. It is hard to know exactly how the collective creative of a band works, but the songs that made up *Shot in The Light* sound as if they were written and recorded out of frustration and a dogged determination. It is the sound of a band open to the prospect of change.

From the opening track, 'Machine', there's a calm coherence about *Shot in The Light*, that makes it an album that is difficult to find fault with. 'Hey! Lucifer' recalls some of the retro kitsch that was evident on their earlier material, and the album's main single, 'I Can't Help You', was the perfect example of what made Engine Alley such a treasure at the time.

If Engine Alley illustrated anything with this album, it was that you could record a really strong album in the mid 1990s without a large suitcase of cash! Trials, tribulations and line-up changes finish so many bands, but at this point in their career of Engine Alley, it brought them a new creative drive, and their strongest album.

For the Record

By Canice Kenealy

Shot in The Light has its own vibe and outlook. The sound is darker, more dense and the arrangements more simple and less quirky than on our debut.

The songs on this album all had a mournful quality, touching on past memories or disappointments, the loss of youth and the threat of loneliness, and then projecting forward, to bereavement and emergency medical situations. The second half is lighter than the first and less angry, with two ballads. That was a natural way of putting it together.

The title is a play on the expression 'shot in the dark' – twisting it for a more optimistic view. The single 'I Can't Help You' may appear to be a negative outburst, but it's really a call to arms to fix yourself your own way, come what may. It means: if you want something done, do it yourself.

At that time in 1995, it was the most accurate reflection of how we were feeling. Thankfully, it wasn't our eulogy.

Sleeve design by Kenealy/Kenealy/Byrne with Dave Monahan and Paddy Tynan

Tracklist

1	Machine	6	So Low
2	Innocent	7	Surprise
3	Hey! Lucifer	8	Steal Your Money
4	The Last One	9	Shot in The Light
5	I Can't Help You	10	I Spy

SLEEPWALKING

Rae & Christian, Grand Central Records, 2000

The mystery of how I came to posses this album still perplexes me. I was working for one of Ireland's fledgling websites during the dot.com bubble. This wonderful album turned up on my desk one morning. I never managed to find out which kind soul left it there, but I have been grateful ever since.

Having Bobby Womack as one of your guest vocalists is always going to spark interest. The man who gave us classics like 'Woman's Gotta Have It' and 'Across 110th Street' brings flair and class to any project or album that he is involved with. Add to this cocktail hip hop royalty The Pharcyde, and you have a potential classic.

The next necessary ingredients are songs – strong songs. *Sleepwalking* is bulging with them, to the point that it is almost an embarrassment of riches. The UK duo does not miss a beat or put a note out of place. 'Sometimes I hear the phone ring late at night, and I wonder to myself now, who could that be?' These are words from one of the album's stand-out tracks, 'Get A Life'.

When you look back at some of the albums that were heralded as classics at the time, it is hard to understand how this wonderfully diverse record did not receive as much fanfare. It is certainly not one that you hear people praising a decade and a half on.

The word 'timeless' comes to mind again here. The songs that Rae & Christian made for *Sleepwalking* do not have an obvious date of origin. Play a track like 'Blazing The Crop' alongside Grandmaster Flash's 1981 hit 'The Adventures of Grandmaster Flash on the Wheels of Steel' and it fits perfectly. Do the same with 'Ain't Nothing Like', but this time with Jungle's 2014 single, 'Busy Earnin', and you find that it sounds just fine.

Whatever genre Rae & Christian steer towards throughout *Sleepwalking*, they do so with style and ease. There is a danger in trying to be eclectic; you can dilute what you are doing and end up sounding confused. Whether it is a reggae workout with guests The Congos, or a delicate ambient piece using the beautiful vocals of Kate Rogers, they just do it right.

Back when it was released, *Q Magazine* summed up *Sleepwalking*, calling it, 'Another triumph, brimming with soulful, languid grooves, deft samples and well-chosen guest singers.' It is not just that the guests are well selected, but both guest and R&C are very much on the same wavelength.

Sleepwalking is an album that was celebrated when it was released, but is not spoken of enough these days. Occasionally, you do come across people who are almost obsessive about it, which will hopefully ensure that it receives the respect that it deserves, all these years after it was released.

For the Record

By Mark Rae

Sleepwalking was our second studio album, and was completed and released two years after our breakthrough *Northern Sulphuric Soul* LP. Bobby Womack and The Pharcyde were the vocal cornerstones for the project, with Tania Maria and Cedric Myton of The Congos adding some tropical spice.

The pressure of sophomore releases is hard to convey. We changed up the style somewhat, and certainly missed the presence of Veba, who was perhaps the greatest vocalist we ever worked with. The album's recording process was also disrupted when Mark was a key witness to a double shooting on the doorstep of the Grand Central Offices, when the album was in the gestation stage.

Despite all the changes and outside forces, we managed to deliver an album that was well ahead of the curve.

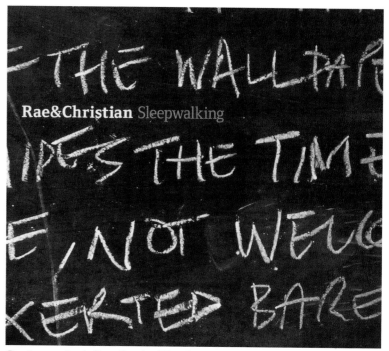

Design and art direction by Blue Source

Tracklist

1 Blazing the Crop
2 Hold Us Down (ft: The Congos)
3 It Ain't Nothing Like
   (ft: The Pharcyde)
4 Get A Life (ft: Bobby Womack)
5 Not Just Anybody
   (ft: Kate Rogers)
6 Trailing In The Wake
7 Vai Viver a Vide
   (ft: Tania Maria)
8 Let It Go (ft: The Pharcyde)
9 Ready to Roll
10 Wake Up Everybody
   (ft: Bobby Womack)
11 Salvation (ft: Siron)

SPEECH THERAPY

Speech Debelle, Big Dada, 2009

Most albums that win the prestigious Mercury Music Prize are guaranteed some sort of special treatment, or respect, at least. Look at the list of some of the recipients of this award: Primal Scream, *Screamadelica* (1992), Suede, *Suede* (1993), Portishead, *Dummy* (1995), PJ Harvey, *Stories From The City Stories From The Sea* (2001), Dizzee Rascal, *Boy In Da Corner* (2003), Arctic Monkeys, *Whatever People Say I Am, That's What I'm Not* (2006), The XX, *XX* (2010) and James Blake, *Overgrown* (2013).

The list is a who's who of music, both past and present. For the acts that were not big names prior to winning, they became substantially bigger immediately after. Why is it that, since winning the Mercury Music Prize, Speech Debelle's career has not followed a similar path?

As I write this, I have the sound of the beautifully melancholic 'Better Days' breezing through my mind. It is one of those songs that sticks with you, like the segment of a book that has made a real impression on you, at a particular point in your life.

Speech Therapy is an honest album. At times, you feel like you are listening in on someone else's conversation, none more so than on the album's title track, where she says, I'm not there yet I'm still trying to fix my faults, trying to pick sense from nonsense, that's what I was taught.

The shortlist for the 2009 Mercury Music Prize was particularly strong; it featured albums from La Roux, The Horrors, Friendly Fires and the three favourites, Florence & The Machine, Kasabian and Bat for Lashes. It would be accurate to say that Speech Debelle had an outside chance.

On the evening of 8 September 2009, *Speech Therapy* was the surprise winner – a pretty big surprise, at that. One of the recurring comments about the album ever since has been its relatively small sales figures, in comparison to those of the other winners. This, of course, misses the point of the award, which rewards quality over quantity.

Speech Therapy is so much more than lyrical styling; there is a gritty beauty to it that you have to admire, and give due respect to. This realism almost runs in contrast to the paced, laid-back vocal delivery, but they just somehow work together.

Part of what gives *Speech Therapy* its rich and organic sound is the live instrumentation. While sampling has its obvious advantages, you cannot always bend and mould them to capture the spirit of the track that you are using them for. The subtle playing glides around Speech Debelle's conversational style delivery, never hindering or smothering the vocal point.

It would not be fair to call this a lost album, or even one that has been forgotten. It has that distinction of being the recipient of a major award, which ensures that the name *Speech Therapy* is written into the record books. It is, however, an overlooked album: not brash enough to scream for attention, but clever and honest enough to impress anyone who has the pleasure of hearing it.

For the Record

By Speech Debelle, from an interview with State.ie

There are no straight pop songs on the record, so it was difficult to get played on daytime radio. We did not have much money for marketing, so it was just put out there, like a teardrop in the ocean. No one really knew that it existed.

I know people considered it to be one kind of record, but I did believe it could go on to sell a lot of copies on its own.

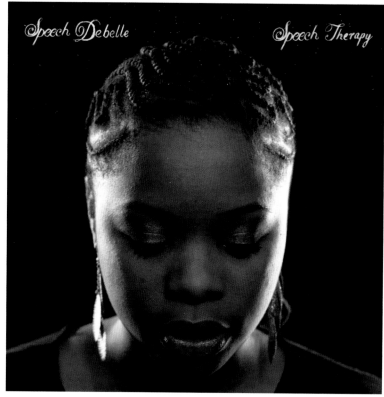

Design and direction by Lewis Kyle White

Tracklist

1	Searching	8	Wheels in Motion (ft. Roots Manuva)
2	The Key	9	Live & Learn
3	Better Days (ft. Micachu)	10	Working Weak
4	Spinnin	11	Buddy Love
5	Go Then, Bye	12	Finish This Album
6	Daddy's Little Girl	13	Speech Therapy
7	Bad Boy		

SPOONS

Jeff Martin, Casino Gravity, 2004

Spoons is one of the best albums that you have probably never heard. It is a shame that more people haven't come across this beauty, from Dublin-based musician Jeff Martin – it is one of those albums that you can quite easily become obsessive about.

It is not a new sound revolution, but it is an album that is hard to draw comparisons with. Even after listening to it innumerable times, finding a suitable comparison is difficult; in all honesty, writing this piece is about it is the first time that I have ever felt that I had to.

It is a pop record, but not in the way you would expect. In a similar way to what Belle & Sebastian have done, Martin made an album that anyone anywhere could relate to in some way. It's like the old saying 'A good song is a good song', and *Spoons* is full of them.

Spoons opens with a warm hum that turns into 'Magnet Line', a song that, to this day, brings a smile to my face. So many people can tell you the deepest meaning to some of their favourite songs, but I could not tell you what I think 'Magnet Line' is about. Quite honestly, I do not care. I just absolutely love the song.

Working with Stephen Shannon as co-producer, Martin has a way of delivering beautifully modest compositions. They could have made this an album full of potential pop anthems, but they let these songs build in an organic way, rather than give them some sort of audio growth hormone.

Self-financing an album in 2004 cannot have been easy, especially an album that was mixed by John McEntire. McEntire's résumé is lengthy, impressive and makes for interesting reading, so do indulge yourself. The album sounds and looks every bit as impressive as one with major label backing. It is unfortunate that a lack of financial clout can lead to music like this (and that of countless other artists) being rendered almost invisible to people that would absolutely love it.

The closing track, 'Augustine', is a beautifully orchestrated piece of music. Some would call it classical and others contemporary, but whatever it is, you will be suitably impressed. Add classy tunes like 'Make Change', 'Anyone's Pocket' and 'Balancing Act', and you have an album that can stand up to scrutiny by anyone.

For some reason, after writing about *Spoons*, names like The Blue Nile's *A Walk Across the Rooftops* and *Breathing Tornados* by Ben Lee pop into my head. It is not be a style-related link, because the three are so different – the thing that binds the three is their creators's attention to detail.

Spoons by Jeff Martin didn't become a world-renowned album, and, more than a decade on, it is highly unlikely that it will. It truly is, in every sense, buried treasure that is waiting to be discovered.

For the Record

By Jeff Martin

Listening to *Spoons* ten years after its release, it almost seems as if it is not my record. Growing up, I used to hear bands talk about a record being a "document" or "snapshot" of a certain time in their lives. While at that time I hadn't made enough records to fully understand this, listening now, I see what they meant.

Making *Spoons* was a big deal for me, and, when completed, it was everything I wanted it to be. It is bursting with hope and ambition, and has an almost naive sense of adventure and discovery, as it works its way towards finding a conclusion and purpose. Listening to it now, it still sounds OK! I'm proud of *Spoons*, and you cannot really ask any more than that from an album. To me, that is musical success.

Sleeve Design by Mike Ahern at D.A.D.D.Y.

Tracklist

1	Magnet Line	7	Shuttlecock
2	Balancing Act	8	Spoons
3	Plays Music	9	Interlude: Tune For A Stranger
4	The Promise	10	Anyone's Pocket
5	Veelow (Pt.1&2)	11	Augustine
6	Make Change		

STEREO MUSICALE

Blind Mr. Jones, Cherry Red Records, 1992

What does it mean to be considered a contender? Maybe the members of Blind Mr. Jones could tell you, for it was this band from Marlow, Buckinghamshire that had more potential than most of their more successful contemporaries of the time.

This band have always been filed under the 'shoegaze' tag, but there was a lot more to them than this. Their debut album, *Stereo Musicale*, arrived in 1992, and brought them much love from highly influential publications like *Melody Maker* and *NME*.

The shoegaze movement, at its height, really only lasted a few years. Sandwiched between the baggy Manchester scene and grunge, it overlapped both for a time. What bands like Blind Mr. Jones and Lush brought to this was more clarity in their vocals and a defined tune.

Blind Mr. Jones also scored a degree of critical acclaim in America with *Stereo Musicale*, as this review from *CMJ* magazine illustrates: '*Stereo Musicale* sets its sights on smashing the "shoegazing" term, making moody, noisy and polished music that seeps and whirls with gracious melodies, lush production (by Radiohead's Chris Hufford) and harmonies that flourish.'

Johnny Greenwood of Radiohead was a fan of the band, and he (playing harmonica) appeared on their *Crazy Jazz* EP, which also appeared in 1992. This was a very prolific year for the band, and one that saw their profile rise considerably. Alan McGee of Creation Records was taken with the track 'Dolores', which appeared on both *Stereo Musicale* and the *Crazy Jazz* EP.

The use of a flute on a number of the tracks really sets this album apart from a lot of what was happening at the time. On paper, it sounds like something that would not work, but when it is placed into the mix, it gives the band a mysterious, trippy sound that must have been quite powerful in a live setting.

Bands that were associated with the original shoegaze wave are not often commended on their lyrics. Blind Mr. Jones showed that they had a strong leaning towards lyrical craft, none better than on 'Henna and Swayed': 'It's me who mists her fallen eyes, and folds and twists her love song lines.'

Stereo Musicale is an album of its time, but that is not a bad thing. It ranks among the best debuts of the early 1990s, alongside *Whirlpool* by Chapterhouse, Lush's *Gala*, and *Just For A Day* from Slowdive. While it was not successful enough to buy each of the band members a mansion in Laurel Canyon, it is an album that they should be, and hopefully are, very proud of.

For the Record

By Will Teversham

Recorded over ten days in the summer of 1992, *Stereo Musicale* was only the third foray in the studio for Blind Mr. Jones, after two EPs. Barely out of our teenage years, I think we were still a bit intimidated by the recording process.

It breaks all the rules of making an album – thirteen songs and one hidden track, over an hour long, five or six instrumentals and with tracks varying from ninety seconds to eight minutes. The first vocals are not heard until six minutes into the record!

Listening to it now, it sounds like a young, experimental band, but I think that is part of its charm. We did not know how to record an album, so we just recorded what we wanted. That comes across in the slightly deranged mix of styles – instrumentals, fast songs, slow songs, from shoegaze to prog rock to a waltz and, to top it off, a dub version of The Fureys's 'Lonesome Boatman' – hardly what you would call coherent.

Released on Cherry Red – a great label but totally skint at the time – it was no surprise that it got overlooked, but I think history has been kind to the record. Although it is definitely still a shoegaze album, I do not think it has aged too badly.

Artwork by Sarah Kersley

Tracklist

1 Sisters	8 Unforgettable Waltz
2 Spooky Vibes	9 Going on Cold
3 Regular Disease	10 Spook Easy
4 Small Caravan	11 One Watt Above Darkness
5 Flying With Lux	12 Dolores
6 Henna and Swayed	13 Against the Glass
7 Lonesome Boatmen	

THE SEVEN STEPS TO MERCY

Iarla Ó Lionáird, Real World Records, 1997

My introduction to Iarla Ó Lionáird and his wonderful album, *The Seven Steps to Mercy*, came in the form of the conversation below.

Record Label: 'Good morning Dan. How are you? Would you be interested in interviewing Iarla Ó Lionáird about his new album?'

Me: 'Sorry, I didn't quite catch that. Interview who about what? What name did you say?'

Record Label: 'His name is Iarla Ó Lionáird, and he's about to release a really beautiful album.'

Mornings have never been my strong point, and pre-coffee conversations are always something like the above, regardless of the topic. However, the interview happened, and the album left a lasting impression.

There is no one on this planet who has a voice like Iarla Ó Lionáird. While he can be called a *sean-nós* singer, which is where his roots lie, he has more vocal dimensions than I could possibly try and tell you about. Whether it is his solo material, or with the Afro Celt Sound System or The Gloaming, Iarla's vocals are unmistakable.

The Seven Steps to Mercy is a wildly progressive album. Radiohead's *OK Computer* ushered in a new perception of guitar music, while Ó Lionáird's debut album for Peter Gabriel's Real World label gave people a new view of Irish music. Like a book, you cannot judge an album by its cover or artwork, but there is something quite mysterious about the artwork on this album. Like its content, the album art is alluring in a very Celtic, and – dare I say it – 'New Age' kind of way.

There's an evident lineage to music like this. It not only links the past with the present, but draws out the relationship between vocal and traditional Irish music, as well as music from other parts of the world. The Chieftains were pioneers in exploring this, and you can hear Iarla's curiosity here, too.

If you play some of the tracks from *The Seven Steps to Mercy* alongside 'If I Had A Heart' by Fever Ray, some of the sounds and imagery are strikingly similar. At this point in his career, Iarla was also a part of the Afro Celt Sound System. As their name would suggest, this collective blended sounds and cultures. There is no doubt that Ó Lionáird's appetite for experimentation and exploration would have grown from the experience with the Afro Celts.

One of the key ingredients that makes this album so intriguing is Ó Lionáird's chemistry with producers and collaborators Michael Brook and Ingmar Kiang. Like many successful artist/producer partnerships, the three come from different artistic backgrounds, but their meeting point finds a rare delicate balance. Brook's experience included work with names like Brian Eno and Nusrat Fateh Ali Khan, while Kiang's CV notes work with Bob Marley and Murray Head.

The Seven Steps to Mercy was an early indication of the talent of Iarla Ó Lionáird. He has underlined his pedigree many times since then, but, as an introduction, you will have to search hard to find a better opening solo account than this.

For the Record

By Iarla Ó Lionáird, for a 1997 interview for News Four

Since I was a child, I was a *sean-nós* singer. A *sean-nós* singer is someone who normally sings on their own, but of course these things have all started to change. My goal on this project was not to use the usual tricks – no *bodhrans*, no *bazukis* and no flutes. I was offered the opportunity by Real World to work with whoever I wanted, and between us we came up with Michael Brook, who had worked with the Nusrat Fateh Ali Khan.

I love the coldness of the treatment of the album. It is all cutting-edge rock 'n' roll treatment, in so far that it is not all drums – it is all guitar loops and samples. I tried to avoid bringing musicians in and saying, 'Can you play along with this?' as much as possible. I want to assemble sounds that reflected what was going on in my head when I was singing on my own.

Graphic design by Anna-Karin Sundin and photography by Steve Pyke

Tracklist

1   Seacht (Seven)
2   Aililiu Na Gamhna (Calling Home The Calves)
3   Caoineadh Na dTrí Mhuire (Lament At Clavary)
4   Abha (River)
5   Aoibhinn Cronan (The Humming Of The Bees)
6   Loch Lein
7   Cuir A Choladh An Seanduine (The Old Man Rocking The Cradle)
8   An Buachaill Caol Dubh (The Dark Slender Boy)
9   Bean Dubh An Ghleanna (The Dark Woman Of The Glen)
10   Aisling Gheal (Bright Vision)

THEY KNOW WHAT GHOST KNOW

Yppah, Ninja Tune, 2009

The year 2009 was very rich for inventive new music. The XX delivered their debut album, Animal Collective served up *Merriweather Post Pavilion* and Fever Ray gave us their self-titled synth-pop masterpiece. With these and many more, it would have been understandable if you missed the curiously titled *They Know What Ghost Know*, from the equally curiously named artist Yppah.

What an unusual name, what abstract album artwork, but, more importantly, what outstanding and unforgettable music engulfs your ears once you set this album in motion. It is My Bloody Valentine collaborating with The Temptations, it is A Tribe Called Quest jamming with Cocteau Twins. It is extraordinary!

Yppah is a musician called Joe Corrales Jr., who has been releasing music under this unusual guise since 2006. There is a joy and a freedom to tracks like 'Shutter Speed', 'Gumball Machine Weekend' and 'Bobbie Joe Wilson' that transport you off into a blissful, dreamlike state. Perhaps this is not the best album to be listening to on a long drive, but there are very few other occasions where this would not be a welcome earworm.

Comparisons can be made between *They Know What Ghost Know* and *Play* by Moby, or even the aforementioned My Bloody Valentine's *Loveless*. Musically, they are all very different albums, but they all possess the most unlikely pop tunes that have a sound and identity different to anything else that was around at the time of their release.

The response to this album was generally very positive at the time, though some reviews were mixed over its diversity. *NME*'s review in May 2009 gave it a strong 7/10. It stated: 'Shoegazing instrumental hip hop might sound like it belongs back in the '90s, but Corrales sprinkles his tracks with a wide range of fairy dust.'

There is always a dominant sound when it comes to pop music; sometimes that is because people are using the same technology to make the music, or one creator spawns numerous imitators. What Yppah did on this album was throw all of his influences and ideas into the mix, and come up with something exceptional. *They Know What Ghost Know* is an album that almost anyone could listen to and take something positive from. It is an album for hipsters, music nerds, daytime-radio junkies and any person with a passing interest in music with a tune.

Tracklist

1 Son Saves The Rest
2 Gumball Machine Weekend
3 Playing With Fireworks
4 Shutter Speed
5 The Moon Scene 7
6 They Know What Ghost Know
7 City Glow
8 Sun Flower Sun Kissed
9 The Tingling
10 Bobbie Joe Wilson
11 A Parking Lot Carnival
12 Southern Sky Tells All

TOMORROW'S LIGHT AND DARKNESS

Will de Burca, Self released, 2014

Some albums, like DJ Shadow's *Entroducing* and Jungle's self-titled debut, capture people's imaginations. This is partially because they stand out from what is around at the time, but it is also because they are inspired pieces of work, created by artists who have disregarded whatever rules or parameters many acts inadvertently confine themselves to.

Dublin DJ and producer Will de Burca hasn't reached the commercial heights that Jungle and DJ Shadow scored with their respective albums, but *Tomorrow's Light and Darkness* nonetheless has a similar 'anything goes' feel to it. Here is an album that didn't have a six-figure budget, but shows no ill effects from the revenue that paid for it.

There are countless genres with which you could define this album – electro, electronica or ambient are three of them. A decade ago, this would have simply been called 'dance music', which was probably the most general categorisation in the history of music. It's at times like these that you realise the limitations of the English language. Electronic music tipping its hat to retro synth-pop is the most accurate label you could give it, if you had to describe it to someone who hadn't heard it.

De Burca clearly knows his music, and you can pinpoint some of his influences in the midst of this tempo-charged record. 'They Gave Us Rock' and 'American Scene' are the most obvious tracks here. They harnessed the kind of power that Death In Vegas brought us with 'Aisha', and could easily be mistaken for a long-lost cousin of Bibio's 'Take Off Your Shirt'.

Prior to releasing *Tomorrow's Light and Darkness* De Burca put together some excellent individual tracks and EPs, but nothing with a duration giving you a full impression of where he was coming from, artistically. This is the beauty of these things we know as albums: they can sometimes give you a glimpse into the world and space that their creator operates in. Even early on, Will de Burca's music had all the facets that film soundtracks and commercials often looked for. This somewhat obvious observation was confirmed after tracks from *Tomorrow's Light and Darkness* featured on Dutch TV, and another was used by a digital marketing company in the UK.

Albums like this will obviously date, but that's not always a criticism, and it isn't one here. What De Burca put together isn't specifically attached to the year 2014 in a stylistic sense, but, like many of the albums from that year that stand out (from artists such as Kate Tempest, Submotion Orchestra and FKA Twigs), it will always act as a mental cue for me, to remember certain events and moments that took place over those twelve months.

The opening track, 'Killer Curtis', sets the tone of what awaits the unsuspecting listener. There are touches of shoegaze on 'Visions We Have Are Fading Away', while '0405' and 'Mandarin Superstar' have an unusual quality to them that echoes acts like Four Tet and Röyksopp.

When we think of DIY music, there is a tendency to presume that it is, in some way, not as well made as commercial music. Moby's *Play* certainly fits this DIY mould, as does *You've Come a Long Way Baby*, by Fatboy Slim. Albums like these have helped change people's perceptions of what can be done when you make music on your own terms.

De Burca may go on to write better songs in the future. He may also record better albums, but, for a debut, *Tomorrow's Light and Darkness* is a huge accomplishment. It's an album that has held onto its place in my iPod for longer than many classic albums from famous names; this, more than anything else written above, is the greatest endorsement that I could give it!

For the Record

By Will de Burca

Tomorrow's Light and Darkness was recorded over a two-and-a-half-year period. I was heavily influenced by Jan Hammer's music as a kid, so I tried to create a more updated sound. The recording programs that I used were mainly Ableton and Reason. Producer Shane McGarvey then brought the tracks to life with his production and mixing skills.

The track 'American Scene' received most radio airplay, but it actually took less than an hour to write! Some of the other tracks were used for syncing, in other words, featured in films, television shows and advertisements. The year was rounded off nicely when Dan Hegarty named the album number six in his Top 50 Irish Albums of 2014.

Artwork by Dylan Madden, logo by Martin O'Brien

Tracklist

1	Killer Curtis		6	They Gave Us Rock
2	American Scene		7	Shattered
3	Visions We Have Are Fading Away		8	Mandarin Superstar
4	0415		9	Big Picture
5	Been & Gone		10	Lionheart
			11	Tomorrow's Light & Darkness

TWILIGHT OF THE INNOCENTS

Ash, Infectious Records, 2007

Though they billed this as their final studio album, the good news was that the band were not breaking up. The Downpatrick trio needed a change, and this album was to be the final step in that part of their career. What happened next was the brilliant *A–Z* singles series, but let's stay with *Twilight of the Innocents* for now.

When you think of the expression 'growing up in public', you might visualise people like Miley Cyrus or Michael Jackson, but this could also be said of Ash. From their teens to their thirties, their career has seen many sharp ascents – and some plateaus – all of which have been in the ever-watchful public eye. It is not that they particularly craved the spotlight, but it did seem, at one stage, that the smallest thing they did would gain some sort of media activity.

Twilight of the Innocents came at a time when Ash were as much a creative force as ever, but music was changing. They were quick to see that, and they took steps both to remain relevant and keep themselves interested. Along with being billed as their swan-song album, it was a fitting cornerstone to that part of their career.

The title track says a lot about Ash as a band at the time. It has all the ingredients that make songs like 'Goldfinger' and 'Starcrossed' as good as they are, but with an added maturity. It also gave those who doubted their ability to write songs of that calibre definitive proof that they could.

One of the things that Ash have always been noted for is their uncanny ability to write catchy pop songs. Looking at the list of tunes, you will instantly recognise 'Oh Yeah', 'Burn Baby Burn', 'Kung Fu', 'A Life Less Ordinary' and numerous others. *Twilight of the Innocents* had its share of instantly catchy songs, but also contained tracks like 'Dark And Stormy' and 'End Of The World', that make you realise how they became a band able to grasp just about every facet that goes into making a complete and well-rounded artist.

If there is a forgotten album in the Ash catalogue, then it is this one. If the more transient Ash fans of years past had heard *Twilight of the Innocents*, they would be amazed at how Ash had developed. Unlike most acts, they managed to hang onto the components that the teenage Downpatrick trio had had – that early-twenties swagger – and mixed in some mature composure, to complete the recipe.

Their *A–Z* singles series was soon followed by a tour. *Twilight of the Innocents* gave us its own A to Z of what Ash are as a band, one that had achieved so much over the years, with much still left to prove.

For the Record

By Rick McMurray

The lead-up to the making of TOTI was a series of new beginnings for the band. We had decided to part with Charlotte Hatherley, who had been a member of Ash since 1997. Tim and Mark had relocated to New York City at the end of our *Meltdown* album tour. As part of their move there, we decided to rent a studio space in New York as our new Ash HQ.

The song was originally known as 'Suicide Girls', and was later renamed 'Palace Of Excess'. It felt like a sort of musical breakthrough. Tim was getting some pretty exciting sounds that felt like they could fill the space left by Charlotte.

Right at the end, Tim gave me this nugget of an idea for an instrumental track that was just a two-note motif, and said, 'We don't have time to put it together, so just record loads of ideas to it and I can chop it up on the computer once you've flown home.' This idea eventually spawned the title track, which is probably one of our most ambitious recordings. It gave us another way of working that we used a lot during the *A–Z* period.

It's strange sitting here listening to *Twilight*, as I type this. It's not something that I do very often – listening back to past albums. In fact, I have probably never done it with this record. There's a few songs on there that I don't have any memory of. I remember driving to Ireland a couple of years ago and 'Princess Six' came on my girlfriend's iPod. I didn't recognise it as Ash until the guitar solo. It was a surreal experience, to listen to your own recording without realising it. It came as quite a relief that I was enjoying it, too!

Art direction by dmh and Mark at Tourist and photography by B plus

Tracklist

1	I Started A Fire	7	Ritual
2	You Can't Have It All	8	Shadows
3	Blacklisted	9	Princess Six
4	Polaris	10	Dark and Stormy
5	Palace Of Excess	11	Shattered Glass
6	End of the World	12	Twilight of the Innocents

THE UNREST CURE

Leo Abrahams, Mercury Records, 2007

Some of the best music that you will ever hear can be from people who are entirely new to you. Although Leo Abrahams had released quite a bit of material prior to 2007's *The Unrest Cure*, this album was my introduction to him.

Listening to it for the first time is like reading a book or watching a film that you are uncertain about. Then, there is that moment of realisation that you have not only been won over, but that this is something you are going to hold close for a very long time.

The point at which this happened for me during *The Unrest Cure* has faded into the ether, but to say that the album as a whole had a pronounced impact may not capture things to the correct extent. '2,000 Years From Now', featuring the extraordinary voice of New York City poet Bingo Gazingo, is a tune that sends your thoughts racing. What's going on here? Who is this guy? Is it a story? Is it a tale?

Brian Eno guests in 'No Frame', while Ed Harcourt shows how versatile his vocals can be when he features on 'Devil's Mouth'. Harcourt's sweet delivery, which he showcased on his song 'She Fell Into My Arms' (from his 2001 album, *Here Be Monsters*) is replaced by a menacing Jon Spencer-meets-Nick Cave delivery.

Albums like this are important, because they shake things up for you. If anyone that you know rolls out the 'music is all the same these days' line, get them to listen to this and they'll change their mind. It is not inaccessible to mainstream-music people either – Abrahams has an ear for melody and harmony like few others.

What can throw a lot of people off certain music is that it sounds too complicated. *The Unrest Cure* has many layers, but, essentially, the songs are simple. It is the little twists and turns that he makes on 'City Machine' that keep you intrigued. The addition of guest KT Tunstall also adds a degree of familiarity, which can never be underestimated.

Reviews at the time were mixed, but a review is just (as this is) an opinion. One of the things about *The Unrest Cure* is you can completely see why people may not be into it. In many respects, it is clearly a superb album, but it challenges you throughout, as it must have challenged Abrahams and his guests to create it.

To go back to the book reference made earlier, not everyone will fully get this album. This is not calling the people who do not get it stupid, but rather stating that this is an acquired taste. If you have a taste for it, *The Unrest Cure* is an album that you will never want to be too far away from. You will come back to it time and time again, and you will never feel let down by what you hear.

For the Record

By Leo Abrahams

The record was really enjoyable to make. Bass and drums were tracked in two days in New York City, with some amazing musicians that I'd met while working on the *Ocean's 12* soundtrack. I had very rough sketches, but everything was totally open-ended, and gradually edited on planes and in the back of buses while I was on tour with other artists.

Some of the vocalists I knew already, and some I had to track down; I made many new friends in the process. My personal highlight was playing the obscure octogenarian poet Bingo Gazingo the backing vocals that Brian Eno had done for him.

Although the record didn't sell, I did get a decent advance from Mercury (what were they thinking?), and good reviews in quality music press. These things are hard to come by now, especially for misfit records like *The Unrest Cure*. So I feel very lucky.

Artwork by Glenn Leyburn

Tracklist

1 Fragile Mind (ft: Kari Kleiv)
2 2,000 Years From Now (ft: Bingo Gazingo)
3 City Machine (ft: KT Tunstall)
4 Banks of Kyoto (ft: Pati Yang)
5 Remote (ft: Conrad Merz)
6 No Frame (ft: Brian Eno)
7 Ultra-Romantic Parallel Universe (ft: Phoebe Legere)
8 Below Ground Pt. II
9 Devil's Mouth (ft: Ed Harcourt)
10 Error on Green
11 All Along
12 Epilogue (ft: Foy Vance)

WAIT FOR ME

Moby, Little Idiot, 2009

Experiencing huge success at a particular point in your career can lead to all sorts of unforeseen complications. Yes, the benefits are obvious, but it can sometimes define your career, eclipsing all that came before it and everything that follows.

There is little orthodox about Moby's career when you compare it with most others. As an artist, he has always operated on a slightly different frequency to everyone else. His 1999 album, *Play*, is an outstanding piece of work, from start to finish. It is a rare example of a body of work that is truly timeless.

It certainly was not his first brush with success, though it did elevate his career to a level that he had never before come close to. People often say that this was his creative peak, but if you look at his career between 2008 and 2011, he was prolific. Moby released three albums during those four years – *Last Night* in 2008, *Wait for Me* in 2009 and 2011's *Destroyed*.

There are defining periods in artists' careers, and 2008 to 2011 was Moby's. You could say that these four years would determine whether he would remain a true creative force, or become a 'greatest hits' artist that relives past glories. *Wait for Me* is an easy album to gloss over, yet it solidified him as a truly relevant artist of the time.

There is a striking emotional and atmospheric beauty to this album. Tracks like 'Scream Pilots', 'Ghost Return' and 'Walk with Me' are touching and fragile, while 'A Seated Night' is spiritual in its hymn-like format.

When compared with other Moby albums, *Wait for Me* has a very different feel about it. Part of this comes from the way it was recorded and mixed – Moby enlisted Ken Thomas to mix the album. Thomas had worked with a broad range of acts over the years, from groups like Sugar Cubes, Public Image Limited and The Damned, to Clinic, Suede and Sigur Rós. The album was mixed using analogue equipment, which allowed it to maintain an organic sound.

Again, you have to go back to the previous point: do you stick to a proven formula? Or do you gamble and adopt a new approach? Moby readdressed how he made his music at this point, opting not to use the big production tricks of the day. If his career could be described as a Saturday night, 1995's album *Everything Is Wrong* was like entering a club, *Play* was the mixture of fear and excitement when you see someone that you really fancy and *Wait for Me* is the calm of 5 AM as you watch the sun come up.

Some albums are like books that you periodically pick up and read segments from. Others simply have you from the minute you start listening, right up until the last note chimes away. *Wait for Me* does the latter with ease from its opening track, all the way through, until it ends sixteen tracks later.

For the Record

By Moby, from moby.com

Mixing the record with him [Ken Thomas] was really nice, as he is creatively open to trying anything – like recording an old broken Bakelite radio and running it through some broken old effects pedals, to see what it would sound like. It is on the record as a forty-five-second-long track called 'Stock Radio'.

Sleeve design by Chris Ritchie

Tracklist

1	Division	9	jltf-1
2	Pale Horses	10	jltf
3	Shot in the Back of the Head	11	A Seated Night
4	Study War	12	Wait for Me
5	Walk with Me	13	Hope Is Gone
6	Stock Radio	14	Ghost Return
7	Mistake	15	Slow Light
8	Scream Pilots	16	Isolate

WEIGHTLESS

Juno Falls, V2 Records, 2007

Can one outstanding song make an album? No – but it can certainly win a following and gain a band the kind of exposure that has become even more elusive in music in recent times.

The song is called 'This Song Is Your Own', and it is one of the great songs that never was. This kind of compliment has been dished out too many times, but even in the context of a book like this, you will not come across a statement like it too often. It is a song of such immediacy that it could have been written by acts like The Go Betweens, Crowded House or Elliott Smith, in their prime

Weightless is an album that saw Myles O'Reilly bring all his years of experience, playing as part of Juno Falls and Blotooth, to make an album that was even better than any of his audience could have expected. The thing about the music that Myles/Juno Falls made prior to this album was that you always felt that time and money had restricted the end result. The debut, *Starlight Drive*, was a fine album, but *Weightless* realised all of its potential.

The songwriting had sharpened, the playing had tightened, and the overall sound could stand up to the scrutiny of even the hardest critic. O'Reilly's vocals are versatile enough to jump from that clean singer-songwriter style to something a little less straightforward.

On the subsequent tour, Myles took Juno Falls on a jaunt around Europe. One particular set took place in a square in Bologna. It is true when you hear people saying, 'You never know who's in the crowd' – on this particular occasion, Brad Pitt was in the audience, and was moved enough to tell Myles how much he had enjoyed the set. The story has blossomed over the years, with all kinds of spectacular add-ons, but Myles tends to play it down.

The adventures that this album led are both exciting and disappointing. For every artist there are ups and downs, but it is the ones that you have no control over that can be the most frustrating. TV appearances, high-profile tour support slots and an impressive amount of radio and media coverage, were all counterbalanced by complications with the album's release.

When the word heartfelt is used in reference to music, it can often bring up images of bed-wetting balladeers. There's nothing that would remotely dampen any bed in *Weightless*, but it is heartfelt to its core. You can really hear how much each of these songs have been nurtured, and cared for in the recording of this album.

Here is an album that had so much potential to appeal to many different kinds of people. The singles 'This Song Is Your Own' and 'The Opposite Of Everything' would hook anyone with an ear for a tune, while others – like 'Dapper Dan', 'The Nova Scotia' and 'Atom Bomb' – become familiar at an alarmingly fast rate. It is both an album to listen back, and have the pleasure of being introduced to.

For the Record

By Myles O'Reilly

Weightless was the culmination of ten years of finding my feet creatively. It started as a major label project. There was a good recording budget and an international release proposal, but on the day that it was physically released on shelves in Ireland, my record company, V2, was bought by Universal. Every artist who had a debt, however small, was dropped.

For many months, my manager and I tried our hardest to keep sales alive from behind the merchandise desk at gigs. In the end, I decided to follow an old love of filmmaking and give up with music. I collected all the *Weightless* CDs from Irish shops, and gave them away for free on Grafton Street.

Artwork and design by Myles O'Reilly

Tracklist

1	This Song Is Your Own	6	The Boy Whose Skin Fell Off
2	The Opposite Of Everything	7	Waxworks
3	Atom Bomb	8	Nova Scotia
4	A Melody Ten Years Long	9	Dapper Dan
5	Slowly Fizzy	10	Double The Part Of One

CONTRIBUTORS' ALBUM CHOICES

ALMOST FAMOUS OST

Various, Dreamworks, 2000

This album was selected by **Aisling Bea,** the award-winning stand-up comedian, actor and writer. Her on-screen credits include ITV's *The Town*, Sky Arts's *The Damned* and the BBC sitcom *Dead Boss*. In 2012, she became the first woman to win the prestigious *So You Think You're Funny?* competition in two decades. Here, Aisling recalls those compilation albums known as soundtracks . . . the excellent *Almost Famous* soundtrack, to be precise.

Photo by Anthony Woods

I have always loved the compilation of songs on the soundtrack of the *Almost Famous* movie, and it is one that I keep coming back to. It reminds me of a particular summer in university, when I was in a sketch comedy group. We were in Edinburgh learning how to be funny, trying to get on with each other while also trying to get on with ourselves, figuring out who we were and how to work the washing machine. There is a coming of age theme to the movie and soundtrack. That's the time that I first listened to it.

Soundtracks used to be a huge deal, like the toy that comes with a Happy Meal! Successful soundtracks used to break new bands, and gave them a huge platform. Recently, the *Drive* soundtrack was pretty special, though. The music had a huge voice in that movie and, similarly to the *Juno* soundtrack, it did manage to sound like how the movie looked.

I came quite late to *Almost Famous*, watching it with a bunch of pals when it was on TV one night. That was a lovely evening, so the soundtrack sort of reminds me of that. I do love the movie - the cast was stunning. I think it captured the dark and light, kaleidoscopic nature of the era, yet ultimately managed to stay a feel-good movie.

I have often found myself belting out Elton John's 'Tiny Dancer'! It reminds me of my little sister, who is a full-grown woman yet tiny, and performs a terrible robot but a mean hip wiggle. It is surprisingly hard to hit those high notes, though.

I think the compilation of artists, and even the ordering of tracks, is pretty pitch perfect. It brings you on the bus journey of the movie from the lyrics 'We've all gone to look for America' to 'The revolution's here . . . we have got to get it together, now.'

Most of the artists on the tracks are some of the biggest, most iconic in the world, but my mother is a retired jockey, so, growing up, I knew more about a horse's rear end than I did about music. University was where I learned about music. This album was a nice starting point for a young lady who grew up listening to dance music and chart hits in nightclubs.

All the songs are obviously from a certain era, but they remind me of scenes from the movie, particularly 'Mr. Farmer', by The Seeds. There is an energy and excitement to the music that sounds like going to the opening the gates of a festival, or the rush of people at the start of something, which is the vibe of the movie.

Any time that I listen to this soundtrack, I think of a pile of university friends working together, some of us going out with each other, ending up calmly watching this film, in a rare moment when a large group of people were all in the same mood. We were draped over one another on couches and dirty bean bags, with cans of beer and cups of tea.

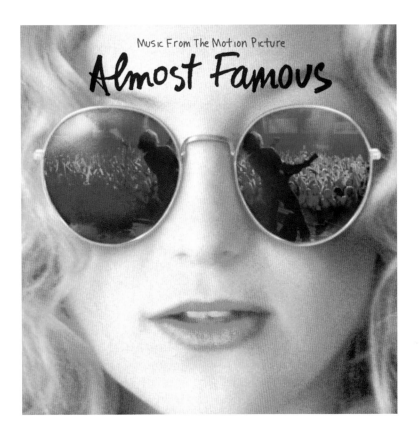

Music From The Motion Picture
Almost Famous

Tracklist

1 Simon & Garfunkel: America
2 The Who: Sparks
3 Todd Rundgren: It Wouldn't Have Made Any Difference
4 Yes: I've Seen All Good People: Your Move
5 The Beach Boys: Feel Flows
6 Stillwater: Fever Dog
7 Rod Stewart: Every Picture Tells a Story
8 The Seeds: Mr. Farmer
9 The Allman Brothers Band: One Way Out (Live)
10 Lynyrd Skynyrd: Simple Man
11 Led Zeppelin: That's the Way
12 Elton John: Tiny Dancer
13 Nancy Wilson: Lucky Trumble
14 David Bowie: I'm Waiting for the Man (from Live Santa Monica '72)
15 Cat Stevens: The Wind
16 Clarence Carter: Slip Away
17 Thunderclap Newman: Some-thing in the Air

APRIL

Sun Kil Moon, Caldo Verde Records, 2008

This album was selected by **Aiden Gillen**, who played the character of Thomas Carcetti in *The Wire*, John Boy in *Love/Hate* and, more recently, he portrayed former Taoiseach Charles Haughey in the excellent *Charlie* series. But that's only scratching the surface of Aidan Gillen's career. Anyone who has seen him present the *Other Voices* TV series will know that he's passionate about music. Here, he talks about Sun Kil Moon's album *April*.

Photo by Rich Gilligan

In my mind, I bought this album in a shop called Sound Garden in Baltimore, Maryland, while working on *The Wire*. I used to listen to it on the train between Baltimore and New York City, as there's a lot of reference to travel on the record. It seemed an appropriate soundtrack to whizzing through New Jersey swampland or run-down Pennsylvanian trackside neighbourhoods on summer nights.

That's in my mind, but the thing is, the reality may be quite different, because I think I'd left Baltimore before the record was released. It's funny the way that the mind does like that. I lived in the Fells Point neighbourhood and they (or He, Mark Kozelek) also had a later record called *Admiral Fell Promises*, and there was the Admiral Fell Inn on the corner of my street. In fact Admiral Fell himself was actually buried in a tomb a few doors down from me, so I'm going to go with Baltimore, Maryland even though I don't think it was actually there at all.

There's a passage that begins many minutes into a track called 'Tonight The Sky' where it really all comes together around the line 'I woke up every morning', that really makes my heart beat. Also, the songs 'Harper Road' and 'Tonight In Bilbao'; I couldn't live without those. There's a long one-note guitar solo on 'Tonight The Sky', that really struck me when I first heard it. The sleeve photo makes me think of a haunted house, and is appropriate.

The songs are very long, and don't have much in the way of choruses. The guitar sounds on it are often dreamy and liquid. Lyrically it is quite dense, and not easily deciphered. It's guitar music, and not a radical sound – what's individual is the lyricism and truth in his voice.

I have seen Mark Kozelek play live a couple of times. The first was at the Academy in Dublin, just around the time that the *April* album was released and, though they played a great set, the atmosphere was so intense and reverential that it got quite uncomfortable. The silence between numbers became unbearable, and I actually left about three quarters of way through because I got so vibed out. There was one song he played that I was convinced was all about paper. It turned out to be 'Tonight The Sky', which isn't about paper. The band played good and loud that night, with some good scuzzy solos. The next time was, I think, at some point in 2013 in the Union Chapel in Islington, London. This was promoting the *Among the Leaves*, album, and wasn't loud at all. It turned out to be an equally intense experience, and Mark's guitar playing was stunning. He was sitting down, and was as laid back as I've ever seen anyone in performance.

I've played tracks from *April* on the radio when I've had the chance. But I also selfishly kind of want to keep it to myself. I have a nostalgic attachment to it because, for me, it's travel music, and I've listened to it travelling to and from some important places, events and people. But I wouldn't have listened to it as often as I have if it wasn't great music.

It doesn't comply with the rules that usually define what an album is. The songs can be very long, and don't always have a verse/chorus structure. It flows in a dreamlike way, both sonically and in mood. It's lyrically dense, and I hear something new every time I listen to it.

Design by David Rager, photos by Nyree Watts

Tracklist

1	Lost Verses	7	Harper Road
2	The Light	8	Tonight The Sky
3	Lucky Man	9	Like The River
4	Unlit Hallway	10	Tonight In Bilbao
5	Heron Blue	11	Blue Orchids
6	Moorestown		

AVI BUFFALO

Avi Buffalo, Sub Pop, 2010

This album was selected by **Dave Fanning**. He would laugh if you called him iconic, but he is! Through his 2fm radio show and numerous TV series, Dave has become the single most important figure for Irish and alternative music in Ireland.

Photo by Marc O'Sullivan

When you called me, what was I listening to? *Avi Buffalo*, and it is as good an album to talk about as any, because I could literally pick five million albums! I was thinking about *Déjà Vu* by Crosby, Stills, Nash & Young, or *What's the Matter Boy?* by Vic Godard & The Subway Sect (which is the best album of 1980), or The Soft Machine's *Third*. You think that you should probably go back to a time when an album meant something.

When I heard *Avi Buffalo*, I liked it in the same way as *The Heartlight Set* by Joy Zipper, because it has great pop songs. 'What's In It For?' is the best song on it, and 'Remember Last Time' is brilliant – they wig out on that. Everything about the instrumentation, everything about the playing on it, is wise beyond their years. They never lose sight of the fact that they are summery. This is not a late-night December album at all – it is a fun sun day album.

I liked this album a lot, in amongst all the other stuff that was there at the time. I played them a lot more than I probably would have been expected to play them. All of the albums that I have mentioned are references as to why I like this Avi Buffalo album.

When you are fifteen years of age and you turn sixteen, the three months of summer can be equivalent to a lifetime. The difference between leaving school at the beginning of June, and then going back in September is huge.

The summer can do something to you – be it that you nail it down with certain music or a World Cup, or whatever. Dragging on every August night, until three o'clock in the morning, with nothing else to think about other than going back to school, is absolutely huge. Those three months seem to go on forever.

The funny thing is, when you are twenty-four, you wake up the next day and you are thirty-four. And do you know what happens the next day? You are forty-four, and then fifty-four! Those summer months can stretch out for ages when you are in your teens, and that is what this Avi Buffalo album can do. It is a complete celebration of the teenage summer, and it is maybe even hornier than I was – in fact, it definitely is!

Now, is it the greatest undiscovered album of all time? I do not know if there is such a thing. There are albums by The Small Faces and The Zombies that I could mention. The greatest song on that level is 'She's Not There' by The Zombies. It is absolute perfection.

I'm not saying that I am always looking for summery sounds. I could have picked *The Good Son* by Nick Cave & The Bad Seeds, which would probably be my favourite album of the 1990s. For instance, in the 1990s, you have a song like '1979' by The Smashing Pumpkins. People call that a great song, but it is beyond a great song. What it is, is Generation X people goofing around, doing what you do in the summer, and that is what this Avi Buffalo album is, too.

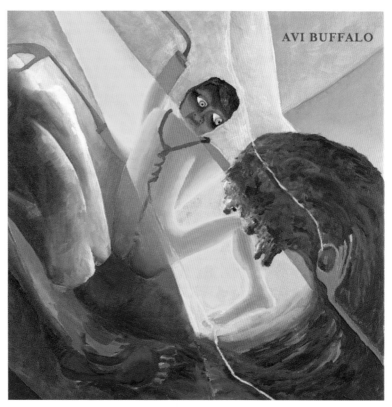

Cover painting by Devin O'Brien

Tracklist

1 Truth Sets In
2 What's In It For?
3 Coaxed
4 Five Little Sluts
5 Jessica

6 Summer Cum
7 One Last
8 Can I Know?
9 Remember Last Time
10 Where's Your Dirty Mind

BEATS, RHYMES AND LIFE

A Tribe Called Quest, Jive/BMG, 1996

This album was selected by **Annie Mac**, one of the main champions of new music on BBC Radio 1. Originally from Dublin, she has been based in London for more than a decade, where she is a much sought after club DJ, in addition to her work on the airwaves.

Photo by Mari Sarai

My LP is A Tribe Called Quest's *Beats, Rhymes And Life*. This was still, essentially, a commercially successful album, but it was generally considered not as good as its predecessor, *Midnight Marauders*. That and *Low End Theory* are lauded as classics today, but this album, to me, is hugely underrated.

It is special for me because it was the first piece of vinyl that I ever bought. I spent a summer in the Lower East Side of Manhattan when I was nineteen. I was in university in Belfast, and was spreading my wings when I came to music.

I ended up working in a vegan cafe, but I lived on St Mark's Place beside a record shop, and this was the record I bought from there. It was my entry point to hip hop, and the first record that made me really understand and appreciate it as a genre. After this, I discovered Nas, Mos Def, Talib Kwali and, of course, Biggie. Q-Tip and Phife Dog will always be my ultimate NYC MCs, though.

It never made me question previous music that I had heard, it more just blew my mind that there was a whole world of hip hop out there to discover. I did not know that much about it – I had previously been into indie, rock and electronic music. I had listened to a lot of Massive Attack, which was pretty much the closest thing to hip hop for me.

The thing about Tribe was their fluidity as MCs. I loved how they finished each other's sentences on the record; you could hear their friendship within their rhymes. For me, they sound like New York City, like Queens on a scorching hot July afternoon. They remind me of walking down Broadway wide-eyed, trying to take it all in. Songs like 'Ince Again', 'Stressed out', 'Keeping It Moving' and 'Jam' were standouts.

I do not feel it has aged at all. To me, it is a nostalgic record only in terms of association, not style, and it still sounds fresh. As I have learnt more and more about hip hop, I always marvel at how Tribe always outshone the rest, seemingly effortlessly. I listen to it still, actually. It's one that I would put on at home on a Sunday afternoon.

As much as I loved Q-Tip and his jazz samples, it was always Phife that I found the most compelling as an MC. I went on to buy the whole back catalogue of A Tribe Called Quest, and I love the other albums, but *Beats, Rhymes And Life* is always the one that I will remember the most.

Album cover by Skam2

Tracklist

1 Phony Rappers
2 Get A Hold
3 Motivators
4 Jam
5 Crew
6 The Pressure
7 1nce Again
8 Mind Power

9 The Hop
10 Keeping It Moving
11 Baby Phife's Return
12 Separate/Together
13 What Really Goes On
14 Word Play
15 Stressed Out

BEAUTIFUL VISION

Van Morrison, Polydor, 1982

This album was selected by **Cillian Murphy**. From *The Wind That Shakes the Barley* to *The Dark Knight Rises*, *Breakfast On Pluto* to his numerous stage appearances, Murphy has proven that he is one of the most versatile and talented actors of his generation. Van Morrison's *Beautiful Vision* captivated him at a young age, and the Cork man still holds the album in high regard.

Photo by Rich Gilligan

As a young boy I spent a lot of time listening to music in cars. We would pack up every summer and head for France. In the back, we were crushed against one another, overheated and cranky. My parents must have quickly realised that music reduced the violence, so we got used to listening to whatever albums happened to be in the car. Some of them became our favourites, and remain so to this day.

Beautiful Vision was released by Van Morrison in 1982. I would have been six. It must have been on one of those extended drives from Cherbourg to some campsite that the album first entered my consciousness. I had never heard Van Morrison before. I suppose I listened to it in the way that only a child can – instinctually rather than intellectually, without the preconceptions or expectations that plague the adult music fanatic. I just loved that album. I remember sitting alone in the front seat of the car after we had arrived and set up camp, listening to it once again.

Generally, the record seems to fall into what may be called his Celtic-mysticism period. During this period, his music was heavily informed by Ireland or, more specifically, by a spiritual version of Northern Ireland – his home. It is an album full of atmosphere, and although it still holds onto some of the groove of those earlier R 'n' B records, it is much more contemplatively soulful. 'Cleaning Windows' is the only exception to this. Traditional elements like the flute and the uillean pipes also feature strongly.

Listening to it now, I feel a great honesty in the lyrics. It seems to me that Van is saying, 'I'm looking for something here, not sure what it is, but it could be an interesting journey.' I think 'Dweller On The Threshold' might be my favourite track, and a great example of how the record works. Such a simple introduction, then straight into this wonderfully ponderous groove. I have sung those lyrics so many times, and despite – or maybe because of – their quasi-religious nature, they never seem to reveal themselves properly to me, but still remain tantalisingly significant in some way. Musically, the interplay between the brass and the rhythm section on this track is amazing: so playful, featuring a gorgeous sax solo (not Van himself here – Pee Wee Ellis). It appears to exist independently of any particular era or genre . . . it is just pure Van Morrison.

'Cleaning Windows' is the only recognisable hit from the record. It is a fantastic musical slice of life. It is slightly at odds with the mood of the rest of the record, but it feels like part of this journey. I am also a huge fan of the closing instrumental, 'Scandinavia'. It feels like it could have been lifted from an Eno album of the same vintage: a beautifully enchanting synth mixing with piano and, again, that slow but genuinely uplifting groove, bringing the album to a positive close.

I realise now that it is impossible to entirely put down in words what this album means to me, so I hope this may serve as an introduction. As Frank Zappa said, 'Writing about music is like dancing about architecture.' Generally, I just give people the record and let them discover it for themselves. Put it on in the car, maybe, and drive.

Cover concept, photograph and design by Rudi Legname

Tracklist

1 Celtic Ray
2 Northern Muse (Solid Ground)
3 Dweller On The Threshold
4 Beautiful Vision
5 She Gives Me Religion
6 Cleaning Windows
7 Vanlose Stairway
8 Aryan Mist
9 Across The Bridge Where Angels Dwell
10 Scandinavia

BLOOD, SWEAT & NO TEARS

Stetsasonic, Tommy Boy, 1991

This album was selected by the charismatic **Chuck D**, who has given us many iconic moments with Public Enemy over the years. Here, he looks back at an album that he still holds in high regard. The year was 1991, and the album is Stetsasonic's *Blood, Sweat & No Tears*.

Photo by Piero F Giunti,
Visionary Rebel Production

I remember hearing this when it first came out, on Tommy Boy Records. Daddy O was the leader of Stetsasonic, and I think his approach to creating a record was sonically flawless. I thought that Stetsasonic, as a performing group in hip hop and also as a recording group, had very few that could match their intensity and ability.

This album came at a point when, for the first time, there was acceptance for hip-hop albums. All the major labels decided to go and make these massive signings of hip-hop artists, and started to release album material. I think that *Blood, Sweat & No Tears* just got lost.

There are so many records out there that it's understandable that people don't talk about this album – I take that into consideration. On Rapstation.com we have a ten-station channel. We have a station that's dedicated to hip hop classics and classic artists, and a lot of the time their art is so very specific and overlooked that you feel that if they released it again now it would be a hit.

There were a lot of hip-hop records in the 1990s that couldn't be released because of sample issues and legal claims. I know that this book covers albums that are in some way obscure, but I think another book in the future about unreleased hip hop would be a good idea! There's a bunch of reasons for it, but the main one is that there is a lot of great music that never saw the light of day.

Anything that Daddy O and Stetsasonic did influenced me, because they had a group of individuals that were skilled to the highest regard. The tracks 'No B.S. Allowed' and 'Speaking Of A Girl Named Suzy' are two amazing tracks that have been forgotten. They did a video for 'No B.S. Allowed', and it was totally overlooked.

Public Enemy have always made sure that we never leave anything in the vaults, so we never did. I think what happened with *Blood, Sweat & No Tears* was very unfortunate. I get sad when I hear this now, because it was the last record released by Stetsasonic. The video, the single, where the group were coming from and what they were trying to convey, was lost in the shuffle.

Art direction by Mark Weinberg, cover illustration by Danny Tisdale, based on photography by George Du Bose

Tracklist

BORED OF THEIR LAUGHTER

The Mary Janes, Hunter S. Records, 1994

He was once the new kid on the block, but **Mundy** has established himself as a name that any music-loving Irish person will instantly recognise. He casts his mind back to when he first moved to Dublin, and he became acquainted with a band called The Mary Janes.

Photo by Mundy

I heard *Bored Of Their Laughter* in the Virgin Mega Stores on Aston Quay one morning in Dublin around 1994. It was one of the only shops that opened early. The album had just been released, and was on one of the listening posts. This was back when record shops were in a good place.

The first thing that I noticed was that this was a three-piece band. The vocals were deep and unique, with a percussive snap. The guitars and bass and acoustics were unusual too – the acoustic guitar was like the high hats and the bass was rhythmic and melodic. The electric guitar playing was phenomenal. It was up there with John Squire or Johnny Marr. The album's artwork had a half-naked half woman/half tree on its cover, which was brave and intriguing.

I loved the tracks 'Short a Few' and 'Lying Down'. 'Friends' was the killer. 'Friends' was kind of their anthem, and Mic would sing it from the pit of his stomach. For a slim man, he could sing like a mountain. I bet that if Kurt Cobain had ever heard that song he would have wanted to cover it. I later found out that Mic wrote the song with Rónán Ó Snodaigh, from the band Kila. Knowing that all these bands were part of a musical tree made me want to start digging and planting.

Bored Of Their Laughter wasn't for mainstream tastes, but neither were Nirvana, Pearl Jam, Soundgarden and so forth. If the right label found them they could have been massive, but it also had cult written all over it. I really thought that they represented Ireland in the world as a great relevant band during the grunge era.

It's one if the most original albums in my collection. It's really hard to pin it down. In later years I heard Richard Thompson and could see a similarity in the voices. Maybe there's a bit of Mike Scott in there, too. This was romantically dark music, with tons of world music in it – touches of India, Africa and Jamaica. It is smoky and hazy, dynamic and ferocious!

It feels like I've seen this band play live a million times, but, in reality, it has maybe only been twenty or so times. Seeing them do gigs was always an event – all the 'heads' went to see them. They had something pure, and everyone respected that. The album is nostalgic to me now. It reminds me of when I first moved to Dublin. It was primarily their music that sucked me in. If I had to make a soundtrack to my life, The Mary Janes would definitely be on it. They've been very significant to me.

There are no drums throughout *Bored Of Their Laughter*, yet it has more rhythm than most bands with a drummer. They weren't trying to be anyone else, which is so unusual. They were in their own magical cocoon. Sadly, that probably went against them in the end. That's what's heartbreaking about the music business. The stuff that reaches the top always has a familiarity to it, because people hate having to think.

It was one of those albums that you swore people to secrecy before you told them about. You wanted them to be yours. They were just like the Verve before they exploded. The Janes were mysterious without trying to be. I mean, anyone that cycles a black high nelly with dreads and leather pants is a mystery to me!

Cover photo by Harry Thuillier Jnr., design by Works Associates

Tracklist

1 Taken In
2 Short A Few
3 Lyin' Down
4 Diamonds
5 Story So Far

6 Friends
7 Talkin' War
8 The Instigator
9 H.U.M.F.R.E.A.
10 Nearly Dead

CHARM AND ARROGANCE

Toasted Heretic, Bananafish Recordings, 1989

This album was selected by **Camille O'Sullivan**. Born in London and raised in Cork, she is a singer who has graced stages worldwide. She has performed alongside Jarvis Cocker and Marianne Faithful, and toured with artists as diverse as Jools Holland and Shane McGowan. O'Sullivan has also scored much acclaim through her acting career. Here, she travels back to her school days and talks about an album she found shocking.

Photo by Sean Breithaupt and Yvette Monahan

I first heard this album back in 1989, when I was in boarding school in Cork city. This cassette was being passed around the dorms, and everyone was talking about. It would not have fallen into the same bracket of music I was into the time (Bowie, Pink Floyd and The Clash), but it satisfied something else in me that wasn't about their music, but more Julian's provocative lyrics. It felt shocking to me at the time, but perhaps it was music that suited who I was then, an inquisitive awkward teenager who wanted clever verses. It made me question myself!

I loved that you could only get the album on cassette. I was already a fan of their first album, particularly because of the 'Galway Bay' song, and the album's cover that looked like a pack of Tayto crisps. The cover on *Charm and Arrogance* was an envelope with their address on it. It felt like this was an underground movement with a cult following.

It wasn't music in a rock sense, but felt very of the time in the 1980s; youthful, quirky, witty, dark and Irish, or 'literary pop', as once described by the songwriter. I had never heard anything quite like Julian Gough, with his pointed Irish delivery and this cult band from Galway. Eccentric poetry was set to music discussing sex, erections (a shocker in '80s Ireland) drugs, Nabokov – the album's title, *Charm and Arrogance* seemed to sum them up perfectly!

The melancholy and darkness of 'Here Comes the New Year', the black humour of 'Drown the Browns', which was very funny, with lines like, 'Their mother had children and thinking she should/She attempted to love them, but my God who could? Kill your children, Mrs. Brown, Do your

bit for Tidy Town . . .' Not to mention 'LSD (Isn't What It Used to Be)', which I found quite sad and melancholic.

I remember seeing Toasted Heretic doing a mad interview with Zig & Zag and Ray Darcy on TV, which was quite eccentric and funny. Julian was holding wads of cash up to the screen, and went into the no-man's zone of the puppet area; I think he got a telling off.

When I think of this album, I have memories of sitting in the common room with my school friends listening to it, as if we had all made a big discovery together. They're very happy memories. It felt like I was on a journey of personal discovery as a teenager with that album. They were of a time. Ireland has changed so much now; it was tantalising and shocking then, but maybe would not be now.

I loved the fact it was like a collector's item only available on cassette – the clever art work, the black humour, the poetry and the fact that they didn't up sticks to go and make it big in London. They were from Galway and worked there. At the time, I hadn't been, but it seemed like an enigmatic wild town, full of singers and artists. They made me want to visit! I loved that they were not rock stars, and even more so that Julian was a sharp, modern-day beatnik poet and storyteller. He was a brilliant personality and seemed destined to perform.

I think the lyrics and singing were so individual. They were so eccentric and authentic. It felt like they had recorded it in their living room, and you were getting direct line to the band, as if they were singing just for you. It wasn't like some record company machine; this band did things their way, and I loved that. It captured a moment in a time when Ireland was changing and, as awkward fun-loving teenagers trying to express ourselves, we were growing up too.

For the Record

By Julian Gough

In 1988, unemployment in Ireland was at 20%. Everyone in Toasted Heretic was on the dole or a student. I worked for the summer in Spain and saved £400 – we used that to make our first album, *Songs for Swinging Celibates*. We recorded it on a four-track TASCAM Portastudio, recording at double speed on both sides of a cassette tape in the living room of our drummer Neil Farrell's parents's house. We used a £55 toy drum machine. We didn't even have a bass guitar, so we tuned down a rhythm guitar and recorded it at double speed, while Declan played the bass lines very fast. When you played it back at normal speed, it dropped an octave and sounded like a bass.

We persuaded Ian Wilson, who produced the *Dave Fanning Show*, to book us a day in the RTÉ studio in Galway, as a session. We mixed the album onto a quarter-inch master tape and made a copy for the Fanning show as payment. We made 100 cassettes, sold them, used the money to make 200 cassettes, sold them, used the money to make 400 cassettes.

By the time we recorded *Charm and Arrogance*, using the same system, we'd made our mistakes and learned how to get the best out of the equipment. We'd even bought a real bass guitar. *Charm and Arrogance* sounds amazing for an album recorded on cassette in a living room. I've changed so much over the years that it's odd listening to it now, like listening to strangers I once knew. I was an arrogant jerk back then, but the album is all about being an arrogant jerk, so at least I'm in complete command of the material! It's honest, so it still stands up. If it has a genre, it's litpop.

Cover art by Neil Farrell, stamps and postmark by Julian Gough

Tracklist

1	Drown the Browns	7	Here Comes the New Year
2	Lost and Found	8	There Goes Everything
3	LSD (Isn't What it Used to Be)	9	Go to Sleep
4	Stay Tonight	10	Charm and Arrogance
5	You Make Girls Unhappy	11	Some Drugs
6	Abandon the Galleries	12	You Can Always Go Home

CHRISTIANIA

Napoleon IIIrd, Brainlove Records, 2010

Paul Thomas Saunders is the man that gave us the aptly-titled album *Beautiful Desolation*. He is a unique talent, and has selected an album that is as steeped in character.

Photo by Dan Curwin

I first heard this album in my house in Leeds. It's one of the few albums that I didn't listen to until the CD arrived. I planned to write a review of it for a magazine that I wrote for. I put it on in the kitchen and just fell into it for the next thirty-five minutes. I then poured my heart out in a passionate, badly written review.

He used to play live with a rack of crazy instruments and a reel-to-reel tape machine playing a backing track. That hooked me initially. That's why I was excited about the album. I think finding an artist who wasn't overzealously hyped, and who was, effectively, just a local musician, was really empowering. The idea that you can be great, with nobody really knowing you, gave me hope. As soon as the album begins, it's Napoleon IIIrd's world. That's the pinnacle of creativity for me. It instantly removes you from a world where all the music you hate is beamed relentlessly from hyperactive prime-time DJs. It's a remedy for reality.

I remember the second track, "Leaving Copenhagen", coming on and building to the line, "Let's all go to Christiania". It's such an anthem of escapism to me. I also remember hearing the track "Rough Music", and thinking that it sounded like a song of primary-colour sunrises and sunsets. All those moments that throw images into your head . . . you remember those forever.

Part of me definitely did think that the album could do relatively well, in a commercial sense. With all its idiosyncrasies, it is also just really immediate. It got great reviews, too. I guess it just didn't tick all the right boxes for the right radio and media movers and shakers to take it to that level.

It's a really uniquely produced record – undeniably a self-produced, home recording. No one who was getting paid to produce a record in a fancy studio would be bold enough to make an album of lo-fi drones and distorted, yelling vocals. It's an album beget of pure ideas, executed by the guy who conceived them. They are not tainted along the way.

I've seen him live a few times. The first time was in a Leeds venue called Brudenell Social Club. There were about ten people in the room, but it was a religious experience. I tell anyone who will listen about this album! He's been a really big inspiration in my whole approach to production. A DIY ethic goes a long way, and there is no greater quality than originality. I namecheck him all the time as an instrumental influence.

It is a genuinely timeless album. It does not concede to many current persuasions of music, and he obviously has scholarly knowledge of the last fifty years of pop music. It is experimental, yet very classic. It is not ignorant of the history of pop music, but it does not rely on it.

I think the fact that it is a really pure, home-made, self-produced record is at the heart of it. Individuality and vision are paramount to creating any art that will not be fleeting. It is how music should be: a pure expression, untainted and gritty.

Photography by Bob Taylor, artwork by John Rogers

Tracklist

1 The Unknown Unknown
2 Leaving Copenhagen
3 The Hardline Optimist
4 This Town
5 That Town

6 Guys Just Wanna Have Sun
7 Rough Music
8 I Try
9 Mtfu

THE CONTINO SESSIONS

Death In Vegas, Deconstruction, 1999

As Nialler9 he is one of the most respected music bloggers in Ireland, and his influence has stretched far beyond his native shores. **Niall Byrne** has championed so many domestic and international acts before they've established themselves. Here he looks at an album that dates back to his final year in school.

Photo by Al Higgins

The Contino Sessions is tied to a period in my life where great change was about to happen. It was my Leaving Certificate year in school in Kildare, and I was starting to go to gigs in Dublin and festivals in Leinster. *The Contino Sessions* was an omnipresent soundtrack to that time.

It is a multi-faceted album. The opening song, 'Dirge', was one of the first songs that I heard from it, an eerie track with Dot Allison singing 'la la la' and a great bassline. The song builds into a buzzing psychedelic crescendo. Apart from that, 'Aisha', with Iggy Pop in serial killer mode, is a perfect weird alternative pop/rock song. Those two songs got me into the album as a whole.

'Soul Auctioneer', with Primal Scream's Bobby Gillespie on vocals, is a malevolent soulclap dub track, 'Death Threat' is industrial slowed-down techno and the closing track, 'Neptune City', is an uplifting, Indian-influenced song, with a denouement based in euphoria.

With Oasis in decline, their grip loosening on the UK media, the likes of DJ Shadow, Orbital and Chemical Brothers were moving things on. Death In Vegas were a part of that. Richard Fearless and Tim Holmes's influences for *The Contino Sessions* were outliers of music, so it was never going to be something that was top of the charts. Members of The Jesus And Mary Chain and The Stooges, Jim Reid and Iggy Pop respectively, appear on the album as a direct link to those inspirations.

Myself and my friends bonded over this. So much so, that I became friends with one of my best mates initially because he had 'DEATH IN VEGAS' written on his schoolbag. Following on from that, I saw Death In Vegas a lot in a few years. I remember going to stay in my friend's sister's apartment on the quays in Dublin, to go see their show in the Temple Bar Music Centre. It was extremely exciting, but one of my friends drank too much and cannot really remember it. I also remember seeing them at Witnness (the extra 'n' was a nod to Guinness) one year. Live, they had full instrumentation and a brass section. Though they were mostly without singers, they always put on a sonic-driven, anthemic show.

It still sounds good to me. It was right on time in 1999 – a palate cleanser of Britpop, and a way in to music of another time, and genres yet to be discovered. The album does one of the things that my favourite albums do – it walks the line between genres, creating something unique that references other styles like Krautrock, electronica, techno, psychedelia and rock.

For the Record

By Richard Fearless

It was a really easy record to make, and it was a really liberating record to make. The first album was quite hard work. With *The Contino Sessions*, we had a studio that we put together, and there was no one breathing down our neck. It was an amazing position to be in, and there was nothing to prove either.

I was a huge Stooges fan, and I managed to get Iggy Pop's address – I can't remember how, but I got it. I sent him a letter and the track 'Flying', because that was the first track that we made off that record, and it became like a mood benchmark. When you do one track, and you nail it, it can set a tone. I wrote him this real kind of fan letter, and he got back to me, and was the first person to come on board.

At that time, I was touring with Primal Scream as their DJ. I had written this track, and I gave it to Bobby. I was quite embarrassed, because I thought that I had put him in an awkward position. Around three months later, we were at something, and he started singing lyrics in my ear – he had written these fantastic lyrics. They were the first two people to come on board for the album.

Sleeve design by Fearlessbeaven

Tracklist

1	Dirge	6	Lever Street
2	Soul Auctioneer	7	Aladdin's Story
3	Death Threat	8	Broken Little Sister
4	Flying	9	Neptune City
5	Aisha		

THE DIFFERENCE BETWEEN ME AND YOU IS THAT I'M NOT ON FIRE

McLusky, Too Pure, 2004

Fight Like Apes have proven to be one of the most inventive Irish acts in many years. They have an uncanny ability to write songs that you will remember, too! **MayKay** (Mary-Kate) talks about discovering McLusky's *The Difference Between Me and You Is That I'm Not on Fire*.

Photo by Loreana Rush

Looking back, it would have been a brilliant concept for radio: four musicians, four bottles of Buckfast, four clipboards, four massive egos and a stack of fifty cent CDs from the Secret Book and Record Shop on Wicklow Street in Dublin. (Word of advice: If you are easily offended, do not go in there to see what price category your own band is in).

The players were Jamie Pockets Fox, Thomas Ryan, Ol Paddy Hanna and myself. The game: Brave New Bands.

We would sit around the living room of my old flat on Lincoln Lane, drink all the Buckfast, egos to the fore, and the chosen MC would play the first record. You were not given an ounce of information on the act you were about to hear, and if you recognised them then you were honour-bound to immediately recuse yourself. We would listen to the bands, mark them under different categories, then tally up everything at the end (taking into account a slight margin of error, what with the Buckfast).

The victor would be revealed, and the MC would have come up with some trivia points on the chosen ones. We would be delighted with ourselves. Some of the bands were absolutely appalling, and some were great (Rilo Kiley, Clor). One even made us start a band.

We were like a pack of rabid, drunk, emotional puppies scrambling around each other the night McLusky won the coveted first prize at Brave New Bands. *The Difference Between Me and You Is That I'm Not on Fire* was the name of the album. 'She Will Only Bring You Happiness' is one of my favourite songs of all time. Being in a band fond of long album titles and lame disses, we were their natural market. They were loud, they were rude but they were witty. They ticked all the boxes.

'The only thing better than discovering this band was discovering that they had bundles of material we had not heard. This was sadly their final album, but there was something poetic about us discovering it that way. These Cardiff boys changed the way I thought about singing and writing. I could shout and scream and curse if that was what I felt like doing, as long as I had something to say and a clever way of saying it.

We ended up supporting the lead singer Andy Falkous's new band, Future Of The Left, at some weird 'festival' in England. We played our cover of McLusky's 'Lightsabre Cocksucking Blues' for him with gusto. Pretty sure he hated it, probably because he said afterwards, 'I heard your McLusky cover there'. That was it, no further comment.

I seized the moment a year later when we played with the lads again. I told Andy all about how he had influenced me in writing and performing, and how much it meant, and so on. He said, 'Ah cool.' I love him. McLusky, R.I.P.

Artwork and cover photography by Victoria Collier

Tracklist

1. Without Msg I Am Nothing
2. That Man Will Not Hang
3. She Will Only Bring You Happiness
4. Kkkitchens, What Were You Thinking?
5. Your Children Are Waiting For You To Die
6. Icarus Smicarus
7. Slay!
8. You Should Be Ashamed, Seamus
9. Lucky Jim
10. Forget About Him I'm Mint
11. 1956 And All That
12. Falco Vs. The Young Canoeist
13. Support Systems

DUBLIN GONE. EVERYBODY DEAD.

The Jimmy Cake, Pilatus Records, 2002

Laura Sheeran is one half of the alien pop duo Nanu Nanu. She has also carved out a solo career that has delivered outstanding albums, like 2012's *What The World Knows*. Here, she talks about being introduced to The Jimmy Cake's *Dublin Gone, Everybody Dead*.

Photo by Laura Sheeran

This came out when I was fifteen, and it was one of the most exciting things that I had ever heard. To think it was an Irish band who had made this music blew me away. But to think that such incredible and innovative music could be getting made, and that hardly anyone would take notice, was even harder to digest. Those guys should definitely have been afforded the ability to live permanently off their music.

I first heard the album in 2002 at home in Corofin, a small village outside Tuam, in Galway. I had been to Dublin for a day trawling through the record shops and was given a tip by my Dad to check out The Jimmy Cake. I bought the album, and could not wait to get home and listen to it.

It was just so different. I loved the fact that it was so engaging but that there were no lyrics. The music is so powerful and driven but equally sensitive and delicate. It is an incredible fusion of sounds.

When I first heard it, it sounded 100% original and brand new to my ears. I had literally never heard anything like it. On reflection, now, I guess there were plenty of influences flying around there, but there are so many people in the band that I am sure the influences could probably span the entire history of recorded music!

I knew it would be an "acquired taste" kind of record, but since I was only fifteen, I kind of felt somewhere, deep down inside of me, that it could be the start of a whole new phase in Irish music. I guess that, in some ways, it was, but on an underground level rather than mainstream.

There is so much going on in it, yet it seems to be very simple: totally exciting and always keeping you on your toes, but not challenging. It is a perfect blend of pushing the boundaries of music but remaining accessible to a wide audience or listenership.

For the Record

By Dara 'Dip' Higgins

In September 2002, at the tail end of a pretty glorious summer, we entered Temple Lane studios to record *Dublin Gone. Everybody Dead*. It was released six weeks later, on 25 October. Every track was a first or second take, live in the studio, with no click track.

We were after a raw, live sound, and we left in the creaks and coughs and studio veritas to add colour. We were tight, back then – limber, younger. The ten of us played together so much, in rehearsals and gigs, that the songs on *Dublin Gone* almost grew organically, as if they wrote themselves.

We were not going to argue with the protean force that drove us to do what we did. Nowadays, we would sit down with the force, interrogate it over a few pints and then ruminate on that for a while. But we are older and wiser now. In 2002 we hadn't a clue. We had no fear.

DUBLIN GONE. EVERYBODY DEAD.

Design by Paul vs. Simon

Tracklist

1	The Opposite of Addiction	5	Eye Of The Cowboy
2	Quartz Cat Waltz	6	Wir Schlafen Auf Den Boden
3	Death Fall Priest	7	Ricky Sound
4	The Width Of The Black	8	Limestone Tiger

FUNK YOUR HEAD UP

Ultramagnetic MCs, Mercury Records, 1992

This album was selected by **Buck 65**, a perfect example of a one-man band. The Canadian alternative hip-hop artist has released some outstanding music over the past twenty years. He (Rich Terfry) is also a celebrated radio host on CBS Radio 2 in his native Canada.

Photo by Rob Campbell

In 1988, Ultramagnetic MCs released an album called *Critical Beatdown*, which is now regarded as a bona fide classic from hip hop's golden age. It took four years for Ultra to get around to releasing a follow up. I was a huge fan, and assumed, with great regret, that they had broken up.

On first listen to *Funk Your Head Up*, I was blown away. It picked up where *Critical Beatdown* left off, and went beyond. The production was incredibly dense and funky and challenging. The beats were hard. It sounded almost as if the Beastie Boys's album *Paul's Boutique* were produced by The Bomb Squad. It is relentless.

Nothing about the production of the album sounds weak, overly slick or corny to me. It is totally raw, classic, turntable-heavy hip-hop muscle. It sounds like it fell to earth from outer space, and landed in the trashiest, stinkiest back alley ever avoided. The rapping on the album is precisely the advanced, experimental lunatic assault I had been waiting to hear.

Four years after *Critical Beatdown*, Kool Keith was still obsessed with brains: 'Your brain is small and very hard to find. I need a microscope to find a two-cent brain that don't think', he raps. And who else could come up with something like, 'I'm so fresh. So fresh, so fresh, so fresh. Better than the rest, yo. Is that true? Does a dog have four legs, two eyes a tongue and a mouth? Think about it.'

There are two stand-out tracks on the album that I truly believe are among the greatest achievements in hip hop history. One is a song called 'Bust The Facts'. This one is a showcase for Kool Keith, and he breaks down the history of the early days of the art form with more vivid imagery and detail than I have ever heard anywhere else. He digs back to tell the stories of the pioneers who came before the three widely-acknowledged 'founding fathers' of hip hop (Kool Herc, Afrika Bambaataa, and Grandmaster Flash). He mentions early pre-hip-hop innovators, like The Disco Twins and Disco King Mario, and even details the equipment they used. It is an important document of how a new musical genre came to be, by someone who was there.

The other stand-out is a showcase for the group's DJ, Moe Love. It is an instrumental sample-and-scratch composition called 'Moe Love On The 1 And 2', and I would argue that it is one of the all-time great works of hip-hop musicianship. It is a masterpiece.

Ultramagnetic MCs released a third album a year later, called *The Four Horsemen*, and I remember that many reviews referred to it as a 'return to form' for the group. I think it sold much better than *Funk Your Head Up*, too. I never understood that. I think it is a pretty good record, but it does not hold a candle to its predecessors.

In 1996, Kool Keith went solo and released an album under the name Dr Octagon. Once again, the hip hop world seemed to be in agreement that Keith helped author another classic. He has barely slowed down since. A few years ago, Ultramagnetic got back together to play material from *Critical Beatdown* on tour. With all that has happened, it is as if *Funk Your Head Up* has been erased from existence. I think that is a crying shame. I cannot think of a more overlooked and forgotten hip hop album. If you ever come across a copy, I highly recommend you give it a good listen. You will be richly rewarded.

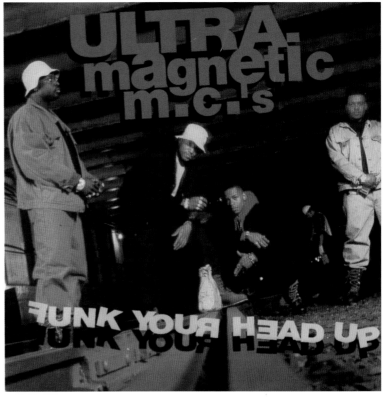

Art direction by Bays & Alli, photography by Michael Lavine

Tracklist

THE GOLDEN HORDE

The Golden Horde, Mother Records, 1991

This album was selected by **Ian Wilson**, who has been a producer for RTÉ radio for more than thirty years. He has produced shows for Dave Fanning, Miriam O'Callaghan, Jenny Huston and me, God bless him! He has been responsible for thousands of local acts getting coverage, by way of 2fms studio sessions. He has also overseen the station's live output at events like Feile, Cork Rocks, Oxegen, The Electric Picnic, Eurosonic, Slane Castle and countless others.

Photo by Kathrin Baumbach

There are undoubtedly better Irish albums, and there are undoubtedly better Irish bands. To be blunt, I was looking after the band at the time, which is completely not allowed as an RTÉ staff member! I had a bit of influence with Mother Records, so pointed them in that direction, and they went on to record this album.

It has two absolutely classic Irish songs: '100 Boys', which holds a place in the top twenty rock singles ever made in Ireland. The other track is 'Friends In Time', and has Maria McKee on it. Everyone knows it. This was the last shot for them, because they had been around for a long time. They had a really good live show, and their infatuation with the Ramones was perfectly acceptable. In terms of actually doing something, I had put Ramones and The Clash as the most important acts of the 1970s.

Maria McKee had just had a huge hit with 'Show Me Heaven', which was featured in the *Days Of Thunder* movie. She was living in Ireland at the time. She came in and sang on the vocals with Simon, and Bruce Brody did the string arrangement.

There was a lot of thought put into the album. It was not an expensive album to make, and it does transfer well when you listen to it now. Daniel Rey, who had worked with the Ramones, came over and worked with the band. The Ramones at this stage had moved to Beggars Banquet, and I remember ringing up Martin Mills directly and getting Daniel Rey's number from him. The band also got in Andy Shernoff, so it was pretty impressive.

As a complete album, it was really very good. It had a range of songs that highlighted Simon Carmody's songwriting ability. I do not know if albums leave legacies anymore, but it has two of the most played songs on Irish radio on it.

The band went on tour with The Cramps around the UK, but the problem was that the album was not available there yet. The band continued to gig, and were one of the biggest touring bands in Ireland, but it just was not going to work out.

Unusually for Irish albums at the time, it has a really exceptional cover. It was a consistent set of artwork that they did with all the releases at the time. Singles? Covers? You can touch it, feel it; you are talking to another generation!

For the Record

By Simon Carmody

That was definitely a very romantic album. It was mostly love songs, because that was the vibe. It was mostly fast songs because fast songs are better than slow songs, mostly. The band was hot, and wanted to create a world of noise and beauty.

It was a kind of defiant rock 'n' roll thing, with some melancholy, some mysticism and a lot of drive. The tunes were nearly all postcards to specific people. Ronan Keating covered one of the songs years later, and did an excellent job. There was a bit of pop there.

We certainly made the record we wanted to make at the time. I remember being pleased at the way it sounded, kind of like an aeroplane, or a jet. That is how musicians think. I remember meeting Alan Vega on Second Avenue and he said, 'Just make a great record man, Don't give in.'

Joey Ramone sent us a note saying that it sounded great, which was very encouraging. It is all a long time ago, but we had a lot of fun doing it and were very pleased when people enjoyed it.

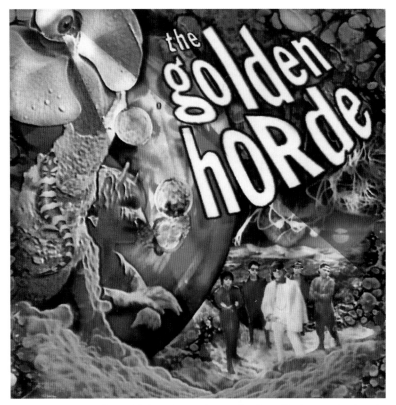

Photography by Steve Pyke, sleeve design by Sam Steiger, paintbox by Charlie Whisker, artwork by Works Associates

Tracklist

1	Endless Weekend	8	I Never Came Down
2	Lisa	9	Now I'm Gone
3	100 Boys	10	Rorschach
4	Hell	11	Over Here
5	She's A Weirdo	12	House of Girls
6	Friends In Time	13	Paula
7	Have A Scene		

HEARTWORM

Whipping Boy, Columbia, 1995

Torsten Kinsella formed the ever-impressive God Is An Astronaut with his brother Niels over a decade ago. They are better known internationally than they are in their native Ireland. Their tours have brought them to China, Siberia, the Czech Republic, Brazil, the USA and far beyond. *Heartworm* by Whipping Boy is his Buried Treasure.

Photo by Derval Freeman – Timeless Imagery

For me, *Heartworm* has an emotional content that you rarely find on most records. There is an angst on it, and a sense that the whole band are battling against the odds. The heartfelt lyrics set the whole album in a very special place.

The first song that I ever heard from it was 'We Don't Need Nobody Else' on a TV show called *The Beatbox*. I thought it was really unusual because he was doing a chant/talk vocal, not your average singing. There was something in Ferghal McKee's timbre that grabbed my attention, and the chorus is a killer hook.

This was different to the grunge sound of a couple years before. At that point and time, everyone was coming out with Nirvana copies, but this was different. It seemed to dive into that shoegaze sound, but it still tipped its hat to the grunge scene in a very subtle way.

I felt that it was extremely original at the time: it was an extra step forward from the whole grunge era. It was a cool sound with great vocals that you could actually hear, which is something that did a lot for me.

When it was rereleased around six years ago, it sounded as if it had just been released there and then. I think it is the best album that I have heard from Ireland; it is that good. The production was just right. There is enough of that contemporary sound, without killing that underground, indie sound that they had as well.

It is still the kind of record that I listen to when I am on tour. There is only so much other stuff that you can take, but I find that this album is one that I can listen to over and over again. This, and Deathcab for Cutie's *Transatlanticism* are two that often keep me going.

When you listen to *Heartworm*, it has the whole package. I think that if the production was considerably less, it would not have aged so well. But the most important thing is the content; the melodies, the lyrics, and the sound of the band really captured something very special.

For the Record

By Paul Page

Writing 'We Don't Need Nobody Else' was a real light-bulb moment for us; the notion of writing honestly about who you were and where you came from had somehow eluded us, up to that point. *Heartworm* was released at the height of the Britpop phenomenon, and it did not fit that whole scene very well. It just got lost.

Although it was a commercial failure, the people that bought it at the time seemed to connect with it in a special way. The album could easily have been consigned to the bargain bins, and quickly forgotten. But that did not happen.

Nearly 20 years on, people are still talking about it, they still hold that record in high regard, for whatever reason. It is nice to know that something that was such a huge part of your life has endured, and is so fondly remembered.

Design by Works Associates, photography by Brendan Fitzpatrick

Tracklist

1	Twinkle	7	Personality
2	When We Were Young	8	Users
3	Tripped	9	Fiction
4	The Honeymoon Is Over	10	Morning Rise
5	We Don't Need Nobody Else	11	A Natural (Extra track)
6	Blinded		

HORSEDRAWN WISHES

Rollerskate Skinny, Warner Bros, 1996

This album was selected by **Glen Hansard**. As the lead vocalist with The Frames, he is one of the most recognisable faces in Irish music. More recently, his fame has spread worldwide, after winning an Oscar with Marketa Irglova for the song 'Falling Slowly'. Glen has selected Rollerskate Skinny's masterpiece, *Horsedrawn Wishes*.

Photo by Flavia Schaub

It was one of those records that someone gave me. I remember bringing it home and listening to it, and thinking that it had a sound from nowhere, or at least nowhere that was recognisable as Irish. Rollerskate Skinny had that sort of thing that Interference had: a mystical presence. I still know very little about the band. I have met Ken Griffin a few times when he played some gigs with us.

Rollerskate Skinny remain slightly Beach Boys – a mysterious band that came together and made a couple of albums. This one in particular is really unusual, because it does not sound American and it does not sound European – it has a place all of its own. With music, like all the finer things in life, it is all about taste. Things either have a tangibility that works with you or that you just dismiss, and it is amazing how quickly we make decisions on records. The first few seconds often decide whether you are ever going to listen to it again or not.

This soup of sound sounded like an acid trip – a bit like what you get off some of the Captain Beefheart records. When you find yourself on your own, with your arms in the air listening to a record, surfing the big sound, then you realise that you are listening to something that you are going to love forever. It is like the first time that you really get into to Pixies and you realise, 'Oh God, I'm changed!' This music has changed everything about what I have liked in the past, and everything that I will like in the future.

For The Frames, this blew our heads off. We heard all these stories, like Ken spending two years with a guitar just playing 'A', and then writing all of his vocal melodies over one chord. I am sure that if you spoke to Ken he would tell you that was bollocks, but those were the kind of stories that we heard at the time! The lyrics are really odd, like in 'Speed To My Side' – 'Speed to my side nobody ever told me that this sort of thing could come alive'. I love the idea that it might look at the sense of love as a beast that rises within him.

The few times that I came across any of the members of the band, they did not have any of that 'indie rock fuck you'. They were just a bunch of dudes who had made this record, and had all moved on by the time we heard it. A lot of bands think about how important they are in the great spectrum of stars. All of that shit will be decided long after you are gone; we have no control over how we are seen and how we are placed.

What also strikes me about Rollerskate Skinny is the song titles, like 'Swab The Temples' – what a beautiful name for a song. 'Cradle Burns', 'Bell Jars Away' . . . when I look at these, I do not know them as song titles. For me, it was one listen straight through. It was all recorded in studios that we have used, but sounds nothing like the studios we used. I would love to go and listen to it now!

For the Record

By Ger Griffin

One journalist described Rollerskate Skinny as a beautiful car crash. Pretentious, I know, but kind of accurate. Sometimes it was an amazing dream, sometimes an amazing nightmare. Making *Horsedrawn Wishes* is the single most intense experience any of us have ever experienced. We had just signed a major deal with Warner Brothers, and we felt that we had something to prove, each of us with a thousand ideas inside our heads.

We then had the finances to totally let rip. Our engineer was advised by his doctor not to work like that again. We burnt the midnight oil, sound engineers, amps, ourselves. I remember leaning over the engineer's shoulder, shouting, "Turn it fucking up", with Stee and Ken backing me up, more, more. It was like a bad scene from Star Trek. Our aim was always to blow our minds and create the most epic sonic peace ever. Sounds arrogant, but that's how it was.

Two intense years of late nights, mad drinking, arguing, laughing. Working like this was the last chance to record ever. We never worked as intensely like that before or since, but that is what is required to make an album like *Horsedrawn Wishes*. You only do this once in a lifetime . . . trust me. Time, of course, will be our judge.

Photography by Eamon McLoughlin, design/photography by Power House Commercial Designs

Tracklist

1	Swingboat Yawning	7	Man Under Glass
2	Cradle Burns	8	Shimmer Son Like a Star
3	One Thousand Couples	9	Angela Starling
4	Swab the Temples	10	Ribbon Fat
5	Speed to My Side	11	Thirsty European
6	All Mornings Break	12	Bell Jars Away

I AM BRAZIL

The Redneck Manifesto, Trust Me I'm A Thief, 2004

Niall Davis is one of Ireland's most successful mountain bikers. He has been ranked as high as number nine in the UCI Espoir World rankings, and has competed at both downhill and cross country World Cup level. He is a big music fan. Here, he has selected The Redneck Manifesto's third album.

Photo by Victor Lucas

The scene that I am from is all biking. I am mainly a mountain biker, but there would have been a lot of BMX guys hanging around with us as well. I think the whole Redneck Manifesto thing came out of some songs that they had being featured on BMX videos. It kind of started from there really. When I found out that they were a Dublin band, I could scarcely believe it because of the style of music. When we found out that they were local, we just started trying to follow every gig that we could.

I think it was in the Voodoo Lounge a good few years ago – the Rednecks and Jape actually played back-to-back, and I have been hooked since then. I think it is a unique sound. It is amazing, really. You could listen to that album, and there are chilled out songs that are the most beautiful instrumental stuff, it is perfect. Then, if you are into something a little more aggressive, a lot of their songs are real builders – they are kind of constantly ramping up, or some start off really heavy and then peter out.

Maybe some people don't get instrumental bands, maybe they are waiting for the vocals to come in, but their songs are so up and down, and Richie is so energetic on stage, and his body language says it all. Maybe it plays on neutral ground or whatever, but the music does more than enough. I do not think it necessarily needs any lyrics with it.

There is a good mix of songs on the album. The title track starts it off – and there are just so many catchy little sections on it – little beats and little hums that stick in your head. Strictly speaking, I tend to listen to them all, but I guess for the sake of this, *I Am Brazil* is a nice blend of the Rednecks. I think the following album, *Friendship*, is probably a little more aggressive and maybe a little bit darker.

I have it on the iPod there now, and if I have a look at my top twenty-five songs, there are probably four or five of them in there that are played all the time. A mix between The Redneck Manifesto and Jape would make up a lot of what I listen to, even now. There is some Rory Gallagher there, too. I listen to other things for a bit of fun, like Eagles of Death Metal, but it could be T-Rex, either, and a lot of Thin Lizzy. I guess it just depends on the mood that I am in at the time.

I love when you see someone who is good at what they do, whether in sport or in music. I would look at Ritchie and think, "Holy shit, he is competent, and he is good at what he does." If you look at Rory Gallagher playing, say, a mandolin or something like that, you think, "Holy shit, he is completely dialled in", and it is a similar thing when you see The Redneck Manifesto play live. It is very impressive, they have got it all well-tuned.

For the Record

By Richi Egan

We recorded *I Am Brazil* at a time of change for our band. We had just recruited Neil O'Connor in on keyboards, and we were moving towards a more groove-oriented sound, away from the heavier aspects of our earlier work.

We decided to record it at Black Box studios in France and work with David Odlum. This proved to be the right decision. The studios are in a rural area, with nothing more than table tennis and some cheap local wine to distract you.

We also had the great fortune to have studio owner and legend Iain Burgess mix one of the tracks. We became close buddies. This fact is very dear to us, because he unfortunately passed away a couple of years later. *I Am Brazil* turned into an album that we are all very proud of, and it opened a lot of doors for us to tour, meet and work with some great people.

Incidentally, the title comes from Niall's son Matthew, who would always say, "I Am Brazil" whenever he played football!

Design and illustration by Matthew Bolger

Tracklist

1 I Am Brazil	7 I Have Not Make It
2 Take On Us	8 Who Knows?
3 We Still Got It	9 Bring Your Own Blood
4 Another Day Of Hunting	10 Paint Your Dilebloa Pink
5 Hibernation Statement	11 Good With Tempos
6 Break Your Fingers Laughing	

IN MY OWN TIME

Karen Dalton, Just Sunshine Records, 1971

Founding member of the much-lauded experimental folk group, Dr. Strangely Strange, **Tim Booth** has left an indelible mark on music in Ireland, and further afield. He has uncovered one of the true treasures of the early 1970s – *In My Own Time*, by Karen Dalton.

Photo by Con Kelleher

Sometime in the early '70s, the late Bill Graham, music journalist and good friend, tapped me on the shoulder amid the superb churning racket of a Rodeo gig, deep in the west Wicklow badlands. He gave me that all-knowing smile, and, from the folds of a battered corduroy jacket, magicked out a Freebird bag, containing a pristine, second-hand copy of Karen Dalton's 1971 album, *In My Own Time*. 'You will come to treasure this . . .' he said, and he was right.

Some years later, in a flat in Dún Laoghaire, I put the album onto the turntable for a group of discerning friends, including the singer Honor Heffernan, and waited for their reactions. Track one, side one: a rocksteady base intro, under looping electric guitars, and then this remarkable voice, swooning in from the ether like honey dripping from a loving spoonful, the voice lilting off into a unique Billie Holiday-tinged dreamland, somewhere between the Oklahoma foothills and Muscle Shoals. The whole structure of the vocals is underpinned and supported by Harvey Brooks's great production, and the really compassionate playing of the backing band, especially the violin. As the track says, 'Something's on Your Mind . . .'

Honor was listening to the album like a hawk, and as the second track, 'When A Man Loves A Woman', slides in, I see her wipe away a tear, head bowed, taking in this remarkable singer. Track three, 'In My Own Dream', features Amos Garret on guitar, and his solo towards the end lifts Dalton's voice into that high, lonesome hill-country mode, perhaps preparing us for the pared down folksiness of the next cut, 'Katie Cruel', recorded with just a frail banjo – most likely that of Dalton herself. Bobby Notcoff's passionate fiddle embroiders her voice. For me, this is the outstanding track, and shows the quality of both the singing, and Brook's production.

You have got to remember that, back then, nobody was singing like this. Nobody was even thinking about singing like this. The year before the recording, Dana won Eurovision and the pasteurised mimsy of Joan Baez was everywhere. We only ever got to hear the real stuff through imported records or from a very few visiting acts, so I never got to see Dalton live.

'Who is that?' Honor asked, and, as 'How Sweet It Is To Be Loved By You' skipped out of the Warfdales, she began to smile. That is the effect that Karen Dalton has – melancholia, underpinned by a childlike joy. Her voice loops across the melody, free as a bird, tuned exactly to the arc and step of the music. The second side of the album is equally as pioneering, and way ahead of its time, but I will leave that to you to investigate. These days, that can be very easily done. This album has now been rereleased, and is available on iTunes, with a couple of bonus tracks.

Karen Dalton died in relative obscurity in 1993, and Bill Graham some three years later. I miss them both.

Album design by Michael Scott, photography by Elliott Landy, direction by Michael Lang/Marv Grafton, reissued design by Kiki Ajidarma

Tracklist

1 Something On Your Mind
2 When A Man Loves A Woman
3 In My Own Dream
4 Katie Cruel
5 How Sweet It Is
6 In A Station
7 Take Me
8 Same Old Man
9 One Night Of Love
10 Are You Leaving For The Country

IN THE NAME OF THE FATHER OST

Various, Island Records, 1994

James McGee is an Irish professional tennis player. The Dubliner competed in the prestigious US Open in 2014, and spends up to thirty-five weeks each year traveling to take part in different tournaments around the world. He talks about the song and soundtrack *In the Name of the Father*.

I have selected the soundtrack album from the movie *In the Name of the Father*. Despite the fact that there are a number of iconic tracks on it, I feel that a few songs on the soundtrack have been overlooked, particularly the title track that Bono performs with Gavin Friday.

In U2 terms it is a buried treasure, but I can understand why, when you consider how many anthems they have written over the years. Some of the other tracks that really struck me when I first heard them were 'You Made Me the Thief of Your Heart' by Sinead O'Connor, The Kinks's 'Dedicated Follower of Fashion' and 'Billy Boola', which is another song by Bono and Gavin Friday.

I first discovered the track 'In the Name of the Father' in 2006, when I was nineteen years old and attending college in Aerica. I came over to the US with a hard drive full of music that a friend had shared with me, and I immediately fell in love with the track. From there, I searched for the rest of the songs on the album. I loved them both individually and as a soundtrack album.

The soundtrack's title track struck me immediately – I thought there might be a religious or spiritual component to it. As I listened to the lyrics and the instruments used, I initially felt that there was an eerie feel to it that slowly builds into an intense, dramatic and powerful track. This song helped me appreciate how musical instruments are used. I had never heard them being put to use in the way that they are on this song before. It begins with what sound like tribal drums and, when the vocals begin, the whole song comes into bloom.

There have been a number of times where I asked friends who are U2 fans if they had heard the track 'In the Name of the Father', and many had not heard it before. I feel they are missing out on a great track, so I always suggest that they have a listen to it.

After meeting Bono in 2011, my attachment to this song grew even stronger. I was attending a dinner at an event in Trinity College, and Bono was one of the invited guests. All eyes were on him for the entire evening. When he got up to use the bathroom, I knew it would be my only chance to get a few minutes of his time. As he was walking by, I put my hand out, and introduced myself and gave him a twenty-second condensed version of my tennis career, telling him what I was trying to accomplish. He looked pleasantly surprised to meet an Irish tennis player, and told me that if I made the quarter-finals of Wimbledon, he would bring Daniel Day-Lewis and Gabrielle Byrne to watch and support me! I was inspired, to say the least.

We had a picture taken afterwards, and as he went to walk on, I told him that one of my key rituals before playing a match was to listen to music, with my favourite pre-match song being 'In the Name of the Father'. He turned his head, smiled, looked at me while raising his clenched fist and strongly stated: 'YOU NEED THAT RAGE!' I'll never forget that moment. It was both funny and inspirational. I still listen to the track on a consistent basis, and any time that I am not in the right state of mind before a match, I think back to that moment and it always psychs me up!

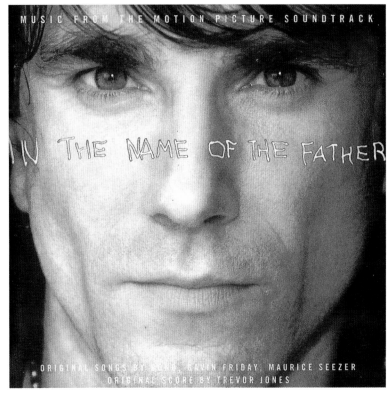

MUSIC FROM THE MOTION PICTURE SOUNDTRACK

IN THE NAME OF THE FATHER

ORIGINAL SONGS BY BONO, GAVIN FRIDAY, MAURICE SEEZER
ORIGINAL SCORE BY TREVOR JONES

Design and art direction by Cally on Art Island

Tracklist

1   Bono & Gavin Friday: In the Name of the Father

2   The Jimi Hendrix Experience: Voodoo Child (Slight Return)

3   Bono & Gavin Friday: Billy Boola

4   The Kinks: Dedicated Follower of Fashion

5   Trevor Jones: Interrogation

6   Bob Marley & The Wailers: Is This Love

7   Trevor Jones: Walking The Circle

8   Thin Lizzy: Whiskey In The Jar

9   Trevor Jones: Passage Of Time

10 Sinead O'Connor: You Made Me the Thief of Your Heart

JAI PAUL

Jai Paul, N/A, 2013

This album was selected by **Daithi**, the fiddle-playing, beat-producing dynamo of energy that gave us the excellent *In Flight* album in 2014. You could say that Daithi brought the fiddle to a different kind of dance floor.

Photo by Conal Thomson

Not only is this one of the most exciting and inspirational electronic albums of this century, but it also has this insane backstory surrounding it. Hell, we don't even know if it's supposed to be an album or not, or whether we are even going to hear a 'finished' version. Even though it was highly praised and made many 'best of' lists that year, the story around the release kind of spun the whole thing out of control, and now we are left with an amazing album that everyone is kind of forgetting about, and it is becoming increasingly hard to find.

I had just finished college when this album came out, I started to spend more time in Galway city, and really enjoying the party scene there. The album reminds me of early-morning house parties and really sticky floors. I was at a friend's house one morning, and heard on Twitter that it had suddenly been released, out of nowhere, on Bandcamp. We bought it and sat there listening, blown away by how different it sounded. It was so rough and ready, and produced in such a weird way.

As we were listening, the rumour had spread, meanwhile, that Jai Paul had not actually released it. Jai Paul's label then announced that the "album" released on Bandcamp was actually a collection of demos released by someone who had stolen Jai Paul's laptop. Mayhem ensued.

The first impression was how amazing the groove was on every track; it felt like Prince had started making modern electronic music. From a music producer standpoint, I could not get over how weirdly it was mixed, but I figured it was intentional. Jai Paul's previous releases had also been rough and ready, and they did not need to be these perfectly produced tracks. I felt that the weird mixes added to the tracks and gave them a load of character, really making them stand out. 'Str8 Outta Mumbai', the second track on the record, felt like it was going to be the hit single, it was so catchy and had us dancing straight away. By the time I got to the cover of Jennifer Paige's 'Crush', I was completely hooked. I still listen to that track so much, to this day.

I definitely felt the album should be huge. I really felt it should have been nominated for the Mercury, but I guess the controversy surrounding it kind of stopped that from happening. Both the artist and the record label said that it was not the official album, so they did not actually do any promotion of their own. Now that it has been taken down from Bandcamp, it is quite hard to find – you can really only find it on torrent sites. I really think 'Str8 Outta Mumbai' could have been a crossover hit. Maybe it still will be. There is still a question hanging over the whole thing. The rumours are that he is still working on the album and that we might see a finished version someday, but I am so attached to this version that I do not know if I will like a 'finished' product.

Blogs are such a big part of our music culture right now, and they are great for showcasing slightly stranger types of music. It is kind of hard to explain, but to me, this record really feels like it came from the Internet. It feels like the sort of music you would come across, headphones on, on some random music blog at 4 AM. That is how our generation finds interesting music these days, I think.

The groove and rhythm of the tracks are what really sets it apart. The weird lo-fi mix, distorted drums and off-kilter synth and guitar sounds gel the whole thing together. I think that is what gives him his distinctive sound. You can tell a Jai Paul track from a mile away.

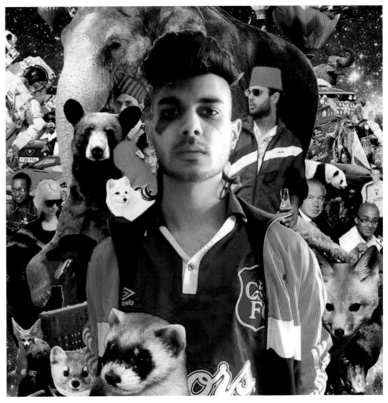

Album art obtained from www.soulmusic.com

JOHN COLTRANE AND JOHNNY HARTMAN

John Coltrane and Johnny Hartman, Impulse!, 1963

Scroobius Pip is the voice that you hear on tunes like 'Thou Shalt Always Kill' and 'The Beat That My Heart Skipped', from his days as one half of the duo that we knew as Dan Le Sac Vs Scroobius Pip. Another duo is on Mr Pip's mind here, and this pairing dates back to 1963.

Photo by Lease Roe –
Joli Studios

When people ask me what my favourite album is, the Johnny Hartman and John Coltrane album is always my number one. It always sounds like a pretentious answer, because it was hugely overlooked and not that well known.

I heard it first through my brother. Most of the stuff that I have gotten into I can trace back to my older brother playing it to me. He lent me the CD many years ago, and I absolutely fell in love with it. Their version of 'Lush Life' is amazing. Johnny Hartman's vocals are sublime. It is a travesty that he is not remembered alongside Sinatra and Dean Martin.

What really blew me away, about that song in particular, is that all the time that Hartman is singing, Coltrane is easing off; there seems to be a huge amount of respect there. When Hartman has a break in his vocals, Coltrane essentially mirrors it, and plays what has just been sung. It is amazing to see these guys each getting a chance to show why they are both such legends, but also not competing in any way. It is a tough thing for a duo coming together, when they have both got their plaudits in their own rights.

It has definitely influenced me in the way that I make music with Dan Le Sac. With the Scroobius Pip stuff, I have more control over how the music is and where the breaks are. Before myself and Dan got together, I was a fan of his work as a producer. So when we play live, the reason that I always have a chair is because I am a six-foot-four bloke with a beard, so even if I am not doing much, I will attract a certain amount of attention just by standing there. For several years now, I have had a chair there, so at the points where Dan is doing his thing, I can completely remove myself from the situation. I can sit down, as if to say, 'There is where your focus should now be'. And this is definitely influenced by this record.

My choice is crazy, in the sense that there is no way that I would have naturally come to what is my favourite album of all time! All the other albums on my list are hip hop or punk, and all have some relation or chain that, even if I had not been introduced to them, I would have somehow gotten to them myself. This album was not that; I was into a bit of jazz, but if I had not had this put in my hands, I would not have had it in my life.

Similarly to Sinatra and Nat King Cole, it is weird that they are so of their time, that, in turn, it becomes timeless. It does not feel dated, because we still replicate that time today. Obviously, it was a while ago, but when Robbie Williams was at his peak, he did a whole album of swing songs and crooning. It is something that is forever there.

I was a big fan of Amy Winehouse. Listening back to people like Johnny Hartman, Martha Reeves and loads of others, it is so clear that, as amazing as Winehouse was, she was heavily influenced by these people, whereas you listen to Hartman, and you know that no one sounded quite like that, and no one could now. Because of the era and the time, accents and language were slightly different – you could not have someone naturally write and sing like that now. If you sung like that now, it would be in homage to those that have come before you.

Original cover design by Robert Flynn

Tracklist

1 They Say It's Wonderful
2 Dedicated To You
3 My One And Only Love

4 Lush Life
5 You Are Too Beautiful
6 Autumn Serenade

JOHNNY GALLAGHER & FRIENDS LIVE & UNPLUGGED IN FIN MCCOOL'S

Johnny Gallagher & Friends, Self-Released, 2002

This album was selected by **Easkey Britton**, a five-time national surfing champion, and the first Irish person to surf the infamous hell-wave Teahupo'o in Tahiti. She grew up in Rossnowlagh in County Donegal, and is from Ireland's first surfing family.

Photo by Robbie Reynolds - Oxfam Ireland

Johnny is this hugely inspirational figure in my life, and one of Ireland's finest guitarists. He is one of the greats in our music world, past and present. He is just an explosive performer, so full of passion for his craft, and that tends to infect others around him and attract other talented musicians to collaborate with him. That is what happened on this album. Johnny has these powerful moments where he will take off with indefinable wizardry, letting his creativity run wild across the guitar strings and kind of leaving everyone stunned and mesmerised in his wake.

I heard the album being recorded live and unplugged when I was a teenager in 2002 at the local pub, Fin McCools, in Ballyshannon. The atmosphere was electric, with a room full of great characters. It was described as, "A great night, dark and plain; Moe poured pints like falling rain, we all sat till early morning, with only one single Garda calling." A time when we were not in such a hurry – when friends could come together for no purpose other than the pleasure of singing aloud to a buzzing crowd of locals. Drinking like fools (I was still on the Britvic 55 mind you!), it was an insight for me, as a young girl, into another world, laughing and joking, and somehow through it all, singing in tune one lively night in June.

What struck me about it was its rawness. It is an upbeat jam between friends, a live acoustic session with a mix of rock and a bit of roll, banjo strumming and belting tunes. It captures the genuine craic, with the background noise of hoots, cheers, laughter and clapping. One of my favourite moments is when Moe, the barman, says in the background, 'Folks, folks will ye just be quiet for five minutes till we get this song on', and there is this instant hush on the album before the musicians get going.

I feel like I have an extra special connection to the album because my Dad, Barry Britton, wrote one of the songs, 'Hard To Be Cool', when he was a drummer in his own band in the 1970s. I thought that was so cool. I still do. I love when Johnny takes off on the track 'Running Up The Hill' – it just makes you want to move, a song where the audience can really express themselves!

The album has a certain nostalgia for me, as a nomad on the road, more often away from home than not. I can feel the pull of home every time I listen to Johnny's version of 'Mr. George'. The album captures such an authentic moment of what makes the Irish music scene so unique. That togetherness, the improvisation and banter among friends, the mix of instruments, rolling from folk to rock, the rough and readiness of it all, strong and simple music-making, stripped bare of all pretension. That is why I think it is an important piece of our music culture, and I like to share it with others when trying to describe the energy and feeling of home. What works really well is the improvised feel – to jam it out. That gives the listener the power to engage. It is music that really connects, that is what it is all about.

For the Record

By Johnny Gallagher

It was 2002. The thought of making a live album had been with me throughout the 1990s while we were travelling through Europe. I wanted to make something powerful, acoustic guitar, box and banjo-driven. It could have been recorded anywhere, but it all came to life sitting with my good 'auld friend Moe McWeeney, who was the owner of Fins at the time.

Fin McCool's is like the centre of the seesaw, it sits perfectly in the middle of Ballyshannon's hill, and is possibly one of the finest wee pubs in the country. When there are twenty people inside, it has the atmosphere of a thousand, and the stout tastes like nectar, poured through its short pipes directly into a man's glass.

This, by all accounts, is not a very well-made album, but it is what was captured on the night that makes it fantastic for me; every mistake, noise, cough and fart made on that night was recorded. As for the twenty-five or thirty people who whistled, roared and clapped in the bar after every recording, sure, they loved being part of it. The excitement and the spontaneity through the course of that evening was magic.

It was brought back to the studio, fixed and mixed, and everything was traditionally recorded, with no editing or computers . . . it was just a very simple recording. I did not get too many albums made, but the ones that I did went to friends and family. It sold well here in the north west, and some copies went to the USA, Germany and France. Sadly, there was no label involved, no sponsor or distributer was interested at the time, so I to put it out there myself. It never had an official release.

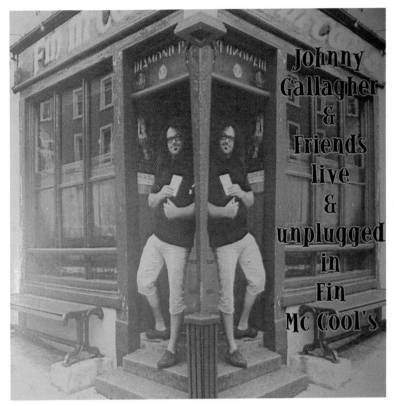

Sleeve design by Patrick Danagher, photography by Philip Mulligan

Tracklist

1	Whatever Is Good	7	Peggy Gordon
2	The Half Door	8	Mary From Dungloe
3	The Restless Mover	9	Running Up The Hill
4	Mystery Mind	10	Murt & Moe
5	The Lonesome Boatman	11	Reel Selection
6	Hard To Be Cool	12	Mr George

JUST PLAIN LONESOME

The Bellfuries, APS Records, 2001

This album was selected by **Imelda May**, one of Ireland's true success stories. The internationally renowned singer has performed on *The Tonight Show*, *Conan* in the US and *Later . . . with Jools Holland* in the UK. Imelda also appeared on RTÉ's *Other Voices* series, and she performed with Jeff Beck at the fifty-second Grammy Awards.

Photo by Barry McCall

I heard one song from this at a club and I was hooked. I had heard people talk about it, so I got the album. It is an amazing album from a great band. It has aged well, and is very simple – it's only three musicians.

The lyrics are great – there is a lot of humour in them. I love the writing on this album, you just cannot help but enjoy it when you put it on. It is one of those albums that, when you listen to it more, you hear more and more what it is that you like about it, and I do actually listen to it regularly.

This is an album that I listen to now, it is not one that reminds me of way back when. I bought it on vinyl a few years ago and, only last week, I think I listened to it every day. I love vinyl, so it is on my turntable all the time!

The band have gone on to do other things since that, that are not quite the same style of music. The guitarist plays beautiful steel guitar on this, which is a very difficult thing to do, and the rhythms are great.

There are lyrics in it like, 'He's gonna know what it's like to swallow this guitar' from 'Your Love (All That I'm Missing)'. There are others in the song 'Up to Your Old Tricks Again', which I love the humour in.

Let alone selling, I am very surprised it is not better known . It is not played anywhere, really, and it is not mainstream by any means. It's known on the rock scene, but apart from that, it's just not well known, which is a shame.

It is quite sad actually. I love this album so much that I know almost every song, and I sing it like crazy. I also make everyone that comes to my house listen to it! This album has not really been forgotten, because it has not been discovered by many people. The people that have heard it love it; it is a hidden gem, not a forgotten gem. Maybe after this, people might check it out and listen to it.

For the Record

By Joey Simeone

Ahhh . . . the little album that could! When it was reissued, I sat down with headphones and listened to it in its entirety, and found myself picking apart all the little things that I wish I had changed!

Although I love to sing, I am not a huge fan of my voice, so I am usually a little embarrassed listening to The Bellfuries in a critical setting. Most artists feel this way about their records on some level, but I think it is best to keep your mouth shut and just let the songs take on their own life.

We were of course not reinventing the wheel, but I think that the combination of influences (heavy metal, '60s pop, early country and rockabilly) set us apart from a lot of what was happening at that time in the rockabilly scene. I get the nicest and most heartfelt compliments about that record. Even though there are lots of songs about loneliness, it seems to make people happy. Connecting with people on that level means the world to me.

Once, I had a couple tell me that *Just Plain Lonesome* saved their marriage, and that it was the only thing they could enjoy together at a time when their relationship was crumbling. I had a doctor tell me that he listens to it while performing surgeries! I have had a few women tell me they had it playing in the delivery room while giving birth. I had no idea that, in years to come, that silly little record would be my ticket to seeing the world.

Cover photography by W. O. Felts, design and layout by Maira Saaverda, logo by Matt Boyle

Tracklist

1. So Sad And Lonely
2. Wasted On Him
3. Teenage Boogie
4. Take It To The Chapel
5. Just Plain Lonesome
6. Gonna Make It Alone
7. Your Love (All That I'm Missin')
8. I Don't Wanna Wake Up Tomorrow
9. Up To Your Old Tricks Again
10. Hey, Mr. Locomotive
11. You Must Be A Loser
12. Stealing Kisses
13. Love Found Me

KALEIDOSCOPE

Siouxsie & The Banshees, Polydor, 1980

This album was selected by **Jacknife Lee**, a Dublin gent now based in Topanga Canyon, Los Angeles. He has produced acts like U2, Robbie Williams, R.E.M. and Taylor Swift, and has written songs with Ed Sheeran and Harry Styles from One Direction. He has also made numerous solo albums, and was a member of bands like Compulsion, Thee Amazing Colossal Men and Casablanca Moon.

Photo by Esme Lee

I rarely hear anybody talk about this album, or even this band, anymore. *Kaleidoscope* (despite selling well on its release) and the group have pretty much dropped from the radar. Our loss; bands should listen to it. It has got what should be fundamental to all records – fearlessness, curiosity, ambition and a desire to do something new.

This was the band's third album, and it was released less than two years after their first punk debut. The progression is huge. Punk agro is out. After losing their guitarist and drummer, they chose not to replace them, and utilised the space left in the sonic structure by the absence. There is a deliberate abandoning of all traces of rock 'n' roll. The electric guitar takes a back seat. It is no longer the foundation, and leaves huge areas empty. It liberates the record. The known rock architecture is gone.

John McGeoch (Magazine's guitarist) guests on the album. He was an extraordinary player, who, like a few musicians of the post-punk era, repurposed the role of the guitar. It chimes and bursts, and is not heavy or distorted. It marks events. Drum machines provide the timekeeping, along with another unorthodox musician, Budgie. He rarely hits the two and four of the bar, as is usual. There is some dub and ethnic rhythm, and smatterings of unusual percussion. It is odd stuff.

No sound is left untouched or straight. Bass is effected everywhere. Yet it all feels spontaneous and immediate. It is a Eurocentric record. I cannot hear any influence of American rock, or the New York sound that was the impetus for the London punk movement. Instead, Kraftwerk and Roxy Music are the parents. Its aesthetic is a big part of its appeal for me. Importantly, it feels like one idea fully realised.

The lyrics can be a weak point – clumsy at times, leaning on spookiness and images of horror that hint at the goth movement that the band would become synonymous with. But with a production that is this inventive, it is easy for me to ignore some of the lamer rhyming and themes.

I forget about the album, but every now and then I put it on and am awestruck by its scope and experimental nature. To achieve this, and have two proper hits, is exceptional: a rare feat.

After this, they returned to the traditional band lineup and produced some fine albums, but this is the one for me. There is so much that shouldn't work with it, but that is why it is wonderful. Perhaps it is no bad thing for bands to lose their guitarists and drummers, and be forced to think differently.

Art direction by Rob O'Connor, sleeve photography by Joe Lyons and illustrations by Rose Harrison

Tracklist

1 Happy House
2 Tenant
3 Trophy
4 Hybrid
5 Clockface
6 Lunar Camel

7 Christine
8 Desert Kisses
9 Red Light
10 Paradise Place
11 Skin

KONK

The Kooks, Virgin Records, 2008

He is one of the most talked-about young rugby players in the northern hemisphere, but **Robbie Henshaw** takes the expectations in his stride – a stride that has helped him become highly thought of on the pitch. *Konk* by The Kooks brings him back to his school days.

Photo by Brendan Moran (Sportsfile)

I really loved The Kooks's first album, *Inside In/Inside Out*. There were some great songs on that album, like 'Naïve', 'Ooh La' and 'She Moves In Her Own Way'. When the second album, *Konk*, came out, they had really cool songs on that too, in particular 'Shine On' and 'Always Where I Need to Be'.

I had been really looking forward the second album. I was blown away by the first, and there was a degree of anticipation for their follow-up. When I got to hear it, I wasn't disappointed. I felt that it was just as good.

I used to listen to *Konk* when I was in school. Any time that I had a free class, or I was in evening study or the gym, I'd have a listen to it on my iPod. I recently came across it when I was shuffling through my old iPod, and it brought back a few memories.

Music has always been a big part of my life. I've played since I was seven years of age, and I still play some gigs and jam with the family, especially around Christmas.

I was taught traditional music by my grandfather, Billy Henshaw senior; he showed me how to play the button accordion and the fiddle. He would whistle a tune, and I would play back what I could.

In my school days I learned the guitar, but I never got around to learning any of The Kooks's numbers –I'll have to at some point in the future when I get a bit of spare time! I haven't had the chance to see them play live yet, but I did see them play at festivals on TV, and was really impressed by their performances.

You definitely get the feeling that *Konk* wasn't as big as their debut album, even though it has some really great songs on it. I always love when I hear their songs on the radio as it brings back fond memories. I haven't heard that much of this album on the radio recently – it's been forgotten about a little, I think.

A few of my friends remember this album, but they're not as familiar with it as I would have thought. You have to search for the songs from it on YouTube, or go through your iPod to listen to them these days.

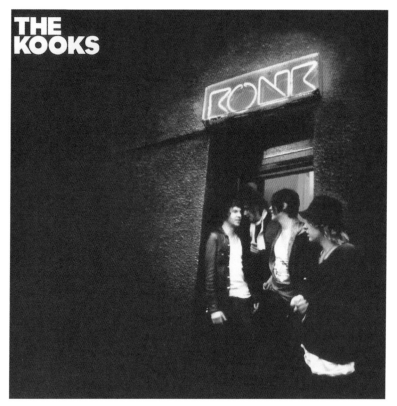

Design by Andrew Murabito, photography by Ben Parks

Tracklist

1	See The Sun		7	Stormy Weather
2	Always Where I Need To Be		8	Sway
3	Mr. Maker		9	Shine On
4	Do You Wanna		10	Down To The Market
5	Gap		11	One Last Time
6	Love It All		12	Tick Of Time

THE LAST RESORT

Trentemøller, Poker Flat Recordings, 2006

This album was selected by **Beardyman**, a beatboxer who can count Bono and Jack Black as fans. He can create more sounds than your imagination could possibly conjure up. Here he tells of his admiration for *The Last Resort* from Trentemøller.

Photo by Juan Jose Ortiz

I have chosen *The Last Resort* by Trentemøller because, for all kinds of reasons, I think it is one of the greatest pieces of electronic music ever made. I do not hear it talked about as a seminal work, but I regard it as one.

I first heard about Trentemøller when he started getting well known in 2007. He had done a remix of Moby's 'Go' that was incredibly complex. He was using samples of extremely distorted and compressed drum kits that would appear for a second and then just disappear. It was just extreme glitch at another level – nobody else had done this before or, at least, not in a solid dance sense.

In the same way that Pixies are loud, here were extreme dynamic shifts that were so well balanced they worked. It is a bit like the genius that it takes to make fusion cooking work, where you have extreme flavours that should not go together, but somehow do.

A lot of the stuff that Trentemøller was doing before he released this album was a bit more extreme, but the dance music he was making had a lot of subtlety and balance in it. When he released *The Last Resort*, it was just so much more nuanced, and the glitchiness was perfect. This balance of little samples of vinyl crackle and the glitches that just come from making analogue devices break a little and having digital things cut badly, done in such a way that the artefacts become elements of the music.

This had been done. There was this whole glitch movement, but it was more a kind of art electronica movement. What Trentemøller did was to take that and work it and make it his own. Skrillex, which is very extreme, probably would not exist if it was not for people like Trentemøller.

It works in the same way that the mid '90s with Radiohead felt: like a galvanisation of all the different lessons you could learn from the different kinds of guitar music that there had been, they seemed to synthesise everything into this perfect kind of guitar-based entity. They made this sort of gestalt guitar band, and then they stopped doing guitar because they thought, 'We've sort of completed that project and we want to move on.'

After *The Last Resort* was released, Trentemøller was one of the biggest artists in Europe, and one of the biggest electronic artists in the world. On that album specifically, there is so much that is subtle and nuanced – it is just gorgeous. You know when you eat Michelin-starred food? I have only had that a few times, but whenever you do, you think, 'Holy shit, that is a work of genius!' The flavours are so balanced, and the textures are amazing. That is kind of the feeling I get when I am listening to Trentemøller. It is not like art for the sake of art, and it is not necessarily stuff to make you dance just for dancing. It is not just music to make you think, either. This is genius at work, and it is utter sonic perfection.

Artwork by Weissraum.de(sign)*, photography (Forrest) by Photocase.com, photography (3D Tree) by Nulleinsbild, photography (Anders) by Dirk Merten

Tracklist

1 Take Me Into Your Skin
2 Vamp
3 Evil Dub
4 Always Something Better
5 While the Cold Winter Waiting
6 Nightwalker
7 Like Two Strangers

8 The Very Last Resort
9 Snowflake
10 Chameleon
11 Into the Trees (Serenetti Part 3)
12 Moan
13 Miss You

LAUGHING STOCK

Talk Talk, Verve, 1991

This album was selected by **Craig Walker**, who came to public attention as vocalist with Power Of Dreams during the late 1980s. He has released numerous albums with POD, Archive and Mineral, as well as a solo record. His buried treasure is the remarkable 1991 album *Laughing Stock*, by Talk Talk.

Photo by Stefano Tiozzo

Power Of Dreams had signed to Polydor in the UK at the very end of 1989 and, as far as can I remember, Talk Talk were signed in early 1990. The A&R guy that had signed them had also signed us. I was in his office one day, and he said to me, 'I can't believe it, I've signed Talk Talk.' It was one of the biggest deals of that era, off the back of huge hits and them playing arenas all over the world. I think that the label were expecting the next Simple Minds or U2 or even Duran Duran, but the album that Talk Talk delivered was anything but.

He gave me a copy of the album, and I loved it. I thought it was the best thing that I had heard in years. I had not heard new music like that ever before, and it blew my mind. It came out around the same time as *Loveless* by My Bloody Valentine. Those were two albums that I played to death while living in London in 1991, working on the second Power Of Dreams album. They were really big influences.

I love everything about it: the flow, the way it builds and the way some of the songs are just built around riffs. You can hear the care and attention that has gone into it, and the detail is really amazing. Through *Laughing Stock*, I got into a lot of different music. It was the first jazzy album that I ever really listened to. Before that I would run from jazz; I thought it was for old farts!

In interviews around the time of its release, Mark Hollis talked about Miles Davis, John Coltrane and all these jazz giants, and he made it sound really cool. After that, I started listening to that kind of music. *Laughing Stock* is not a jazz album, but it has that spirit.

Even now when I stick it on, it transports me back to the time when I first heard it, which all great albums do. I can hear Talk Talk's influence in a lot of post-rock bands. People like Mogwai in particular were definitely fans of that album. I can understand why it was not a huge success at the time, but I think that it is still going to be listened to in forty or fifty years, and you cannot say that about a lot of music.

For the Record

By Mark Hollis, from the 1991 Polydor Records promotional interview 'Mark Hollis Talks About Laughing Stock'

With this one, there has been a very conscious effort to get away from conventional songwriting. If you look at the first track, 'Myrrhman', there is no part that will ever repeat itself. If you move into the second track, each verse that you move through cuts by a bar, it gets increasingly shorter as the bit that is going on in the back gets longer, and the vocals are shifting their position with reference to the bar. It is just to get away from this frustration that you get of fitting into moulds.

Cover illustration by James Marsh, sleeve by Russell Uttley at Peacock Design

Tracklist

1	Myrrhman	4	Taphead
2	Ascension Day	5	New Grass
3	After The Flood	6	Runeii

LINK WRAY & THE WRAYMEN

Link Wray, Edsel Records, 1960 (reissued by Hoodoo Records, 2011)

Jim Fitzpatrick has worked as an artist in Ireland for over forty years. His Celtic Irish artwork is known worldwide, and his 'Viva Che' and Thin Lizzy pieces are, in every sense of the word, legendary. Jim talks about the electrifying feeling of hearing Link Wray.

Photo by Jim Fitzpatrick

People will probably laugh, but it was electrifying when I heard it first. You cannot imagine the environment we grew up in, and it is not just Catholic Ireland, the whole world was very much into jazz and little else. Some music was frowned upon. This was before Bill Haley & His Comets, who I saw live in the Theatre Royal.

I heard Link Wray on AFM – I used to listen to a programme called American Armed Forces Network. This was after the war, obviously, and AFM was a brilliant station. You got music you had never thought of or heard of before. I heard this music, and it was 'Rumble'. It was Link Wray, and I did not know who it was. It was extraordinary because of the image it created in my mind.

There was a film out around the time called *Blackboard Jungle*, and it was banned in Ireland. Link Wray's music was subversive; it was associated with juvenile delinquents. So, when Cliff Richard and The Shadows came along, it was all very cool and white. You know what I mean?

Now when Link Wray's music came along, it was just dangerous. We knew we were listening to some kind of forbidden music. If you can imagine this, there was a restaurant in town called The Rainbow, and opposite it was the Broadway Café. These were our hangouts, for me and my mates from school, during the summer holidays. They had jukeboxes, and we used to play 'Rumble', and the place would come alive. People's hair would stand on end with this kind of music. It was primarily instrumental.

Across the road in The Rainbow, they had a jukebox with a video screen, if you can imagine that! You put in your shilling, and there was a video of a performer, in full colour. The one we played over and over again was of a guy called Vince Taylor, in a black leather jacket and a bebop haircut, singing 'Brand New Cadillac'. and I do not want to say that it drove us crazy, but it certainly got the testosterone going. Girls would be there, and we would literally be bopping.

'Later on, we started going to tennis clubs, which were the equivalent of night clubs, where you got great music. It all came from the very back of the power chord, created by Link Wray. That is my own belief. I could be totally wrong, but I think it is a fairly accurate description of it. Eric Clapton was a great proponent of Link Wray, and a great supporter of him later as well.

They are very heavy bass power chords, but that was not the only thing he sang. He had a great song called 'Ain't That Lovin You Baby'. His other hit was called 'Jack The Ripper', which is more the same as 'Rumble'. It was considered degenerate, though, and his music was banned. It was banned in New York City, for heaven's sake – that is how dangerous it looked.

This was a time where *Blackboard Jungle* came out, and then *Rock Around The Clock*. I cycled up from Portrane with my mate (we were on holidays) to see *Rock Around The Clock* in The Carlton in Dublin. It was just sensational, we were standing up on the seats, and that was considered delinquent behaviour. The name 'Rumble' came from *West Side Story*, which, at that time, was a big musical. A 'rumble' was a street fight. So it was what it was – it was street fighting music.

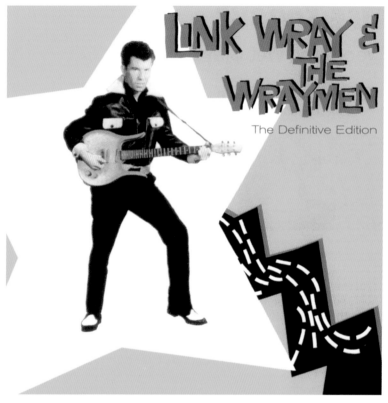

Cover Photo by X, design by Jettoki DB

Tracklist (2011 edition)

1 Caroline
2 Slinky
3 Right Turn
4 Rendezvous
5 Dixie-Doodle
6 Rumble
7 Hand Clapper
8 Raw-Hide
9 Lillian
10 Radar

11 Comanche
12 Studio Blues

Bonus Tracks
1 Mary Ann
2 Trail Of The Lonesome Pine
3 Rumble (Alternate Take)
4 Golden Strings (Based On a Chopin Etude)
5 Ain't That Lovin' You Baby
6 Comanche (Demo)

7 Slinky (Alternate Take)
8 Radar (Alternate Take)
9 Mary Ann (Alternate Take)
10 Ain't That Lovin' You Baby (Alternate Take)
11 Walkin' With Link
12 Danger One Way Love
13 Johnny Bom Bonny
14 Roughshodl'm Countin' On You
15 Right Turn (Alternate Take)

LIFE SPARKS

Woodstar, Wet Clay Records, 2003

This album was selected by **Blindboyboatclub**, who creates laughter and fear in equal proportion as one half of the Rubberbandits. However, Blindboyboatclub knows his music. Woodstar's *Life Sparks* is his album of choice.

Photo by Steve Ullathorne

Woodstar's *Life Sparks* is a savage album full of savage songs. My brother was the lead singer and co-songwriter in the band, so I first heard a lot of the songs played on acoustic guitar in our living room. I was only a teenager, but it was the first time I learned that a professional piece of music only needs good chord structure, melody and lyrics.

It was only when EMI got involved, and Woodstar took those songs to legends like Stephen Street and Ben Hillier, that I understood the value of a producer: someone who can take a good song to the next level. Because all these bigwigs in England were interested in the band, I think everyone assumed the album would be huge. The songs were too good. The album has no filler.

When the album was recorded, I was asked to make the artwork for it. I had to listen to it every day, to get a feeling for the paintings and photographs I took for the album art. It was that repetition and absorption that got me deep into the album, and also, inadvertently, shaped me as a musician and producer.

I love 'Time to Bleed'. What Ben Hillier did with the production was amazing. Sounds were introduced that you cannot really hear unless they are pointed out to you and, if you take them away, you long for them. 'Suicide Way' is another cracking hard rock tune.

Listening to the album was very important for my musical education. When I would say to my brother, 'I love that "Time To Bleed" song', he would say to me, 'Then you should check out Burt Bacharach'. So I'd go and discover Burt Bacharach for the first time. Hillier wore his influences on his sleeve, which led me to discover albums like *Scary Monsters* by Bowie, and musicians and bands like Neil Young and America.

The album has a very American sound, with nods to acts like Wilco and Sparklehorse. But it was the snakey bits of David Bowie or Bacharach that got me excited: how the feeling of Bowie was evoked with just a guitar lick or a synth line that sounds like it's from *Low*. Woodstar really had their own thing going when it came to the songwriting. The use of dark, visually rich lyrics over Bacharach-type pianos was unique.

I was only a nipper in secondary school when they used to play, so I couldn't go see gigs even though I'd created the album artwork. I managed to sneak into the album launch gig before a bouncer spotted me, and I had to leave halfway through or the venue would have lost its licence. By the time I was eighteen and could go to a gig, the band had split up, which was a terrible loss to Irish music.

It is a cracking album and I still listen to it regularly, like I would any album that I consider a classic. However, for me it represents two things. I learned how to write songs and become a producer by observing the process from bedroom recording to finished song. I also learned that a song is like a painting: it's something anybody can do anywhere, using only talent. It's talent and creativity that determine the quality of the work – not equipment or money. That gave me confidence to become a songwriter.

An album is only of its time when it relies on a type of sound that is popular at that moment. *Life Sparks*, at its core, is about solid, good, songwriting. They are songs that are just as good with one voice as with an acoustic guitar. When a song has that, it will always be timeless. Every musician should aspire to that.

For the Record

By Fin Chambers

I have very fond memories of making *Life Sparks*, in particular around the demoing of the songs, when we would sit around working on arrangements in 'the shed' in Mungret – a makeshift studio we had built from scratch at the end of a field. That time when a band gets together and sits down to work on songs – no pressure, just partying and jamming, but also having material that you know has worth – is an extraordinary experience.

The energy between the players, creating a unique sound that cannot be heard anywhere else, is a lovely thing. We had that chemistry in Woodstar, and the songs and sounds could have come from any era, and therefore still feel relevant today. Eventually, other things such as the business, the demands of life and the emotional baggage that we all carry with us into any system we enter, finally catch up and the magic somehow gets obscured. But if it even happens to you once in your life as a musician, it is all worth it. I am very grateful to have been a part of Woodstar: *Life Sparks* is a wonderful tribute to that time in our lives.

Photography, sleeve artwork and design by Dave Chambers

Tracklist

1	Sorry Skin	7	The King
2	Dumb Punk Song	8	Can't Let Go Of Anything
3	Control	9	These Scars
4	Life Sparks, Red Flame	10	Time To Bleed
5	Suicide Way	11	The Sky
6	Through Our Lives		

LIVE

Donny Hathaway, Atlantic Records, 1972

With two albums, and countless tours and plaudits to his credit, **James Vincent McMorrow** is on the right path to becoming a national treasure! Here, James talks about an artist and album that not only has shaped his career, but inspired him to write and sing.

Photo by Emma J. Doyle

I could have picked any record from Donny's catalogue – they are all equally important to me, all masterpieces in their own right – but I think this was the record that got me. It resonates with me on every level. It was such a musical statement from someone who, I think, is one of the most important musicians of all time, and who I believe deserves to be spoken about in the same sentence as the other R 'n' B greats, but who a lot of people just do not know that much about.

I was reading an article in *Rolling Stone* with Pharrell Williams; I grew up completely obsessed with the Neptunes production. In the article, they asked Pharrell which was his favourite rhythm section of all time, and he cited this record. I had never heard of Donny before, but I figured that if Pharrell was that into it, then it was something I needed to hear. There were not a lot of Donny CDs in the shop, just this album and one of his Roberta Flack duets records. I brought it home, really just thinking that I would dig the drums and bass section, but his voice totally blew my mind. To this day it is still the best that I have ever heard.

The record opens with a cover of 'What's Goin' On' by Marvin Gaye, and it is just an absolute groove machine. The clarity of the recording, the definition in the instruments and his voice . . . for a live album it is almost impossible to understand how they got it all so right. My experience of live albums, up to that point, was a lot of overly compressed, under-recorded works, but there is so much air in this mix.

The audience is the thing that makes this album doubly special. You can hear them almost all the way through the record, shouting out at all the right moments, encouraging the music the whole way through. Right before the second track, 'The Ghetto', they play this beautiful instrumental segue coming out of 'What's Goin' On'. There is a little lull right before Donny's about to sing the first intro line, and this woman in the crowd yells out, 'Alright, this is it!', and the crowd just loses its mind and goes into this unbelievably tight soul clap, that perfectly predicts the tempo of the song.

I tell everyone who I can about Donny Hathaway: in interviews, walking down the street – it does not matter. I feel compelled to speak about him, as he is such a huge part of my musical background. I have always felt a really strong urge to speak to people about his work, and I am continually amazed at how relatively unknown he is.

This album, this artist, he is so deep in my musical story, that every time I hear this album, I think of being eighteen, and hearing it for the first time: hearing a voice that made me want to sing, hearing songs that made me want to write. At the end of the day, I am both a musician and a music fan, my brain is divided clean down the middle like that. What I want from the music I love is for it to hit me at my musical core and my emotional core at the same time.

There is a magic to this record that cannot be understood, and probably could not be repeated, even if you tried a thousand times. Having a different crowd, one musician in there who is off their game, Donny not feeling it, and this album would not work. There is a moment towards the end of the record, on a song called 'Voices Inside', when Donny breaks the song down into movements, and during each movement, another musician takes a solo, and is highlighted. On one of the last sections, the bassist Willy Weeks takes his moment, and he starts doing this bass run that keeps going up and up and up, and, out of nowhere, Donny just starts laughing on the mic, and you can tell that even he is wrapped up in this thing, and cannot believe what is happening. It is completely perfect.

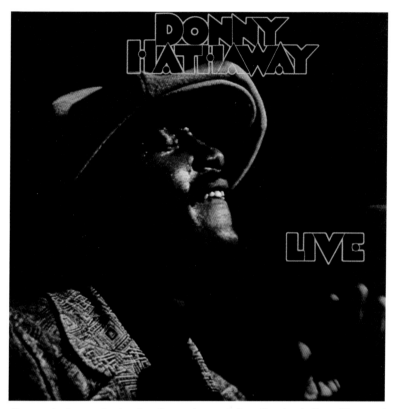

Cover photography by Jim Cummins, art direction by Jeffrey Blue and typography by Terry Dale

Tracklist

1	What's Goin' On	5	Little Ghetto Boy
2	The Ghetto	6	We're Still Friends
3	Hey Girl	7	Jealous Guy
4	You've Got A Friend	8	Voices Inside (Everything Is Everything)

A LOVE SUPREME

John Coltrane, Impulse! Records, 1965

This album was selected by **John Kelly**. As a radio presenter, he is known for his exquisite taste. He has also had a very successful TV career with *The View*, *Other Voices* and *The Works*, and is a celebrated novelist. Here, he talks about *A Love Supreme*, a classic that many may not yet have sampled.

Photo by Barry McCall

To call *A Love Supreme* a buried treasure would not be quite true. For jazz fans, it is a very well-known album, and its first hearing is often something of a rite of passage. That said, jazz is a minority sport, and many people may well not have heard of it at all, or might be put off by the very word 'jazz'. While it is not exactly a hidden treasure, not everyone has been lucky enough to find it.

It comes in four mind-blowing parts, all of them recorded one evening back in 1964. Coltrane had been leading his quartet for the previous three years, but when this record appeared, it was clear that he had moved into a whole new dimension. What you call your God is your business, but Coltrane is aiming for the realm of the divine here, and you can hear it. It was a liberating and welcome sound to me – a mind-opening expression. I must have been hungry for it.

I was at university. I had been listening to jazz – and Coltrane in particular – since I was at school, because I could borrow records from the local library. But back then, I was listening randomly, often choosing discs simply by the look of the cover or on the basis of an artist's name I had picked up on the sleeve notes of some other record. I had also seen a television documentary on Coltrane, and I suspect that is what really woke me up to his music and made me realise that the term 'jazz' did not quite cover it. This guy was beyond anything I had ever heard. So, the first place of hearing was probably in my less than salubrious student digs in Belfast.

To borrow an image from Heaney, it blew the heart open. Here was someone seriously embracing the spiritual and, by the sounds of it, actually connecting with something. The musicianship, the relationship between the musicians, that unique, in-the-moment interplay and, of course, Coltrane just doing what he does. Elvin Jones, the drummer, once said that John Coltrane was an angel – and he meant an actual angel. It was his only was explanation for what Coltrane could do.

It is not an easy record, and sure, it is not for everyone. But in the right circumstances – in peace and, especially, on your own – *A Love Supreme* will deliver something you will never get from any amount of drink, drugs or dogma. It takes an open mind, musically, and every other way to just go with it. I guess it is, necessarily, a private record. To have heard this music live, in a communal setting, must have been something very special. Possibly overwhelming.

Nothing under the sun is new, but this is an utterly unique record. The inspiration and genius of Coltrane is the source, but, of course, he is playing with a very special group of people. Elvin Jones, Jimmy Garrison and McCoy Tyner come together to create a truly extraordinary sound, and between them all, something mind-blowing happens. They all bring their influences with them but put it all together. On this one evening in '64, and you get a sonic miracle.

It is timeless. There is nothing like it. The emotion and the intention within it, however, is as old as human history, and that is why it works. So much of the '60s legacy has turned out to be fraudulent hokum, but *A Love Supreme* is basically the sound of four remarkably gifted human beings, transfigured by the music, and hitting the very heights. And the listener gets lifted up too. Elevated, transported and healed.

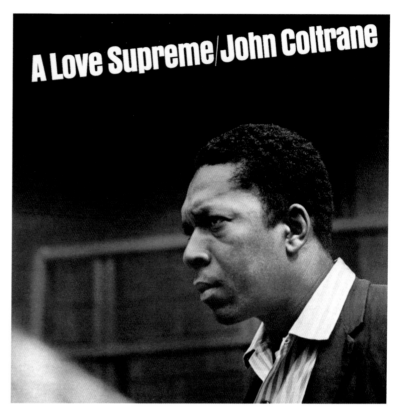

Photo by Bob Thiele, art direction by Hollis King, graphic design by Jason Clairborne, photography by Joe Alper/Lee Tanner

Tracklist

1   Part 1 – Acknowledgement
2   Part 2 – Resolution
3   Part 3 – Pursuance/Part 4 – Psalm

MIRRORS

Peggy Lee, A&M Records, 1975

This album was selected by **Gavin Friday**, who is perhaps the best-dressed man in Ireland. Whether it is solo or as part of Virgin Prunes, Gavin Friday has always made music that stands out. Mr Friday uncovers the unjustly overlooked *Mirrors*, by Peggy Lee.

Photo by Barry McCall

Mirrors, by Peggy Lee, of all the long-lost, forgotten-about albums, wins outright for me. Most of us are, or, dare I say 'should be', aware of the Peggy Lee masterpiece, 'Is That All There Is?', which was written and produced by the legendary rock 'n' roll pioneers Leiber and Stoller. An out-of-the-blue and off-kilter hit from 1969, the extraordinary song kick-started a revival in Ms Lee's career. Its success provided the impetus for a full album, though not until six years after it appeared in 1975.

I was torn between so many options and, with a dislike for 'best of' lists, it was at first a battle to decide between Wire's *154* and Kate Bush's *The Dreaming* as favourite unsung hero of an album. But then, in my own quirky way, I went with Peggy Lee *Mirrors*, as it is a profoundly brilliant and timeless masterpiece that is not that well known. I first heard this album in 1990, via the great producer Hal Willner, who gave me a very rare vinyl edition of the album. I had no previous knowledge of its existence.

Mirrors is, in my humble opinion, a masterpiece. To the learned ear, this album is most definitely a direct musical homage to one of the twentieth century's greatest composers, Kurt Weill. And indeed, there is no debate that the influence of Weill is, musically, the album's touchstone, but what makes it extraordinary is where this album takes the listener. It is as if Leiber, Stoller and Lee were making their own 'De Profundis'. The 'team' of Lee/Leiber/Stoller let loose together, and created what could be, for all three of them, the perfect swansong.

It blends the best of all the worlds these giants were involved in, from jazz to pop, from classical to psychedelic. It is a beautiful, tragicomic, challenging and surreal work. Seriously, one of the weirdest and one of the most beautiful albums that I have ever heard. It is not just a collection of songs, it is a world of its own. This album is very much out of sync with most things. Some of the songs bring to mind The Beach Boys and the later day Beatles, as if they were hanging out with Kurt Weill. It almost has a classical psychedelic feel to it, both musically and lyrically, beautifully and dangerously surreal.

From the prozaced bluesiness of 'I've Got Them Feelin' Too Good Today Blues' (the title alone says it all) to the slinky, sexed-up jazz of 'Some Cats Know' (with lyrics that Nick Cave would die for), to the Sgt Pepper circus on steroids of 'Professor Hauptmann's Performing Dogs' Then there is the gothic end of the world melodrama of 'Tango' to the Nosferatu-meets-Baby Jane 'Ready To Begin Again'. It goes on and on like a magic spell, ending and beginning, and never ending. I am making a show of myself here, as I inarticulately rant and rave! But surely that is what true greatness does to us.

Art direction by Roland Young, design by Junie Osaki, photography by Hans Albers, illustration by David McMacken

Tracklist

1 Ready To Begin Again
2 Some Cats Know
3 I've Got Them Feelin' Too Good Today Blues
4 A Little White Ship
5 Tango

6 Profesor Hauptmann's Performing Dogs
7 Mary Jane
8 I Remember
9 Say It
10 Longings For A Simpler Time

MONA LISA OVERDRIVE

Trashmonk, Creation Records/Poptones, 1999/2001

This album was selected by **Alan McGee**, the man who ran the iconic Creation Records. He signed acts like Oasis, Primal Scream, My Bloody Valentine and The Jesus & Mary Chain. He also had his autobiography, *Creation Stories*, published in 2013, not to mention a new label – 359 Music.

Photo by Dan Hegarty

Mona Lisa Overdrive by Trashmonk is an album that I managed to put out twice, once on Creation, and then with a new sleeve on Poptones. Trashmonk is a guy called Nick Laird-Clowes. He used to be in The Dream Academy, and wrote songs with Brian Wilson and Pink Floyd.

He had been around and written for a lot of people, and finally decided to make his definitive solo album, with Creation, at the height of Brit pop. There's amazing YouTube footage of him making it in his kitchen – it's actually insane! It's just 15 minutes long, but it's incredible.

It's a genius record. He did the vocals in his bathroom. He opened the window, letting Notting Hill pass by, and got all that ambience onto the tracks. He started making it in 1996 and we put it out in 1999. We then re-released it on Poptones between 2000 and 2001. It's just an incredible record.

People would ask, 'What is a great lost Creation album?' And I would reply, '*Loveless*', but eventually, someone found it. And now, people are finding Slowdive as well. Trashmonk's isn't as good as *Loveless*, but it is as good as Slowdive. It's different. This is a real DIY album, made by a guy with out-dated equipment going digital, if that makes any sense? If somebody found it, it would be their favourite album.

Go on Amazon. It is probably for sale now. You could probably find it for one cent because everybody has sold their record collections. You go on the Amazon second-hand section, and you can buy everything for a penny.

I know the record inside out – it's timeless. It's weird that this record has never been discovered. I mean, the film that his music was featured in, after that, was *Invisible Circus*, which was big. It had people like Cameron Diaz and Christopher Eccleston in it.

It is an album of any time. I have got to be honest, though, and admit that I haven't listened to it in a couple of years, but that is only because I cannot be physically putting on a CD, shutting the actual box and pressing 'play'. We have all become lazy fuckers, because you go on YouTube and it's all there – we are living in such an easy world.

For the Record

By Nick Laird-Clowes

The album had turned into a sort of 'do-it-yourself' *Sgt. Pepper's Lonely Hearts Club Band*, woven together over many months in my front room. The original idea had been to make a simple, stripped-down album of songs, using the newly emerging digital recording technology, but somewhere along the line I got distracted.

I had been using the MPC 3000 (sampling drum machine) to fill with recordings I had recently made on a trip to Nepal and India, to study Tibetan Buddhism with the great Rinpoches. A lot of times, it was the extraneous noises behind the main recordings that interested me – the slamming of doors, coughs and so on . . . by slowing them down or reversing them, new worlds emerged, into which I played my songs. Often, these sounds seemed to make a sort of inadvertent comment on the lyric (many of which were an open letter to a failing, long-term relationship).

When Alan McGee first came to my flat, there was very little space left that was not covered by equipment, instruments or objects from my travels. He was wonderfully enthusiastic when I played him some of the tracks, and he asked what I wanted to call the album. I said *Trash Monk Phenomena*. 'I don't know whether it is phenomena or phenomenon', he replied, 'but you are Trashmonk!' I looked around, and realised that he was probably right.

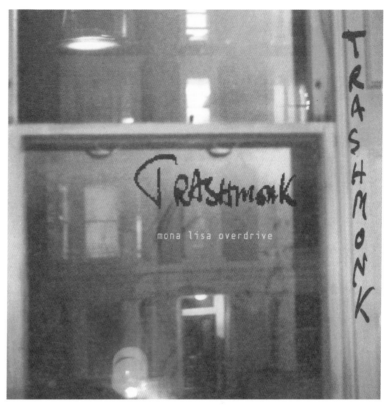

Design by Trashmonk/Renata Sverak, cover photography by Niloo Tehranchi

Tracklist

1   Girl I Used 2 Know
2   Polygamy
3   Sapphire
4   High Times
5   Amaryllis
6   All Change
7   Inner Brownstone Symphony
8   N.W.O.
9   It Won't Be Long
10 Dying Day
11 On The Way Home

MY SANCTUARY

Autamata, Lefthand Records/RG Records, 2002/2004

Michelle Doherty has balanced a career that includes work as an actress, model and broadcaster. Her radio and television work includes a show on Phantom FM, RTÉ Two's music TV show *Under Ether* and *Xposé*, on TV3. She delves into the recent past, selecting Autamata's debut album.

Photo by AM London

Sometimes when you are bored you cannot pick anything, so you put the old iPod on shuffle, and a song will come on, and you say, 'Oh my God, I forgot completely about this.'

My Sanctuary is one of those albums that I can listen to over and over and over again. I am a big fan of electronic music anyway, but I think the vocals from Cathy Davey and Carol Keogh add another dimension to it. It is one of those albums that I forget about, but every time I hear it, I say to myself, 'You definitely have to keep that in your top choices.'

It was probably 2006 when I first heard it. I was living with a friend, and she gave me that and Alphastates's first album. I hadn't heard of Automata before that. It was the best thing ever. I am very vocals-driven, and Carol Keogh's vocals, to me, are very Kate Bush – very ethereal. I know this probably sounds really insulting, but sometimes when you hear something of that quality, you actually first assume that it is not Irish, that it has to be from somewhere else in the world, you know?

I think *My Sanctuary* is timeless – it still holds its own. As I said, I could listen to it from start to finish and I throw it on all the time. I do not think it has aged at all. It is just that vision that he (Ken McHugh) had, that still holds its own. I love that he mixed the sounds that he made in studio, and that it was mixed with live instruments as well.

I think there is something in it for everybody. It is slow, and then it picks up with 'Jellyman'. I know, at the time, that *My Sanctuary* was critically acclaimed, but it does not get as much appreciation as it maybe should. He was just years ahead of himself.

For the Record

By Ken McHugh

My Sanctuary was the very first album of music that I officially released to the public. Previous to this, I had completed a couple of albums under my own name that I just passed around to friends. I was working as a producer for other artists at the time in my Dublin studio, Area 51. David Kitt's *The Big Romance* was one memorable album from this period.

I never thought that *My Sanctuary* would be released, so there were no rules or expectations when creating it. Each track was its own sonic experience, and performing it live was not a consideration. It was created with whatever was at hand – guitars, synths, percussion, drum machines and samplers. There were no obvious samples that I had to get clearance for – I was mainly sampling my own sounds and using that process as a tool.

The two female guest collaborating vocalists on the album, Cathy Davey and Carol Keogh, were two singers I was working with at the time. I was a big fan of their voices and songwriting abilities – Carol on a film *Saltwater,* with her band The Plague Monkeys, from an engineer's respective, and Cathy as a producer, developing her solo career that led to her deal with EMI. I played the girls completed instrumentals and they chose which ones they liked, and worked on writing songs over these that we then shaped into final songs as a collaboration.

In my eyes, the album was a success. It may not have sold a million copies, but I stayed true to what I believed in as an artist at the time, and put my name on the map in certain circles. Perhaps I will re-release it again someday to shine a light on it.

Design by Rob Crane, cover photography by Martin Yates

Tracklist

1	Fragments	7	Jellyman
2	Jive County	8	To Be A Robot
3	Out Of This	9	Onward
4	Registered User	10	Postscript
5	Little Green Men	11	Hide And Seek
6	Let's Normalise		

MUSIC IN A DOLL'S HOUSE

Family, Reprise Records, 1968

This album was selected by **Larry Gogan**, who is the reason that many people listen to the radio, and that numerous people chose radio as a career. Everything good that you've heard about Larry Gogan is, more than likely, true! He is, as the saying goes, 'one of a kind'. Larry's album of choice dates back to 1968.

Photo by Jenny McCarthy

I've chosen an album by a band called Family. It's not the American band The Family, who recorded 'Nothing Compares 2 U' that became a big hit for Sinead O'Connor – this is a British band. Their heyday was between 1968 and 1973, and they had around seven albums that have been almost completely forgotten.

The one that I like the best was their very first. It's called *Music in a Doll's House*. Roger Chapman was their lead singer. He was quite eccentric, famous for throwing tambourines into the audience, so you had to be able to duck very quickly!

They had about four hit singles, but no one ever talks about them anymore. I particularly liked the song 'No Mule's Fool', which was one of the tracks on that album.

They stood out at the time but, for some reason, they never made it really big. They were a rock band, but were different from a lot of the other stuff at that time. They did have a few hit albums and singles, though. They had a great sound – a very good sound for radio, too.

Very few radio people played them, but John Peel played them a lot. I remember thinking, 'Well, if he likes them, then I'm going to have to have a good listen and see what it's like.'

It was Roger Chapman's voice that struck me first. He had an incredible voice. I really liked their sound and the way that they presented things, but unfortunately never got to see them live.

I remember reading that Chapman was a very charismatic figure. The line-up changed a number of times, though, and eventually it all fizzled out in 1973. They only had a five-year window, but they had seven albums in that short space of time.

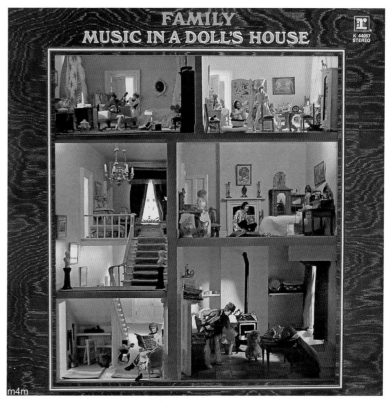

Cover photography by Julian Cottrell, design by Peter Duval

Tracklist

1   The Chase
2   Mellowing Grey
3   Never Like This
4   Me My Friend
5   Variation on a theme of Hey Mr. Policeman
6   Winter
7   Old Songs New Songs
8   Variation on a theme of The Breeze
9   Hey Mr. Policeman
10 See Through Windows
11 Variation on a theme of My Friend
12 Peace of Mind
13 Voyage
14 The Breeze
15 3 X Time

OH MERCY

Bob Dylan, CBS Records, 1989

Iarla Ó Lionáird is an extraordinary vocalist whose career has seen him perform as far afield as the Sydney Opera House to New York City's Carnegie Hall. He has worked with Robert Plant, Peter Gabriel and Sinéad O'Connor, as part of the Afro Celt Sound System and, more recently, The Gloaming.

Photo by Feargal Ward

Bob Dylan's *Oh Mercy* was released in 1989, and it was the first album he worked on with Daniel Lanois as producer. It is a kind of step-change for Dylan in lots of ways. The sound of the record is very influenced by the producer, the pace of the songs is remarkably slowed down and the whole thing is immersed in a sort of unusual, warm ambiance, which no doubt is the product of Daniel Lanois's production.

I think there is an unusual focus on the songwriting. Dylan is the pre-eminent songwriter of the age, but in these songs there is a tremendous focus, tremendous economy and a new approach to the sound of his voice, quite brittle and up-close. That, combined with the production, gives the album a unique and beautiful sound.

There are a number of things that I would dispute about Dylan. The arguments that people make about Dylan being a great songwriter but not singer, I just find completely ridiculous. His timing is beautiful – he moves words around the bar line, the way he understands the way words can and should work with music.

Everything comes together beautifully in this record. His songwriting is immensely powerful, like on 'Most of the Time'. The album is quite reflective, quite dark, really, and very touching. I am not sure if he is talking about his father on 'Shooting Star', but he's definitely looking back and judging himself through the eyes of others. There's another song, then, that I love, which deals with a familiar enough Dylan trope, one that contains a lot of kind of prophetic imagery. It's 'Ring Them Bells'. It's so beautifully done.

Dylan made a lot of bad records in the 1980s, but there are some exceptions. Dylan purists would say that by then he was well past his vintage, citing earlier records like *Blood On The Tracks* and *Blonde On Blonde* and other records like that, which are, of course, immense. The quality of production – the sort of thoughtfulness with which Dylan makes this record – could, to some extent, be laid at the feet of working with a producer so committed to recording and to the process.

I think *Oh Mercy* was the beginning of Dylan's resurgence that brought him into the '90s and right into now. He has made ten good records or so since then. They are tremendous, and have won him many awards and a whole new generation of listeners. Records like *Mississippi*, *Love and Theft* and *Modern Times* come to us from a Dylan who was influenced, whose rudder had moved and changed by making *Oh Mercy*. That is how I read it, anyway.

There is a gorgeous sound field enveloping the whole record. It is very beautiful to listen to. The songwriting is very, very strong. The problem with Dylan is that he has been around for so long, that when we refer to him in terms of what is a classic album and what is a seminal album, there are so many to choose from and, invariably, people go back much further than 1989, which I think is unfair. A lot of people have stopped listening to him for a long time now, and they do not know anything about his output in the '90s and the 2000s, but I think he has remained very strong creatively.

This is an important album for Dylan. It is a new step, a step into a different kind of sound awareness, a different type of disciplined songwriting, where only the best make it across the finish line. There is not a single weak song on this record, and that could not be said about some of the records that came before.

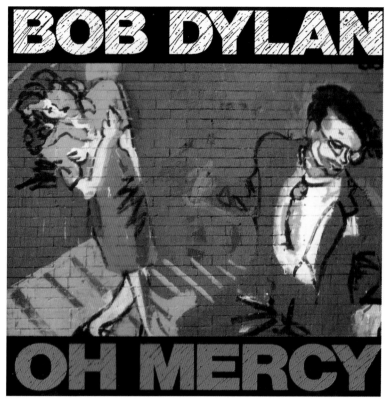

Album design by Christopher Austopchuk, type by Mark Burdett

Tracklist

1   Political World
2   Where Teardrops Fall
3   Everything Is Broken
4   Ring Them Bells
5   Man In the Long Black Coat

6   Most of the Time
7   What Good Am I?
8   Disease of Conceit
9   What Was It You Wanted
10 Shooting Star

ON THE TURN

Kerbdog, Fontana/Mercury, 1997

This album was selected by **Brian Cash** of the Irish band Halves, which has given us two studio albums and one live album. Call them alternative, call them ambient; they make wonderful music. Cash shares his love of Kerbdog's 1997 album, *On the Turn*.

Photo by Fiona McSorley

To date, I can count on one hand the number of records that have not only floored me, but have also truly mystified me. By age fourteen (in 1997), I had already fallen hard for the likes of Nirvana, Faith No More and Soundgarden, but the first record that ingrained itself into me so completely came out of nowhere. I say nowhere, but the cherry on top was that this was also an Irish album. The bad news? Mere months after the release of *On the Turn*, my new favourite band announced that they were calling it a day.

I spent the next few years checking every record shop and mail order listing (there was not the convenience of eBay back then) for any single, EP or white label promotion that I could get my hands on. My copy of *On the Turn* lived in my three-CD changer, until it simply wore down with age. Three years were spent converting classmates to the cause, and it did not take much to get them hooked. It was raw, home-grown and perfect, so giving it anything less than our full attention was not an option.

From the immediacy of the opener, 'Sally', to the droning finale of 'Sorry for the Record', each of these twelve songs could have been a single. The track order almost does not seem to matter. I have always felt that the album's secret weapon was Cormac Battle's vocal melodies; the intros, verses and bridges sound just as memorable and vibrant as the choruses. Add to that the relentless grinding guitars and pounding drums, and it is easy to see what sets *On the Turn* aside from the landfill of glossed-over post-grunge records. It is almost twenty years on and Garth Richardson's masterful production has not weakened one bit – when 'Severed' kicks in, it shatters.

In recent years, Biffy Clyro have often hired Richardson as a producer. Interestingly, they attribute this choice to the record they say influenced them most: *On the Turn*. There is even a confidence and daring that extends to the artwork. Having a *National Geographic* portrait of three elderly swimmers as a front cover instantly sets it aside as something unique.

In the years since it was released, it is amazing to see Kerbdog's legacy grow. I never meet people who simply just like this record, only those who flat out adore it. Now with their ongoing reunion, and a new generation of devotees, it is a testament to the band that *On the Turn* is still relevant, with no sign of waning. Tracing the chronology of this piece, I realised that six months after I bought *On the Turn*, I started my first band, so it is that little bit more important to me now. I still hurry towards the 'K' section in second-hand record shops, just in case.

For the Record

By Cormac Battle

So there we were, set up with all our gear in Sound City Studios, Los Angeles, wondering, 'How the fuck did a bunch of guys from Kilkenny get to make an album in the same room as Nirvana's *Nevermind*?' Well, after four months (meant to be six weeks), we walked out with Kerbdog's second album, *On the Turn*.

The level of detail and perfectionism expected in making the record was something we did not expect. It left us exhausted and nearly broke up the band. Producer GGGarth was used to working with professionals like Rage Against The Machine, so he had his work cut out with us and we had to learn super fast.

Commercially, it failed to deliver. Nevertheless, I still believe that it is one of the best Irish albums that never was. Do seek it out!

Design by Kerbdog/Peter Curzon, photography by Michael O'Brien

Tracklist

1	Sally	7	On the Turn
2	J.J.'s Song	8	Secure
3	Didn't Even Try	9	Lesser Shelf
4	Mexican Wave	10	Pointless
5	Severed	11	Rewind
6	Pledge	12	Sorry For The Record

OUR LIFE

Noise Control, NC Recordings, 2010

Shahin Badar has one of the most powerful and moving voices that you are likely to hear. She provided the remarkable chant on The Prodigy's 'Smack My Bitch Up'. Here she talks about Dublin act Noise Control, and their album *Our Life*.

Photo by Pinkkie Makhajani

I could have picked a lot of albums, but I chose *Our Life* by Noise Control, an Irish band from Dublin. There is a track that I really love on it called 'Catch The Race'. I felt the track in itself sort of portrayed a message about how we are all racing through life, and it has a hidden theme, I think, of spirituality. I feel that the whole album is powerful, it is positive and it is using a lot of electronic dance hall and those sorts of sounds. There is a great vibe off the album, and some tracks that I felt had great potential. It is different. They also used elements of some theatrical sounds that I found really interesting. I love the production.

The band were actually chosen by The Prodigy to be the opening act of the Irish leg of their tour, and they performed at a lot at festivals. They also supported acts like Underworld, Tricky, Calvin Harris and lots of other people. I think that one of the things I really like about *Our Life* is the fusion of electric guitars, bass, big beats and drums.

One of the things that I found about artists like Noise Control is that a lot of record companies could have picked them up. I felt like this band had a lot of potential. I never found that the record companies were giving artists like them a chance. They could have, and this is one of the things that I find quite frustrating with the mainstream.

I collaborated with them on a track called 'Take It'. Noise Control were in touch with me because they heard my vocals on the track 'Smack My Bitch Up', by The Prodigy. They sent me a sample of an instrumental and asked me if I would be interested in featuring on this track. I heard the track, and in it I found a lot of spirituality. That really interested me. I got back to Declan and said that I would love to work on the track, and was going to compose something. I decided that I wanted to get something different with the Asian vocals chant – something that had a very spiritual message.

I think *Our Life* is one of those great albums to keep and to have, because it has all sorts of different elements going on within it. But you have to take time out, sit down and listen to it.

I think that a lot of artists who have potential, like Noise Control, really need to be out there doing their thing and making a mark. I totally believe in this band, I really do, and I hope that they continue to make great music.

For the Record

By El Byrne

It was important to us that we capture the energy and live sound of our gigs as much as possible in making this album. All instruments were live takes. The production and sound of the album was very important to us.

Our Life was recorded in Grouse Lodge, Beechpark Studios, and Sun Studios, between 2008 and 2009. We headlined festivals for about four years, and paid for the album with the money from the gigs. A big portion was funded from licensing two songs to the Playstation game *Pure*.

Recording 'Take It' and working with someone as talented as Shahin Badar was an amazing experience. Being self-managed, coupled with the whole process of forming a label, put a lot of pressure on us. Do not get us wrong, though – we had a great time doing it. We got the album made, and it cost a lot of money. We do not think that anybody really heard *Our Life*, and it is a pity that it got overlooked. But it is now being picked up by *Love/Hate* and couple of other things.

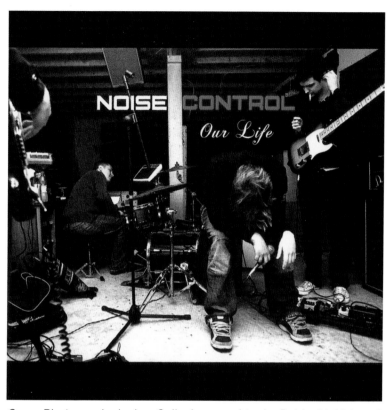

Cover Photography by Lee Gallagher, graphics by Bobby McMahon & Niall Byrne

Tracklist

1 TV Screen
2 Culture
3 Our Life
4 Steel
5 We Like Music
6 Solar Star
7 Catch The Race
8 Take It
9 Cities Of Dreams
10 Mudbath

PARALLELOGRAMS

Linda Perhacs, Kapp Records (reissued by Sunbeam Records), 1970

JD Beauvallet is an editor at the highly influential French culture and music publication, *Les Inrockuptibles*, or, as it is sometimes known, as *Les Inrocks*. JD talks about the once lost and now rediscovered *Parallelograms*, by Linda Perhacs.

Photo by Renaud Monfourny

The fans have perpetuated the life of this album, telling people over and over again that they should listen to it and becoming ambassadors. There have been some amazingly strange ambassadors of this Linda Perhacs album. Daft Punk are not at all musically in that vein, but they did a film called *Electroma* and, in the soundtrack, there was a track by Linda Perhacs, and that really contributed to the popularity of Linda Perhacs, and the rediscovery of the album. I really do not have a clue how Daft Punk discovered her, but they wanted to have one of her tracks on the soundtrack.

I love this sort of folk music from the late '60s and early '70s, and, for years, this was something you could not hear, because these records were not available. They were mentioned only by musicians. It is always quite a good sign when musicians have hidden treasures, and they say, 'This is a record that made me want to start music.'

For years and years, I kept on hearing about Scott Walker, Tim Harding and Tim Buckley from musicians, and I thought these must be great. So something happened with Linda Perhacs, and lots of musicians kept mentioning her name in interviews. It could well be snobbery sometimes, like, 'I'm the only one who knows these records, I am cleverer than you.' When I finally heard *Parallelograms*, it was just absolutely astonishing. It was like discovering a new continent, a new sound.

There was something very strange about it. I did not know the history of the album, which was already a great story, but the album itself is absolutely astonishing. Basically, it is folk music with something very eerie in the background, almost David Lynch-esque. You do not know what is going on

in the background, and I have found out since that she actually used the studio as an instrument. She kept on slowing down tapes, accelerating tapes, playing tapes backwards – that is what makes the sound so peculiar.

So, it could have been quite a straightforward folk album like in a Joni Mitchell kind of way. She has got the quality of voice to do that. The more you listen to it, the richer it sounds, which is always a great find. Listening to albums like *Parallelograms* by Linda Perhacs, or Vashti Bunyan's *Just Another Diamond Day*, you might feel annoyed that these albums had been kept secret from you – you think, 'Those bastards from the music industry, you know you should not hide treasures like this from us!'

Linda worked in a practice in Los Angeles as a dental hygienist in the late 1960s, making musician on the side, and one of her customers was Leonard Rosenman. He was a very famous film music director, and actually did the soundtrack for James Dean's *Rebel Without A Cause*, and the Star Trek movies too. He kept on telling her, 'Play me your demos, play me your songs.' She was very shy about it, but finally did.

He encouraged her to record a song, but the mastering was such a disaster that she gave up. The record was released and disappeared almost in the same week, and she went back to being a dental hygienist. The album got deleted, and disappeared, but then with the Internet she realised that there were a lot of people talking about the record, and she was absolutely amazed.

Linda Perhacs just thought it was a lost album, and that it was a very small part of her life. She had largely forgotten about it. When she was contacted to do another record, she decided that she would. She recorded her second album some forty-four years later, in 2013, which is absolutely amazing.

For the Record

By Linda Perhacs

As you know, *Parallelograms* was recorded during the highlight of so much going on in the world of the early 1970s. All the songs on the album were a reflection of my thoughts and innermost dreams for a better world. Like most songwriters or poets, I felt a deep need to share with the world, in the hope that my dreams would, in some small way, help with getting us all through it all. I even added a bit of irony to the album with 'Porcelain-Baked Cast-Iron Wedding' and 'Paper Mountain Man'. Both songs were based on true events.

Photography by Bob Flick of Vortex Associates, album design by Virginia Clark

Tracklist

1	Chimacum Rain		7	Hey, Who Really Cares?
2	Paper Mountain Man		8	Moons and Cattails
3	Dolphin		9	Morning Colors
4	Call of the River		10	Porcelain Baked-Over Cast-Iron Wedding
5	Sandy Toes		11	Delicious
6	Parallelograms			

PAUL'S BOUTIQUE

Beastie Boys, Capitol Records, 1989

This album was selected by **Cathal Pendred**. Mixed Martial Arts (MMA) is big business these days, and Pendred is one of Ireland's most successful MMA fighters. He received huge exposure from his appearance on the UFC's *The Ultimate Fighter* season nineteen in mid 2014. Cathal's album of choice is Beastie Boys's *Paul's Boutique*.

Photo by Alex Hutch

The album *Paul's Boutique* was the first piece of work that I heard from the Beastie Boys, and it is what turned me into a fan. I have always considered it one of their best albums, so I was shocked to hear that it was seen as a commercial flop when it was released, in comparison to the group's first album.

I came across it by chance. I remember getting a Walkman for my birthday when I was eight or nine (sometime during the mid 1990s). I had this Walkman, but no tapes, so I went to an Oxfam store close to my house and bought £10 worth of cassettes. I could not tell you the names of any of the other tapes I bought, though I am pretty sure they were all horrendous or else just not to my taste. But I did buy one that I loved, and it was *Paul's Boutique*.

The album was my first real introduction to hip hop. I was immediately drawn to it and, to date, it is still one of my favourite genres. I had never heard of the group, and neither had my parents. I think at the time I thought it was music that would only ever be popular in America, because it was like nothing I had heard on the radio in Ireland before.

I think that the Beastie Boys are an acquired taste. If anyone ever mentions that they are a fan, I will always enquire whether they have heard this album. If you like the group, this album is a must. They played Electric Picnic in 2007, but I was living in San Diego at the time. That is the only time I had ever heard of them playing in Ireland.

I think that the group have their own unique sound. This album had more of a rock sound than their first, which sounded more exclusively like hip hop. I think they were one of the first acts to successfully blend rap and rock together. In that sense, they were pioneers in the genre of rap rock. Massive acts like Eminem and Rage Against the Machine have cited Beastie Boys as an influence in their music.

This album was not only my first taste of hip hop, but, as it was the first album that I actually listened to on my own music device, it was really my first introduction to music itself. Any time I hear any of the songs from this album, it reminds me of being young and walking to primary school with my earphones in, thinking I was the coolest kid around!

Cover photo by Nathaniel Hornblower, with assistants Mathew Cohen, Jeremy Shatan and Dominick Watkins

Tracklist

1 To All the Girls
2 Shake Your Rump
3 Johnny Ryall
4 Egg Man
5 High Plains Drifter
6 The Sounds of Science
7 3-Minute Rule
8 Hey Ladies

9 5-Piece Chicken Dinner
10 Looking Down the Barrel of a Gun
11 Car Thief
12 What Comes Around
13 Shadrach
14 Ask for Janice
15 B-Boy Bouillabaisse

PERFECT STRANGER

The Chapters, 3ú Records, 2009

This album was selected by **Danny O'Reilly**, the face and voice of one of Ireland's most popular bands, The Coronas. From filling small venues around the country, they've grown into a group that have released three double-platinum-selling albums and a fourth – *The Long Way* – that has seen their international profile grow substantially. Danny tells us about The Chapters – a band that had a huge impact on The Coronas.

Photo by Gavin Leane

We came across The Chapters gigging in Dublin around the same time that we had started out (between 2006 and 2007). We couldn't believe how tight they were as a band. They had these amazingly infectious songs that I was instantly drawn to. With hooky pop choruses, great harmonies and a groove that reminded me of Fleetwood Mac, Talking Heads and Springsteen all at once, I couldn't get enough.

All this sits alongside Ross's raspy voice, which definitely has something original and special about it. I must say, first of all, that over the years I have become great friends with the band. Simon Eustace (guitar) has directed a handful of The Coronas music videos, Tully (piano) has written with us and, at the time of release, they were signed to our label in Ireland, 3ú Records. All this bias aside though, *Perfect Stranger* really is a masterpiece. It's hit after hit, in my opinion. It's just a pity that it didn't turn out that way.

We got to know the guys as they had begun to think about recording the album. Tully sent me a rough demo of a song called 'Moving', and it made the hair on my neck stand on end. Subtle and melodic, it is just a gorgeous song. To this day, I think that the early demo of that song had something that maybe even the finished, properly recorded album version didn't have. Anyway, not long after, 3ú signed them up, and the album's lead single, 'Videotapes', got a decent amount of airplay. I remember Tony Fenton in particular getting behind the song. It was a great lead single, and I couldn't wait to hear the finished album.

I was at the album launch in the Odessa club, and the songs sounded great live. The record didn't disappoint, either – songs like 'Looking For Love', 'Trying To Get Ahead' and 'Moving' inspired a writing burst for me personally, and a few of the songs on our second record (namely 'Won't Leave You Alone' and the outro, 'All the Luck in The World') are definitely derivative of moments on *Perfect Stranger*.

Unfortunately, the album didn't catch on as much as we all thought it would. Radio didn't really take to the next singles, and the band parted with their manager and the label soon after. Tully and Simon went on to do their own things, but Ross, Murph (bass) and Ciaran (drums) continued as a three-piece, and released a much more stripped down, almost country-sounding album a couple of years ago.

My mother always told me that there are millions of amazing acts and great pieces of music that don't get to where they deserve to be. For whatever reason, *Perfect Stranger* didn't take off. To me, it's simply an album of great songs. We all loved it. It made us want to be a better band, and I think that's the best compliment you can give to any piece of music.

For the Record

By Ciarán Fortune

Although a debut release, *Perfect Stranger* was by no means our first body of work. It was born from a love of high-energy live shows, an appreciation of classic pop hooks as well as 1970s and '80s sounds. Artists like Fleetwood Mac and Bruce Springsteen were key influences. We insisted on live recordings, playing to our strengths, making sure not to stifle any song with too much production. Our creative approach was always democratic. We learned not to take ourselves too seriously. The plush atmospheric material of our earlier work gave way to synth-driven catchy tunes, and we aimed to visually represent these accordingly with Simon directing our videos himself.

It was also our first experience of record company backing. Curve Management and 3ú Records signed us almost immediately after being dropped by a promising 360 deal that failed to materialise, due to the economic downturn. We were hugely fortunate to have their support and trust, allowing us the creative freedoms that not too many artists are afforded on a debut record. The album saw us leave Ireland to showcase in Italy, Germany and the UK, but as work began for the follow-up ('Blood Feels Warm') two members left. This album was completed and self-released following collaborations with a variety of artists.

Artwork by Inputout

Tracklist

1 Juice	7 Ukiyo
2 Videotapes	8 Looking For Love
3 Moving	9 Trying To Get Ahead
4 Automobiles	10 Black Room
5 Ukrainian Gymnast	11 Home
6 Perfect Stranger	

POST-NOTHING

Japandroids, Polyvinyl Records, 2009

Let's not mince words – And So I Watch You From Afar are a monster of a band. Prolific, powerful and the owners of a relentless touring schedule, ASIWYFA's **Rory Friers** has much love for *Post-Nothing*, by Japandroids.

Photo by Graham Smith

When you love something enough, it is sometimes heartbreaking that everyone else in the world does not see what you see in it. But maybe that is what makes it so special to you in the first place. Maybe if everyone loved it, it would not be the same. Who knows. I thought long and hard about this, and decided that I would talk about *Post-Nothing*, the first album by two-piece Canadian noisies Japandroids, which came out in 2009.

I chose *Post-Nothing* because it is unlike some of the weirder, more obscure or inaccessible albums that I had considered writing about, so niche or bizarre that it is completely understandable that I am the only one who thinks they are great. The songs on *Post-Nothing* could have sold a million copies each. From the beginning to the end, this album is full of amazing songs that are perfectly crafted. It's as simple as that. The band are two anti-virtuosos that record live, warts and all, as loud and as hard as they can. Trashy, ferocious drums are on the brink of being left behind by the charging track, like a skier trying to out-ski the avalanche. All this, alongside fuzzy electric guitar, forced out through a Vox AC30 at as loud the speakers permit, passionate vocals in both content and delivery with lyrics to match.

The recording is not great – they sometimes do not play completely in time with each other and there is even the occasional questionable note. But what it culminates in is an album so sincere, stirring and anthemic that it makes you feel like running barefoot up a snow-covered mountain and punching a lightening bolt out of your fist at the top. It sounds like Jawbox and Rites of Spring having a 'Who can play the fastest Bruce Springsteen covers' competition.

I first heard about the album after a show we played with Adebisi Shank in The Lower Deck in Dublin. I was chatting with a guy outside. We were swapping album recommendations, and he told me that I should check them out. So, the following day, I stole the record off the Internet, as I was/am skint at all times. I played a track at random: 'I Quit Girls'. Its hypnotic loop of clangy, shellac-esque guitar tone came in, and I quickly stuck the album on from track one. Once it was over, I put it back to the start again.

The whole thing jumped out with instant, urgent sincerity. It was not over-thought or micro-managed or perfect in a technical or sonic sense. Instead, it was infectious and carefree. It soundtracked a year-long road trip of shows for us; its battered CD sat on the dashboard of every van. It travelled with us on every tour.

By no means is the album musically groundbreaking – almost the opposite, in fact – but that is the beauty: it is timeless. They would have been amazing songs in the '70s, '80s or '90s. They are songs played with the means you have to hand, in a garage with a friend. Every musician has been there – there is no mystique to it. It is instantly relatable, and almost nostalgic when you hear it, yet simultaneously so urgently in the present. Everyone who I made listen to it loves it. You can't not. *Post-Nothing* is one of those albums that, if somehow, magically, everyone in the world got an MP3 player or iPod in the post one morning with a set of headphones, it would probably solve everything. Well, for at least thirty-five minutes, and maybe thirty-five more after that.

For the Record

By Brian King, from an interview on an-themmagazine.com, May 2012

When we recorded our first album, we were just a local band in Vancouver, playing shows around for fun. We did not have any fans, we did not have an audience, we did not have a record label. Nobody cared who we were, or cared about the band at all. So, when we did that record and we were writing those songs, we were doing it strictly for ourselves. It was strictly for fun. There was no pressure or expectation, other than that which we put on ourselves.

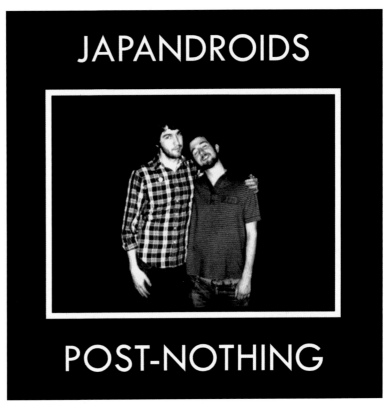

Photography by Konrad Jandavs and Steve Louie

Tracklist

1	The Boys Are Leaving Town	5	Heart Sweats
2	Young Hearts Spark Fire	6	Crazy/Forever
3	Wet Hair	7	Sovereignty
4	Rockers East Vancouver	8	I Quit Girls

PURPLE HAZE

Cam'ron, Roc-A-Fella Records, 2004

Lethal Dialect is a rapper, a lyricist and one of the most talented vocalists Ireland has heard in many years. He has blazed quite a trail in a relatively short career, that has seen him bring people's attention to a thriving Irish hip hop scene. *Purple Haze*, from the flamboyant Cam'ron, still does it for Lethal Dialect.

Photo by Al Higgins

It's a strange one, because most people would never put me and this album together. It's hard to listen to it objectively now because of the nostalgic value attached to it (it was my soundtrack to the memorable summer before my last year in school), but it's definitely one of the few that I still play regularly to this day.

The video for 'Girls' was on heavy rotation on MTV. That was the first single off the album. A friend of mine was selling bootleg CDs at the time and that album was there, so I took it. I went and bought a legitimate copy then, of course!

I remember reading a review of the album where it was described as a 'dystopian day-glo fantasy land'. That is exactly it. The instrumentals were a mix of bouncy, pitched-up soul samplers and operatic bangers. Cam just breezed through them with this slick, quirky, arrogant, multi-syllabic flow. At the time, Cam was in the news getting a bit of slack for wearing a pink fur coat and hat with a matching pink phone to an award ceremony or something like that. It summed up what the album was about: tongue in cheek, colourful and not giving a fuck. Think Conor McGregor meets Action Bronson meets MF Doom. And this was in the mid 2000s!

I think the tracks 'Killa Cam' and 'Get 'Em Girls' were the clinchers. They both sample opera singers, singing the words 'Killa Cam' in full opera voice. Who does that? I thought that the album was going to be an acquired taste at first, but then they released 'Down And Out' as the follow-up single and video to 'Girls', produced by and featuring Kanye West in his prime. Once that started getting airplay on MTV, I knew it was going to be fairly big.

It is definitely influenced by the Rocafella, sped-up soul-sampling era in hip hop, because Rocafella was the label it was released through, but the overall sound of the album was – and still is – very individual. The operatic samples, chanty hooks and Cam's delivery added that trademark Harlem twist.

For me, *Purple Haze* encapsulates the mid 2000 era of hip hop. It is my favourite era in hip hop, partially because it soundtracked the end of my school days, but also because Cam was so ahead of his time. A lot of the modern-day rappers (Action Bronson, A$AP Rocky) have listed this one as a major influence. It also had a huge effect beyond music. Shortly after Cam appeared in the matching pink fur get-up, auld lads in the local boozer were wearing pink T-shirts.

What makes this album work so well is the larger-than-life Harlem attitude that seeps through it – with braggadocio, arrogant and impartial. Cam's flow and delivery set a precedent in hip hop thereafter, as did the overall ridiculousness and hilarity of the concepts (the Mizzle skits, and Cam's infamous 'I get computers 'puting' line.) Add to this the fact that it is ten years old this year, and does not sound dated.

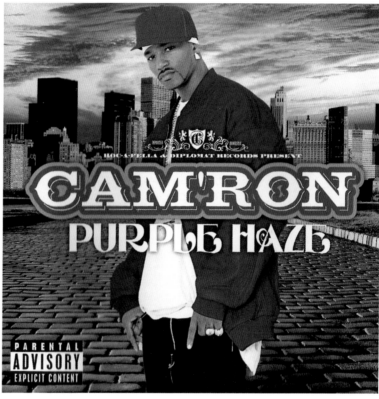

Creative Direction by Rick Patrick, art direction by Robert Sims, photography by Oluwaseye, styling by Monica Morrow

Tracklist

1 Intro
2 More Gangsta Music (ft: Juelz Santana)
3 3Get Down
4 Welcome To Purple Haze (Skit)
5 Killa Cam
6 Leave Me Alone Pt. 2
7 Down And Out (ft: Kanye West & Syleena Johnson)
8 Harlem Streets

9 Rude Boy (Skit)
10 Girls (ft: Mona Lisa)
11 I'm A Chicken Head (Skit)
12 Soap Opera
13 O.T. (Skit)
14 Bubble Music
15 More Reasons (ft: Jaheim)
16 The Block (Skit)
17 The Dope Man (ft: Jim Jones)
18 Family Ties (ft: Nicole Wray)

19 Adrenaline (ft: Twista & Psycho Drama)
20 Hey Lady (ft: Freekey Zekey)
21 Shake (ft: JR Writer)
22 Get 'Em Girls
23 Dip-Set Forever
24 Bonus Track
25 Take Em To Church (ft: Juelz Santana & Un Kasa)

RED HOUSE PAINTERS

Red House Painters, 4AD, 1993

He is the impressively tattooed and more-often-than-not bearded lead vocalist with Biffy Clyro. **Simon Neil** has fronted the Scottish three-piece for two decades and, in that time, they have become a truly massive band. Simon talks about the impact that Mark Kozelek and Red House Painters have had on his career.

Photo by Andrew Wilsher

People often call this album 'Rollercoaster' because of the artwork, or 'Grace Cathedral Park', after one of the songs on it. In my opinion, Mark Kozelek (the singer and songwriter in Red House Painters) is one of the most underrated musicians and songwriters ever. I think that it is a crying shame that he is not held up as an icon of songwriting and modern American music.

I got into this record when I was around 17. Up until that point, I had only listened to heavy music with distorted guitars, because until then I had thought that heavy guitars equalled intensity. When I heard this Red House Painters record, it made me realise that sometimes you can make something that is even more intense just by using space and silence.

It has this ominous feel to it, because it is so slow. The lyrics are so pure and honest that you really feel that you are almost getting into Mark Kozelek's life. That is what I feel that his lyrics are about; he has always been very straight up, so you know if he is singing about a particular lover, or a particular friend or part of his life.

His lyric writing on that album has influenced how I write songs in a huge way. I might have been singing about dragons and castles if I had not discovered Red House Painters! It is fourteen of the most beautiful songs ever. My favourite is 'Katy Song', which has one of my favourite lyrics of all time: 'Glass on the pavement under my shoe, without you is all my life amounts to.' I actually have that tattooed across my stomach.

This was such an unusual record for its time. When you go back and listen to what was around then . . . perhaps there is a bit of the Cocteau Twins about it? Mark Kozelek was raised on AC/DC, Iron Maiden and classic metal bands, but in listening to his music you would have no idea.

If you have an understanding of the rock dynamic – as ridiculous as that may sound – when you listen to this record, I think he really understands about teasing an idea out, and getting the listener to fever pitch. The way the songs unfolded, they were not verse/chorus/verse/chorus, rather, it was a much more natural development of the song. Biffy Clyro takes its own love of the song outro from Red House Painters. A good example of that is on 'Things Mean A Lot', which has a chorus that just goes round and round. It is one of those songs that you never want to ever end.

For the Record

By Mark Kozelek

This album was mostly recorded at place called Razor's Edge studio, on Divisidero and Fell in San Francisco, from 1992 to 1993. This was our first album recorded with record company money, and knowing that our music would be heard around the world was both exciting and frightening.

We started recording this twenty-three-song record that, in the end, was released as two different self-titled albums, at a studio (that was out of our league, price-wise) called Coast, on Mission and 9th. We had a $40,000 budget that was quickly running out, so we went back to Razor's Edge where we could be more comfortable.

The studio was near The Panhandle, and I was dating a girl over there near Haight Street. My nights were mostly spent at her place, not sleeping; I was too over-whelmed to get any sleep. The band would work four long days a week in the studio, Monday through Thursday, and I'd spend the weekend listening to rough demo mixes on cassette.

Getting to the finishing line was excruciating, but after nine months we had completed the twenty-three songs. My favourites made the cut of the self-titled album that became known as *The Rollercoster Album*, and the rest became known as *The Bridge Album*. 'Katy Song' and 'Mistress' remain two of my most requested songs, and I still play them, from time to time.

Images by W.K.V.I.

Tracklist

1	Grace Cathedral Park	8	Rollercoaster
2	Down Through	9	New Jersey
3	Katy Song	10	Dragonflies
4	Mistress	11	Mistress" (Piano Version)
5	Things Mean a Lot	12	Mother
6	Funhouse	13	Strawberry Hill
7	Take Me Out	14	Brown Eyes

RESEARCHING THE BLUES

Redd Kross, Merge Records, 2012

This album was selected by **Kim Shattuck**, who has been the voice of US alternative rock band The Muffs for over two decades, and was a touring member of Pixies when they visited Europe in 2013. Here, Kim Shattuck tells of her obsession with Redd Kross's 2012 album, *Researching The Blues*.

Photo by Kim Shattuck

It is really aggressive in a way that I like, and it's hard for me to talk about music, for some reason. Words escape me a lot when it comes to music. I fall into music more than I can verbally communicate. What I like about *Researching The Blues* is that it is super melodic, but it still has a lot of edge to it. There are certain songs on there that I am not as into, but also certain songs that I am 100% behind. They gave me an unmastered copy to listen to, and said, 'Oh, what do you think?'

I was obsessed with it for a year. I just listened to it straight. I love Jack McDonald's voice on it. He has a John Lennon-like timbre to his voice. I had it on my iPhone when I was touring with the Pixies. I listened to it a lot then. But I get obsessed with different things at different times – I did not even listen to the mastered version after it was released until later. I just had the unmastered CD in my car that did not even have any titles on it.

I think that if a band waits for a while they can redis-cover their old influences. I am kind of doing that right now. It means that you will keep your edge. I think Redd Kross waited long enough from when their last album came out to when they put out their new album. I think they were truly inspired when they wrote this album.

Red Kross just have such a hardcore, loyal following. It just stays kind of in-house that way. Their fans are just really intense. I don't know, I just think that it might be a slow build-up for them on this album, because it is so good. It is such a good album that not everyone has caught on fast enough.

Any time that I get freaked out about an album it is always because of the melody, and the melody here always just knocks me out. They have this song called 'Stay Away From Downtown' that is sing-songy but, in a way, not goofy. It just kind of hit me really hard – when I hear songs that I like in that way my upper lip sweats! It is super weird, but it only happens once in a while, and I'm like, 'Oh my God, that's the best album ever.'

For the Record

By Jeff McDonald, from an interview with Guitar World *magazine*

We got together and rehearsed the songs, and then went into the studio and just laid them all down. Then I worked on the tracks from home quite a bit. Things are a lot different now. This is the first album that we recorded using Pro Tools. I tried to shake things up and make it feel more spontaneous, by mixing in some random gear and pedals.

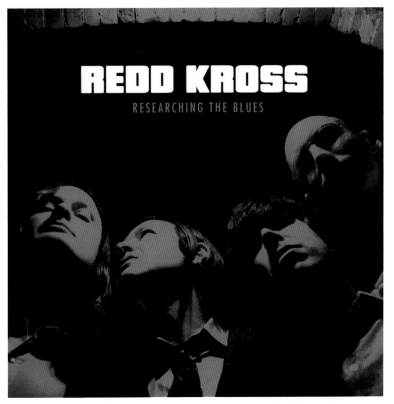

Photography and logo by Jonathan Krop, design by Maggie Fost

Tracklist

1	Researching the Blues	6	One of the Good Ones
2	Stay Away from Downtown	7	The Nu Temptations
3	Uglier	8	Choose to Play
4	Dracula's Daughter	9	Winter Blues
5	Meet Frankenstein	10	Hazel Eyes

SK1/SIMPLE KID 1

Simple Kid, 2m Recordings, 2003

This album was selected by **Jerry Fish**, the frontman for An Emotional Fish, and ringleader of The Mudbug Club. He has had a long and decorated career in music. Simple Kid's debut album *SK1* is his buried treasure.

Photo by Celine O'Sullivan

I had a very lucky introduction to this record, because I was the presenter of the second series of the TV show, *Other Voices*. Simple Kid was one of the guests on the show, so I got to meet him and interview him. His brother is Auliffe, the bassist with Sultans Of Ping. They would go on to be contemporaries of mine, so there was an immediate rapport.

On that series of *Other Voices*, Simple Kid and The Handsome Family really stood out for me. Simple Kid/Kieran looked fantastic. He looked like a 1970s tennis star! When I heard the album, I knew it was one of those records that you never want to turn off. There is a bit of Beck in there, and then you listen to it more and you hear The Beatles and Damon Albarn, and a there is a country flair in there, too – maybe Neil Young. It has got incredible taste, with riff and lyrics to die for.

I guess if you are a fan of music, you do not even need anyone else to hear what you have heard. In my mind, he is right up there with Keith Richards and The Rolling Stones. For me, Kieran is a massive star because of those two albums that he made, but, in particular, the first one. I expected him to be huge, but there are so many factors to a successful record. You have a lot of successful UK acts that I do not get,

but they have a massive industry behind them.

The opening track, 'Hello', just invites you in. The whole record is like being at a show, or you feel like you have just been at a festival performance. I would love to be able to bring him back, in some guise or other. I still have a lot of friends in Cork, but finding Simple Kid is a challenge, because he just kind of disappeared!

He's almost in DJ-mode on this album – there is crafting and programming there, which I would do a bit of in my own material. There is even a bit of Daniel Johnston on it; if he wants strings, he just has strings. An artist really has to dig deep to create something of worth, so he has obviously spent a lot of time over each song.

I have always been a fan of that Cork thing. Someone just reminded me of when I was in An Emotional Fish – we used to do a gig, and then stay for two or three weeks! I have had a lot of fun in Cork, and I love the humour. I am a big fan of The Frank & Walters, and The Sultans Of Ping. When An Emotional Fish and Something Happens were around in the 1990s, against all odds, these bands from Cork got on *Top Of The Pops*; they had a formula that we had not yet figured out!

There has always been a certain kookiness to Cork, or an air of anarchy, like in Manchester. There is a sharper tongue to it, or it is not as slick at the capital. Although it is quite Beatles-esque and flowery, *Simple Kid* has that anarchic quality too, that helps it not to be too sweet.

For the Record

By Kieran Mac Feely

My overwhelming memory of writing and recording *Simple Kid 1* was that I was tired of trying to 'do it the right way'. I had, by that point, worked with a multitude of producers, engineers and A&R persons of differing levels, and there always seemed to be complicated reasons why you could not just record a song simply, in one go, and be done with it.

I had zero knowledge of production or theory back then, but I bought a mic, a laptop and a tape machine, and read some manuals and experimented. I rapidly developed my one theoretical position: point a mic at something, and press record. If it sounds nice, keep it; if it sounds horrible, point the mic a bit differently and try it again. To this day, this is still the only thing I have learned, and I think it is all any musician needs to do . . . close your eyes and listen.

Design by Martin & Anthony at Redgiant, photography by Phil Nicholls

Tracklist

1	Hello	7	Loves an Enigma
2	Truck On	8	Supertramps and Superstars
3	Staring at the Sun	9	Kids Don't Care
4	The Average Man	10	Breakups Breakdowns
5	The Commuter	11	No News
6	Drugs		

SOLO IN SOHO

Philip Lynott, Phonogram, 1980

He is one of the new generation of Leinster Rugby players, and has become a familiar figure in the green of Ireland, too. **Marty Moore** has won trophies with both country and province. Here, he talks about discovering Philip Lynott's *Solo in Soho* album.

Photo by Brendan Moran (Sportsfile)

I first heard this in my grandparents's house about three years ago, when I was looking through some old records in the attic. I had just gotten a record player as a present, and between Grandad and Dad there was a great collection of old vinyl, which I was searching through when I came across *Solo in Soho*.

I had always been a big fan of classic rock for the guitar playing, and Thin Lizzy in particular. I also loved Lynott's work with Gary Moore on 'Parisienne Walkways', so hearing Phil Lynott solo for the first time was incredible.

I think that Thin Lizzy were probably responsible for my initial interest in classic rock, but the *Solo in Soho* album led to me being interested in more vocal pieces from that era. I think the clincher was definitely 'King's Call'. When I first listened to it, Grandad told me about Lynott writing it as a tribute to Elvis Presley. Although the guitar playing on the track was a lot softer than most of the Lizzy stuff, Knopfler's style is evident, and makes it all the better!

I was about 30 years behind on getting into this album. I remember thinking to myself, 'How have I never listened to this one before?' I suppose it may have been overshadowed by the more successful Thin Lizzy albums. Most people of my generation would be familiar with hits like 'Whiskey In The Jar', 'Dancin' In The Moonlight' and 'The Boys Are Back In Town', but may have never been exposed to Lynnott's solo pieces, as they are not generally something that is played on the radio these days.

Obviously, being Phil Lynott, the album will be likened to Thin Lizzy, but I found it to be a softer version of the classic rock stuff, though still keeping with it through the great instrumental pieces. Being twenty-three, I have never had the pleasure of seeing Phil Lynott play, but in 2007 I went to see Thin Lizzy in the Olympia with John Sykes on vocals. I felt that this was a chance to experience a band that had influenced the music that I had listened to for many years, albeit without the main man. I was not disappointed, and was grateful to at least have gotten a taste for what they were like in the 1980s.

I have a strange nostalgic attachment to the album. I spent days learning to play Thin Lizzy tracks on guitar in my grandparents's house growing up, and never knew that the *Solo in Soho* album was in the house, and I would not hear it for almost another ten years!

Photography by John Swannell, artwork & design by Linda Sutton & Roger Cooper, art direction by Chris O'Donnell

Tracklist

1 Dear Miss Lonely Hearts
2 King's Call
3 A Child's Lullaby
4 Tattoo (Giving It All Up for Love)
5 Solo in Soho

6   Girls
7   Yellow Pearl
8   Ode to a Black Man
9   Jamaican Rum
10 Talk In '79

STAND BY YOUR MAN

Candi Staton, Fame Records, 1971

Laura Izibor introduced herself to the world in 2009 with the release of her debut album, *Let the Truth Be Told*. It achieved tremendous international success, entering Top 30 on the Billboard Top 100 in the USA, and reaching number six on the billboard R 'n' B/hip hop chart. She has shared the stage with Aretha Franklin, John Legend, Al Green and James Brown. Candi Staton's *Stand By Your Man* made a lasting impression on the Dublin singer.

I have selected *Stand By Your Man*, by Candi Staton. I'm a big fan of her vocals and the raw lyrics on the album. It really hit me from the first time I heard it. When I was seventeen, I was working with Stuart Mathewmen (who you may know from his work with Sade) in New York. He played 'Too Hurt To Cry' in the studio one day, and it blew me away. I then followed up, and listened to the album.

What struck me about it was that this was the same women who sang 'Young Hearts' – I could not believe it. There is such intensity in her voice on this record. I love the way the songs are written, like she is just telling you what is going on with her. The musicianship is so gritty, it has a really live feel!

You could say that this album appeals to soul lovers, or people who appreciate authentic music. I have always liked old school music since I was a teenager, but I'm not sure what the age demographic would be for Candi.

The songs 'Too Hurt To Cry' and 'Freedom Is Just Beyond The Door' are in a great key for her voice. These are two of my favourites; both songs really peak the album for me. I hear a lot of blues in her music on this album. There is some Muddy Waters and BB King influence there, but there is a real original flavor to this record. At the time, I was very surprised that so few people had heard of it.

She was such a great soul artist before her disco success and I feel grateful to have discovered this period of her career. I have never seen her play live, but my mate Murray James went on tour with her and said she is still incredible. Seeing her perform live is on my list of SERIOUS things to do!

Stand By Your Man is a great piece of work – a hidden gem, if you ask me. I think that it was of its time, but perhaps the reason that it isn't as well known as it should be is because there were just so many incredible artists doing similar things at the same time and in a more commercial way. It brings me back to being so young, when my head was buzzing with all this new music that I was being introduced to. It was an amazing time of my life.

The songs have the sentiment of classic blues: stories of heartache sung in simple, hard-hitting lyrics. Candi's voice hits you right inside, it is so strong and full of distinction – all this, along with some great soulful chords and progressions. It's really an all-rounder!

Design by Roy Kohara, photography by Bob Wortham

Tracklist

1 Stand By Your Man
2 How Can I Put Out The Flame
3 I'm Just A Prisoner (Of Your Good Lovin')
4 Mr. And Mrs. Untrue
5 Too Hurt To Cry

6 He Called Me Baby
7 Sweet Feeling
8 To Hear You Say You're Mine
9 What Would Become Of Me
10 Freedom Is Just Beyond The Door

TELL IT LIKE IT IS

Candi Staton & Bettye Swann, Honest Jon's Records, 1986

This album was selected by **Bronagh Gallagher**. Along with a successful music career, she has appeared in numerous major movies, like Quentin Tarantino's *Pulp Fiction* in 1994, George Lucas's *Star Wars: Episode I – The Phantom Menace* (1999) and *Sherlock Holmes*, in 2009. You will also have seen her in that excellent 1991 film, *The Commitments*. She talks about the Candi Staton and Bettye Swann compilation, *Tell It Like It Is*.

Photo by Conor Masterson

I have picked an album called *Tell It Like It Is*, which is a two-sided female soul compilation by Candi Staton and Bettye Swann. These songs were recorded in Fame Studios (Rick Hall's studio), in Muscle Shoals, Alabama, during the late 1960s and early 1970s, but they only really came to light in 1986, as far as I can make out. A lot of this stuff went into vaults when different record companies took over the smaller labels, and the recordings from Fame Studios were scattered among a lot of different soul collectors and fanatics.

This record changed my understanding of how music was recorded, because they are so simple. They are so brilliantly played and so cleverly produced – that is what Rick Hall was famous for in Muscle Shoals. I first got a cassette copy of it from a mall in Belfast in 1986, and I actually still have it.

I was about fifteen, and I had collected soul music. My Mum and Dad had also been collectors, so from about nine years old onwards I was collecting quite seriously. I would know exactly what was what from the records that Mum had – 'Can we look at this musician? Can we look at that musician?' This came out of the blue, though. It was basically the sound of it . . . it was just that Muscle Shoals sound.

It was different from the Jerry Wexler productions. It was different from motown. There was something just completely raw and new about it – the way the guitar sounded, and the way the female vocals sounded. It has these sort of tired, raspy, very honest, painful soul singers. It was not like the sort of manicured production of Berry Gordy and the great artists that we know, who also made exceptional records. There was a difference. There was something about Candi Staton's voice, especially. And the flip side of the record was Bettye Swann's voice – that, to me, was just the sound of Alabama.

The sound of the South was totally different from the thriving communities, I suppose. It is just the way the records make you feel. There is a longing to them, and I just love that about music. And then, there is also an attitude to them, where the women are talking about how they are the ones in charge. 'I'd Rather Be An Old Man's Sweetheart (Than A Young Man's Fool)' is one of those songs. It is brilliantly provocative soul singing, and very sexy.

All the recordings that Candi Staton did at that time have since been released in the entire Fame Studio collection. So, they are all available again now, but for years they never were. It was Honest Jon's label – this fantastic reggae, blues and African Caribbean music collectors in London – that got the rights to it, and they released it on their label. Then, the entire collection was subsequently released.

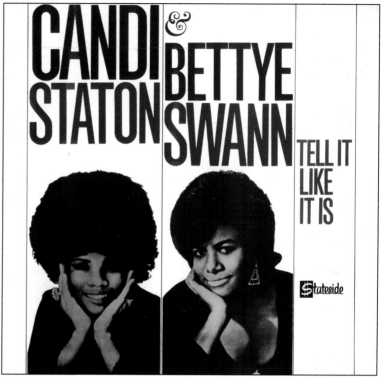

Design by Phil Smee at Waldo's

Tracklist

Candi Staton
1. Someone You Use
2. I'd Rather Be An Old Man's Sweetheart (Than A Young Man's Fool)
3. Evidence
4. Sweet Feeling
5. I'm Just A Prisoner (Of Your Good Lovin')
6. Do Your Duty
7. Get It When I Want It

Bettye Swann
1. Tell It Like It Is
2. These Arms Of Mine
3. No Faith No Love
4. Cover Me
5. Don't You Ever Get Tired (Of Hurtin' Me)
6. You're Up To Your Same Old Tricks Again
7. Today I Started Loving You Again
8. Willie & Laura Mae Jones

SWEETBACK

Sweetback, Epic, 1996

This album was selected by **Jim Carroll**, the fast-talking, no-bullshit journalist who has graced the pages of the *Irish Times* for many years. Since July 2009, he has helped the 'Banter' sessions become the celebrated forum that it is today. Here, he jumps back to 1996 with *Sweetback*.

Photo by Shane Serrano

The attic is calling. Up here, amidst the eaves, beneath the rafters and beside the chimney breast, there is a selection of boxes that contain dusty grooves of all kinds. These pieces of vinyl, CDs, minidiscs and cassettes are survivors from the old days, the days before digging in the crates was replaced by typing a name into a search engine, Spotify or YouTube.

Up here, amidst acts no longer remembered, even by the record labels to which they are still in the red for unrecouped advances – if those labels still even exist – you will find a couple of twelve-inch singles, and an album by a band called Sweetback. The sleeves are still intact, though rather weather-beaten, as a result of years of late-night living when you used to DJ for a living in clubs. The music still works, though. The music still sends you.

We will get to the hook in a moment, but here is some more preamble for the extended twelve-inch. The music still sends you: 'ain't that something? Isn't that an incredible attribute, for something emerging from the imagination of an individual or collective?

That is what we want from art, isn't it? The trip, the odyssey, the journey, the excursion, the grand tour. We want music to take us away from whatever world, mood, mindset or environment that we are currently in, and transport us to the other side. It is a wild thing to ask from a simple piece of music. It is wilder to consider how much music actually does this.

Here comes the hook. When the Sweetback album starts to play, I see colours forming. This is not about synaesthesia or anything like that, but rather about how those first lazy beats and that ridiculously sexy bass pulse on 'Gaze' send me back to a house in Dublin, with a late-winter sun creeping up the wall outside the back window, casting a glow as the album played. That was the where and when of discovering Sweetback for the first time.

The shorthand with *Sweetback* was that they were Sade's band – namely Andrew Hale, Stuart Matthewman and Paul Spencer Denman – and this was an album they wrote, recorded and released when she was not making music or touring. Vocals came from Maxwell, Amel Larrieux (from Groove Theory fame) and Bahamadia.

It was 1996, and it was one of the first albums out the gap to sit down that new-school R 'n' B class, and make sense of it all. You listen to the album now, and you can hear elbow room being made in the stalls for the likes of Jill Scott, Erykah Badu and D'Angelo.

It was prescient, it was neat, it was – yes – ahead of its time. It was lush music for the azure hours of your life when things are still and even, but you are still keen to paint another picture or spin another tale to use up the ideas in your head. The narcotic dub and the slow-motion, shimmering sway of the beats were truly al dente. Here was music which had a well-lived, seasoned, experienced veneer to it: seductive, not sassy, a tease instead of titillation, a haze rather than a heat.

At this stage, I could continue to make like a tout outside a dodgy restaurant in that holiday resort you visited last summer, and sell this album for all kinds of reasons not related to what you will get in reality. But you have got eyes and ears of your own. It is a small amount of time for a big return to dig this out and dig in. Unlike those radio advertisements hawking banks and financial services, the value of your investment here will go up, rather than down.

Design by Alan Aboud, photography by Donald Christie

Tracklist

1	Gaze	7	Chord
2	Softly Softly	8	Walk Of Ju
3	Sensations	9	Hope She'll Be Happier
4	Au Natural	10	Come Dubbing
5	Arabesque	11	Cloud People
6	You Will Rise	12	Powder

THIS IS THE TOMB OF THE JUICE

Republic Of Loose, Big Cat Records, 2004

This album was seleted by **Bressie**, the former vocalist with The Blizzards, who has become a well-known face on Irish TV screens, for his honest – and often blunt – views, as a judge on *The Voice Of Ireland* and, more recently, for his *Bressie's Teenage Kicks* series. Now a solo artist, Bressie has seen the music business from both sides. His album of choice is Republic Of Loose's 2004 debut.

Photo by Barry McCall

There are lots of reasons why I chose this, but one of the main ones is that The Blizzards had started gigging in Dublin. We were being helped at the time by Marcus Russell, who was Oasis's manager, but he also owned Big Cat Records, who signed Republic Of Loose. I went to Dublin to meet Marcus one day, and he brought me to Eamon Doran's to see them.

Up until that point, Ireland had been the kind of country that produced singer/songwriters or guitar-driven stuff, but Republic Of Loose were totally off the chart. It was full of personality and, more than anything, I was attracted to how good a frontman Mik Pyro was. At that time, I had not heard the record. Marcus said, 'Look you just have to listen to it' – I think what he said was, 'It is just pure sleaze.' I had never heard an album described that way, so I had to listen to it.

Even to this day, when I go running or cycling or even turn on an iPod, it is one of the albums that I listen to the most. It just has this outlandish personality to it. I remember listening to the bit where Mik goes on an absolute rampage, on 'Fuck Everybody', in the middle of the album, and thinking that it oozed charisma in a way that I had never heard before.

Another thing that I liked when I watched them live was that the two guitarists, Dave and Bres, were doing things with guitars that I had never heard done. It was very clever, but very subtle too. At the time, everything was about distorting your guitar, making everything loud and hiding the fact that you really were not a very good guitarist! The interplay between the two lads was amazing – the rhythm section was really simple but driven, and then you had this frontman who was possessed.

I had retired from another career, and then spent two years playing with The Blizzards, until something happened. At that time, Republic Of Loose had just come out, and music for me was really raw, so I did not question it. I did not think too much about radio or record labels, and it was really enjoyable. At that time, there were bands around like the Loose and Director, and it was when I enjoyed being in a band the most.

It was the liveness of the album that really got me. At that time, they were the anti-music scene in Ireland, and I loved that. There was a madness to the band when they performed live. Mik would just stare at people, sometimes even verbally abusing them. I remember thinking, 'Should I try that, or will I end of getting the head boxed off me?'

When I moved to the UK, people used to ask me about Irish music, and Republic Of Loose were always one of the Irish bands that I would push. I used to say to people, 'Listen to the album, not just the individual songs.' On an album, it can be very hard to create and define a definitive direction, but this certainly has one.

For the Record

By Mik Pyro

I was disappointed with the album at the time immediately after its conception, mostly because it veers too wildly in tone and we were not grooving with quite the R 'n' B bounciness that we were trying to emulate. However, I listened to it last week, and it sounded pretty fantastic. I was delighted by how organic, warm and plain weird it was.

It was the first album that I ever made, and I tried to get a bit too much religiosity into the lyrics, but, at the time, I actually believed I had hellhounds on my trail and that I was not long for this earth! You can hear that in the music. It is the feverish energy of men in their late twenties, who never thought they would get a chance to record an album, pouring every ounce of invention and passion they had to make this grotesquely beautiful oddity. I'm glad it exists. We deserve that, if nothing else.

Illustrations by Max Keane, colour and design by Dave Pyro

Tracklist

1	Intro	9	Sweet Cola of Mercy
2	Kiodin Man	10	Six Sober Sounds
3	Hold Up!	11	Fuck Everybody
4	Girl I'm Gonna Fuck You Up	12	Ride with Us
5	Goofy Love	13	Dial Jesus for Sweetness
6	Something in the Water	14	Black Bread
7	Tell More Lies	15	Lawn Child
8	Slow Down		

THREADS

Now, Now, Trans Records, 2012

Beginning as a talented mid-teen prospect, Bridie Monds-Watson, who we know as **Soak**, has developed into a singer and musician making music that has been embraced by both alternative quarters, and the mainstream. Her career has been on an upwards trajectory, and it looks set to stay on that course.

Photo by Joshua Hailing

This album is really original in the way that it is written. All the songs are like little stories and truths, and the music is just amazing. It is the kind of music that you would expect to be in the movie *Juno*. It is a brilliant, brilliant album.

I first heard about it on the Internet – one of the bands that I liked when I was thirteen shared the link. When I first heard it, I thought that a lot of people would like it, but I did not think that it would be very mainstream, mainly because it is not really something that you would hear on the radio, unless it was weird radio! But I imagined that they would do a load of amazing shows and tours that would do well.

This album is something that I have posted about a few times on Twitter, and people have replied, saying, 'Wow, I have never really met that many people that like this band.' I have a few Spotify playlists on my phone that have an unbelievable number of albums and songs. Some I have not listened to in a long time, but I have them there so that if I want to play them to someone, there they are.

I think it took quite a while for *Threads* to grow on me. I can be quite critical of music, so when it takes me a while to get into an album, that is a good thing, because the album will stay with me for a very long time. If I like something straight away, I may get bored of it, or play it until I hate it!

I listen to music as a musician and a fan, depending on how long I have been following the band, or if they are friends of mine. If I have been following the band for a long time, I would probably say, 'Ah, they have just released a new song!' If it is a friend, or something that I have just heard, I would probably look at it from a more artistic point of view.

I think that a lot of Now, Now's structures, instrumentation, melodies and hooks have inspired me and my music. A lot of those tiny bits in their songs really make them what they are. That is what you remember the most about a certain song.

For the Record

*By Cacie Dalager, from an interview with
AV Club*

We were so, so nervous going into the studio, because it was the first time that we had ever been in a real recording environment, working with a producer, and our first time going out of town to record. We had recorded almost all of our prior music in Brad's basement, whenever we felt inspired, and with no real timetables. We would try to set deadlines for ourselves, but no one was enforcing them.

We were definitely freaking out a fair amount by the time we got to Vancouver. As a band, we never feel fully ready to record, and are always working on the songs until the very last minute, because we like to have every layer and part written before we ever hit record. In the case of this record, it was crazy; we were literally writing it for years, and the months right before we went into the studio were insane.

Tracklist

1	The Pull	7	Separate Rooms
2	Prehistoric	8	Thread
3	Lucie.Too	9	Wolf
4	Dead Oaks	10	School Friends
5	Oh. Oh.	11	Colony
6	But I Do	12	Magnet

TWO NUNS AND A PACK MULE

Rapeman, Touch & Go/Blast First Records, 1988

This album was selected by **Andy Cairns**, who has been the voice and face of Therapy? for over two decades. The band brought us anthems like 'Teethgrinder', 'Nowhere' and 'Screamager'. Here, he talks about one of the albums that had a huge influence on his career.

Photo by Tom Hoad

This is a record made by what is commonly referred to as a "power trio", but unlike any other power trio I had ever heard up until that point. It is never talked about much in rock or avant-rock circles, even though it is a project of Steve Albini. Not surprising, really, given the name of the band.

I first heard this album the month it was released in Larne with original Therapy? drummer, Fyfe Ewing. We were both fans of Albini's previous band, Big Black (Fyfe fanatically so) and the line-up also featured two from Scratch Acid, who we also liked. Fyfe had the album delivered to his house via mail order, and got it before it became available in Belfast. We had gathered with the purpose of playing it through several times very loudly.

What I liked most about it was the punch of the whole thing. My head was nodding and my limbs were twitching as they would if I were listening to James Brown or Can, not a so-called noise rock band. We listened to it again and again that evening, singling out parts that we liked and, over the following months, the album became something of an obsession.

Right from the off, the band all coming in at once alongside the drum, filling into a fantastic head-winging groove, and then the opening line of, 'Why don't you snuff it then? Plant-eating pussy?' on a song called 'Steak And Black Onions'. I was a vegetarian at the time, but just took the whole political-correctness baiting in my stride. The lyrics were not the most important thing about this album – the sheer physical heft was. 'Hated Chinee' (again, more PC baiting) had the

most perfect metallic funk guitar riff set against a drum pattern, seeming to pull back from syncopation just before lurching into it. There is a ZZ Top cover on there, too. 'Just Got Paid' brings scalding white funk to the blues riffery, and my head starts nodding all over again.

We knew that the album would never break over in the style of Sonic Youth or Pixies. It was too smart to ever appeal to a jock audience in the way that some dubious rock songs could. I also think the name and subsequent picketing of some UK gigs by enraged social groups did not help its cause. I did, however, think that it might become a classic in the same vein as 'Spiderland' by Slint or 'Goat' by Jesus Lizard.

When the album came out, myself, Fyfe and Michael (McKeegan, Therapy?'s bassist) told everyone who would listen how majestic it was. Most, though piqued by the involvement of Albini, baulked at the name of the band. A lot of Therapy?'s early material has elements of that album running through it. It would certainly clear a room at a party, as we found out several times.

I will forever associate this album with friendship, inspiration and the early days of Therapy? It soundtracked so much of the time we spent together, and was also played loudly in my car on the way to work shitty nightshifts in a factory. The little tricks that I picked up as a musician listening to this record have stuck with me to this day.

I initially saw this record as paving a new possibility for the three-piece. It was not Motörhead and it was not The Police – it was a strange new noise altogether. The power in this record was not about being stomped on, it was about allowing yourself to be swallowed. Stupid name, though.

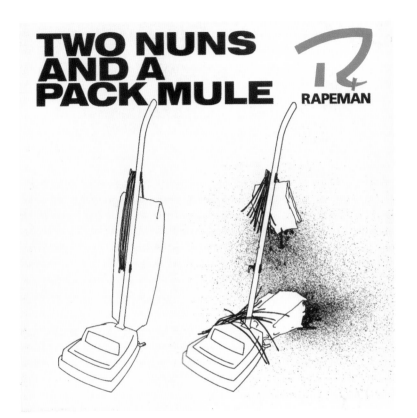

Tracklist

1 Steak And Black Onions
2 Monobrow
3 Up Beat
4 Coition Ignition Mission
5 Kim Gordon's Panties

6 Hated Chinee
7 Radar Love Lizard
8 Marmoset
9 Just Got Paid
10 Trouser Minnow

A WORLD IN A GRAIN OF SAND

The Magic Lantern, Hectic Eclectic Records, 2011

Wallis Bird has had music in her life from an early age. Her energetic style of playing has won her fans all over the world, and drawn comparisons with Ani DiFranco, and the great Janis Joplin.

Photo by Jens Oellermann

This album made me go stupid. It is one of the most intelligent and subtle albums that I have ever heard, and it makes me act neither subtle nor intelligent. I will tell you why in a second.

The album is called *A World In a Grain of Sand*, from the band Magic Lantern. The writer Jamie Doe is mega young for such talent, and hails from Dalston, East London. He writes modern-day sea shanties in a traditional English folk style, wrapped up in Afrobeat, meticulously arranged by some kind of all-hearing god in heaven.

It is a ridiculously beautiful album, so careful, and then so demented and heart shattering, so well performed, recorded and mixed with love, in a gorgeous tactile packaging. For almost the whole year of 2012, it was actually all I played all day. I have heard it about 500 times now, I would say. I can critique and decipher everything about the album, but I simply cannot explain the reason why I love it this much. It is like a good best friend.

I first heard *The World In a Grain of Sand* in November 2012, at around midnight. I was relaxing, sitting on the floor against the bed, and my partner at the time put it into the player. The first chord came in, beautiful and close, and then came his voice, masculine, odd, cumbersome and pinched, all at the same time. I sat there motionless, with my head turned towards the player for the entire show, only opening my mouth occasionally to say 'Wow'. When it had finished, I leant over, and pressed play again. And so began my 'repeat sessions' of Magic Lantern!

It turned me into a teenager. I made a T-shirt based on a message I asked my ex to pass onto him at a gig I could not attend – it reads: 'I've had amazing sex to your album'. When I was hammered one night, I sent Jamie a phone recording of me singing a piece from his song, and we became pen pals of the deepest kind, and we have still never met.

We swap song demos at their most fragile stages like secrets, and I leave notes in guestbooks and messages with other musicians across the globe for him to find. They sometimes get returned! And over the years, his sea shanties have sewn their way into my life and my friends' lives. He is a muse without knowing.

But aside from all this silliness, his album has changed songwriting for me. He writes because he must. The kind, genial, true and patient hand taken to record this beautiful music, just for the sake of his expression, regardless of how few or how many people consume it, means the world to me. It instilled in me my belief in art.

I giggled like a child when I heard that his second album is almost finished! More T-shirts!

For the Record

By Jamie Doe

A World In a Grain of Sand sums up a really huge part of my life. It was the first The Magic Lantern album: the product of all my songwriting up to that point, and of four years playing with the band, working on developing a sound. When I look back on it now, the overwhelming feeling I have is of innocence, of not knowing any better, and of working it out for ourselves. We made the only record we could make, we made it our own way, and I would not change a note. If I had known what I know now, I would have done some things differently, but all the love we had in the world went into that album, and I have been amazed at how, in its own quiet way, it continues to have a life of its own.

Sleeve Design by Ollie Hammick, painting is by Nicky Peart

Tracklist

1	Somebody Told Me	7	Patriots
2	Cut from Stone	8	A Man & His Dog
3	Laura's Song	9	Karachi
4	The Ship That Washed Away	10	The Bridge
5	Guilty Hearts	11	Romeo and Juliet (III)
6	Shine a Light On		

THE YEAR OF HIBERNATION

Youth Lagoon, Lefse Records/Fat Possum Records, 2011

She is one half of electronic pop duo Young Wonder. Like Beth Gibbons of Portishead, Bjork and Kate Bush, you could never confuse **Rachel Koeman**'s vocals with anyone else's. As Young Wonder, Koeman and Ian Ring have brought us some incredible tunes in a short career thus far.

Photo by Rebecca Naen

The album that I have chosen is the debut from an act called Youth Lagoon. The album is titled, *The Year of Hibernation*. I adore it. The lyrics to me are more than just lyrics – I hear them as poetry. They resonate with me, bringing me back to the nostalgia of childhood, to the uncertain feelings of growing up. For me, it is an absolutely magical collection of songs.

My boyfriend introduced me to this album; he knew that I would love it. I do not specifically remember the very first time I listened to it. I think it was comfortably familiar, almost like an old friend. Most albums for me take time to grow.

I really loved how tastefully the indie-pop sound was portrayed. To be honest, I had never quite heard anything like it. It was minimalistic, but, at the same time, totally catchy. The lyrics were ear-catching. They totally encompass how it feels to grow up, that feeling of uneasiness is explored, which really struck me, as it is something I like to write about myself.

I really love the imagery and the tone of the track 'Seventeen'. It is about the sheer innocence and joy of childhood imagination. It reminds me so much of myself. He talks about how his mind races with thoughts, imagery and detail that he cannot put a stop to. There is something so innocent and so truthful about it, I cannot help thinking that everyone else secretly feels the same as him.

Being involved in music has made me aware that a lot of people just do not get music that is not so commercially viable. I never really think of anything in terms of, 'This is going to be massive', because I think you can never predict what is going to be big. Music is completely subjective and, for me, I look for lyrics that I can relate to. Not everyone else is going to relate to the same lyrics the way that I did.

The album has that lo-fi indie-pop sound, which was quite relevant a few years back, and still is. I guess I hear many elements of bands such as Wild Nothing, and perhaps Beach House, but it is a lot more stripped back. He has definitely developed his own style. Sometimes, I think I can almost hear some Irish-sounding riffs.

I rarely feel compelled to tell people about the music I am listening to at the time. I am actually quite strange when it comes to listening to music. It is quite a personal thing for me, and I do not really like suggestions from other people very much. I think it is nice to discover music for yourself. There is something quite satisfying about that!

I guess the album is of its time, but something in me wants to say that it is quite retro. Most lyrics deal with childhood or young adolescence, so it feels old, in a good way. It seems to document not only his childhood, but everyone else's, too. I really like to think back on my childhood as an adult. I think we have a lot to learn from it.

For the Record

By Trevor Powers, from an interview with pitchfork.com

I just wanted to write honest songs. So much music nowadays is really shallow. There is not much heart or emotion in it. Another thing is that I really do not want to fit myself into a box. There are a lot of subgenres right now, but I do not want to peg myself as this or that.

Tracklist

1	Posters		5	July
2	Cannons		6	Daydream
3	Afternoon		7	Montana
4	17		8	The Hunt

YOU CAN BE ANYONE THIS TIME AROUND

Timothy Leary, Douglas/Rykodisc, 1970/1992

This album was selected by **BP Fallon**. Musician, writer, photographic artist, DJ, gentleman: he has done so much in his distinguished career. It is a career that has seen him work with John Lennon, Led Zeppelin, Marc Bolan, Johnny Thunders, U2, Jack White, BP Fallon & The Bandits, BP Fallon & The Ghost Wolves and many others.

Photo by Christopher Durst

Mind your mind and your mind will mind you. It is a meeting of minds here, of those who are spectacularly, beautifully and undarkly out of theirs. Stoned, immaculate, effervescent, relaxed and paying attention.

Ah, Dr Timothy Leary, apostle of LSD, truth-seeker, rebel outlaw, man of intellect, former professor at Harvard. 'Turn on, tune in, drop out', Marshall McLuhan had said, and Lear enthusiastically proselytised McLuhan's message as the medium. I was – and am – a disciple. Suddenly, this black-and-white Dixon of Dock Green world went glorious Technicolor, and beyond.

John Lennon was a huge fan, writing 'Tomorrow Never Knows' after reading Leary's *The Psychedelic Experience* . . . on acid. He name-checks Leary in 'Give Peace a Chance' (Leary is singing along on the record), and wrote 'Come Together' from the sketch of a song he had composed for Leary's latest gambol, his 1969 run for governor of California against the actor Ronald Reagan. Of course, for Leary, political success was hopeless, and by the time this album came out in 1970, our hero Dr Tim – who Nixon called 'the most dangerous man in America' – was in jail.

The promo for this record proclaimed, 'This is a dangerous album'. It could be stickered, 'Do not do this at home' – a 'trip-with-Tim' self-help item. Or, 'Do this only at home'. It is also, at times, unintentionally hilarious, like when our narrator tells us, in the title song, accompanied by sitar and suitable samples, that this time around, off our trolleys, we can be John and Yoko, Allen Ginsberg, the Maharishi, Country Joe & The Fish, The Grateful Dead,

Jefferson Airplane . . . even The Rolling Stones, if we are particularly lucky.

The centrepiece is 'Live and Let Live', where you hear Dr Leary's speeches from his 1969 campaign for governor, propagating such ahead-of-their-time schemes as making marijuana legal and sales of it, the very same principle now recently adopted, with great success, in Washington and Colorado, some fifty years later.

In amongst this spoken-word spiel, weaving around it, pushing it, floating above and below it, there is this band of miscreant musicians painting added pictures: Steve Stills and John Sebastian on scratching guitars, Buddy Miles on the drums and Jimi Hendrix on the most spectacular throbbingly perfect bass guitar.

Now famous, Jimi still gifted his guitar playing to records by other people; the eponymous album by Eire Apparent, which he produced; *The Everlasting First* by Love; some dodgy recordings with Curtis Knight and some fine ones with King Curtis; 'Old Times Good Times' on Steve Stills's first LP; the *McGough & McGear* album by Scaffold members Mike McGear and poet Roger McGough; sexy funk licks on 'Doriela Du Fontaine' by ahead-of-his-time rapper Lightning Rod, also known as Jalal Mansur Nuriddin of The Last Poets. And now, here comes Jimi on slinky, muscular and fluid bass guitar, backing up the wisdom and/or ramblings of 'the high priest of possibilities', aided by a Buffalo Springfield, a Lovin' Spoonful and the leader of The Buddy Miles Express.

Later, Jimi and Buddy would enlist Jimi's pal Billy Cox on bass and form Band Of Gypsys. But here they are more than happy to plonk and bash away behind the enthusiastic exhortations of the exalted cosmicist Dr Timothy Leary.

Sleeve by Kelley/Mouse Studio – Alton Kelley and Stanley Mouse

Tracklist

1   You Can Be Anyone This Time Around
2   What Do You Turn on When You Turn On
3   Live and Let Live

PHOTOGRAPHY CREDITS

Aisling Bea by Anthony Woods
Alan McGee by Dan Hegarty
Andy Cairns by Tom Hoad
Annie Mac by Mari Sarai
Blindboyboatclub (Rubberbandits) by Steve Ullathorne
BP Fallon (& The Bandits) by Christopher Durst
Bressie by Barry McCall
Brian Cash by Fiona McSorley
Bronagh Gallagher by Conor Masterson
Cathal Pendred by Alex Hutch
Chuck D (Public Enemy) by Piero F Giunti (Visionary Rebel Production)
Craig Walker by Stefano Tiozzo (stefanotiozzo.com)
Daithi by Conal Thomson
Easkey Britton by Robbie Reynolds/Oxfam Ireland
Danny O'Reilly (The Coronas) by Gavin Leane
Dave Fanning by Marc O'Sullivan
Gavin Friday by Barry McCall
Glen Hansard by Flavia Schaub
Ian Wilson by Kathrin Baumbach
Iarla O'Lionaird by Feargal Ward
Imelda May by Barry McCall
James Vincent McMorrow by Emma J Doyle
JD Beauvallet by Renaud Monfourny
Jerry Fish by Celine O'Sullivan
Jim Carroll by Shane Serrano
John Kelly by Barry McCall

Larry Gogan by Jenny McCarthy of PHOTOSBYJEN
Lethal Dialect by Al Higgins
Cillian Murphy by Rich Gilligan
MayKay (Fight Like Apes) by Loreana Rushe
Michelle Doherty by AM London
Aidan Gillen by Rich Gilligan
Camille O'Sullivan by Sean Breithaupt, Yvette Monahan
Marty Moore by Brendan Moran (Sportsfile)
Robbie Henshaw by Brendan Moran (Sportsfile)
Buck 65 by Rob Campbell
Jacknife Lee by Esme Lee
Dan Hegarty by Ken Heffernan
Niall Byrne by Al Higgins
Niall Davis by Victor Lucas
Paul Thomas Saunders by Dan Curwin
Rachel Koeman by Rebecca Naen
Rory Friers by Graham Smith
Scroobius Pip by Lease Roe - JoLi Studios
Shahin Badar by Pinkkie Makhajani
Simon Neil by Andrew Wilsher
Soak by Joshua Hailing
Tim Booth by Con Kelleher
Torsten Kinsella by Derval Freeman
Wallis Bird by Jens Oellermann